"America's frontier spirit is alive and well in the United States, even in the center of its biggest metropolis. Anna Maria Bounds breaks tired old stereotypes about Northeastern urbanites and their politics, and brings to life the New Yorkers who have been scarred by crisis, lost faith in government, and band together to prepare for survival. It is exactly what you want from a great ethnography: a vivid, engaging picture of a world that existed right in front of us, yet somehow remained invisible to the collective imagination. Essential reading for the sociology of politics, community, culture, and the city."

Joseph Cohen, Founder of the award-winning Sociocast

"New Yorkers preparing for the worst, a rapidly growing social phenomenon, is traced and tracked by this terrific book profiling the 'prepper' movement. Written with novelistic skill, Dr. Bounds turns a sharp sociologists' lens to what the rich, the poor, and the middle are doing: whether bugging out, or bugging in, joining a group or going it alone, *Bracing for the Apocalypse* takes you inside this important but seldom studied area."

Andrew A. Beveridge, President and Cofounder of Social Explorer

"Anna Maria Bounds's account of the culture, work and context of the New York Prepper subculture offers a fascinating, often hilarious reversal of stereotypes about the tribe of doomsday preppers in the city. As a participant ethnographer in the network, as an urban sociologist, and as a New Yorker who has experienced urban disaster herself, Bounds writes with equal measures of expertise, curiosity, and solidarity. She connects the urban phenomenon of doomsday prepping with the social origins of city life as well as new narratives of normalized emergency, different versions of the apocalypse, and varieties of zombies. This book offers insight, transparency, and an apt sense of the will, the vulnerability and the resilience of 'all in' contemporary urban life."

Meg Holden, Simon Fraser University

Bracing for the Apocalypse

Increasing American fear about terrorism, environmental catastrophes, pandemics, and economic crises has fueled interest in "prepping": confronting disaster by mastering survivalist skills. This trend of self-reliance is not merely evidence of the American belief in the power of the individual; rather, this pragmatic shift away from expecting government aid during a disaster reflects a weakened belief in the bond between government and its citizens during a time of crisis. This ethnographic study explores the rise of the urban preppers' subculture in New York City, shedding light on the distinctive approach of city dwellers in preparing for disaster. With attention to the role of factors such as class, race, gender and one's expectations of government, it shows that how one imagines Doomsday affects how one prepares for it. Drawing on participant observation, the author explores preppers' views on the central question of whether to "bug out" or "hunker down" in the event of disaster, and examines the ways in which the prepper economy increases revenue by targeting concerns over developing skills, building networks, securing equipment and arranging a safe locale. A rich qualitative study, *Bracing for the Apocalypse* will appeal to scholars of sociology and anthropology with interests in urban studies, ethnography and subcultures.

Anna Maria Bounds is an Assistant Professor of Sociology at Queens College, City University of New York, USA.

Bracing for the Apocalypse
An Ethnographic Study of New York's 'Prepper' Subculture

Anna Maria Bounds

Routledge
Taylor & Francis Group

LONDON AND NEW YORK

First published 2021
by Routledge
2 Park Square, Milton Park, Abingdon, Oxon OX14 4RN

and by Routledge
605 Third Avenue, New York, NY 10017

First issued in paperback 2022

Routledge is an imprint of the Taylor & Francis Group, an informa business

British Library Cataloguing-in-Publication Data
A catalogue record for this book is available from the British Library

Library of Congress Cataloging-in-Publication Data
Names: Bounds, Anna Maria, author.
Title: Bracing for the apocalypse : an ethnographic study of New York's 'prepper' subculture / Anna Maria Bounds.
Description: Milton Park, Abingdon, Oxon ; New York, NY : Routledge, 2020. | Includes bibliographical references and index.
Identifiers: LCCN 2020006636 (print) | LCCN 2020006637 (ebook) | ISBN 9780415788489 (hardback) | ISBN 9781315225258 (ebook) | SBN 9781315225258 (ebook)
Subjects: LCSH: Survivalism--Social aspects--New York (State)--New York. | Preparedness--Social aspects--New York (State)--New York. | Subculture--New York (State)--New York. | New York (N.Y.)--Social life and customs.
Classification: LCC GF86 .B725 2020 (print) | LCC GF86 (ebook) | DDC 306.4/613--dc23
LC record available at https://lccn.loc.gov/2020006636
LC ebook record available at https://lccn.loc.gov/2020006637

ISBN: 978-0-367-50954-5 (pbk)
ISBN: 978-0-415-78848-9 (hbk)
ISBN: 978-1-315-22525-8 (ebk)

DOI: 10.4324/9781315225258

Typeset in Garamond
by Taylor & Francis Books

Contents

PART 4
Urban prepping as a new reflection of citizenship   171

Preface

When I first discussed this study with Andrew Beveridge, my chairperson at the time, he chuckled and said, "You need to check out Alison Lurie's funny novel about a sociologist who studies a cult that believes in aliens. The researchers get sucked up in it. You don't believe in that prepping stuff, do you?"

Right away, I shook my head no, but inside I was thinking yes *and* no. I was born on the coast of the Gulf of Mexico and I grew up in a beach town on the Atlantic Ocean. Prepping for hurricanes was routine for my family (okay, my father, and we all just observed it.) That hardly qualifies me as a head case. Preppers are stereotypically seen as suspicious sorts who are very wary of other people. I am way too friendly, after all. Still, I decided to give Lurie's book *Imaginary Friends* (1967), a quick read.

The first few sentences of chapter one gave me pause. The narrator, a fellow professor, introduces the story of Professor McMann's research project to a group of zealots who believe in a different universe and purport to exchange messages from aliens:

> Could any group of rural religious cranks really have driven a well-known sociologist out of his mind? Or were they just, so to speak, the innocent flock of birds into which we flew our plane? And is McMann really mad now, or not? What does 'being mad' mean, anyhow?
>
> (p. 2)

Okay, this was an intriguing first page, but this was just one person's assessment of McMann's mental well-being. Studying preppers isn't going to make me go crazy. I am not crazy for studying this group. New York preppers aren't crazy; they have just been through a lot. Yet, reading a conversation between students in McMann's fictional department made me reflect again (Lurie, 1967):

> 'Listen, what happened to Professor McMann, I was planning to take his course?' asked one student.
>
> 'Well, you know what I heard,' the other student said, 'he took off in a flying saucer.'
>
> (p. 2)

Now, I thought, *Oh no! Flying Saucers. Is this flying saucerish research? Am I drinking the Kool-Aid from a saucer? My interest in preppers doesn't mean that I am going to transform into a survivalist and start wearing camo, does it? Sure, Lurie's novel is funny, but it has no bearing on my reality.*

But then, I heard it later that week:

"That's Professor Bounds. She's the one who studies prepping," said a professor talking with two students. She nodded her head toward me down the hall.

Hearing my name, I smiled as I unlocked my office. My expectation was that the students would walk down to talk with me.

"That's her?" asked the first student with wide eyes.

The two students looked at one another and then they turned to stare at me.

Their gaze told me everything.

I had become the oddity.

"Oh … prepping. I am really into that," whispered the second student. "I always secretly watch those shows."

The other student nodded in agreement.

As the students disappeared down the hallway, they slipped into a hushed conversation about this secret thing, prepping.

Prepping and the image of preppers—why does it arouse so much fascination and anxiety in people? Lurie's narrator again gives some insight into this:

> … I think that people can be divided into those like me who are more secure with a nice long word between them and a phenomenon, and those who are less so—who aren't reassured but frightened when the doctor tells them the technical name of that funny feeling in their stomach. Maybe that's how you tell the intellectuals from the sheep—or from the goats.
>
> (Lurie, p. 23)

For me, this book is about exploring how we deal with that "funny feeling in our stomachs" that stems from our past experiences with disasters or from dark places in our imaginations. This book is about how groups of people seek to gain control over the unpredictable in their lives. In other words, I'm interested in the "doings of [people]" (Berger, 1963, p. 17) in planning for extraordinary circumstances.

Acknowledgements

My sincere and deep gratitude is given to the New York preppers who shared their world with me. In particular, I am especially grateful to the members of the New York City Prepper's Network. Your knowledge and your camaraderie are important pillars of this book. To not just survive but thrive after a disaster? I'd bet on each of you.

I also thank to my colleagues in the Sociology Department at Queens College, City University of New York, for their support and encouragement. Thank you to the Andrew W. Mellon Foundation for financial support. A special thanks to Andrew Beveridge, Joseph Cohen and Suzanne Strickland for contributing constructive comments throughout the research and writing process. My students were also terrific guides in helping me to imagine the future of New York.

As always, I am indebted to Robert A. Beauregard for his scholarship and his guidance.

My deep appreciation is also given to my editor, Peter Heap. He has offered tremendous insight in guiding this book to fruition. Chelsea Randall's incisive reviews of my work have also strengthened its focus and its depth. Josephine Barnett, a scholar-in-making, offered invaluable feedback and stellar wordsmithing. My research assistant, Kimberly Pogorelis-Palmiotti, was masterful in tracking down elusive sources. My thanks to Damon Rowe as well for helping me follow up on a lead or two. Thank you to Taylor & Francis, especially Neil Jordan, for your expertise.

I wish to acknowledge Michael Mills of the University of Kent. My conversations with Michael about our respective research interests in prepper subcultures were very important in conceptualizing this project.

This book could not have been written without the insight and boosterism offered by Meg Holden of Simon Fraser University. Meg's thoughtful critiques have been crucial to my work. However, her most important contribution has been the sense of freedom that she has encouraged in my thinking. Since our days together at the New School, Meg and I have sought to focus on projects that speak to our minds and hearts as urban citizens. I learned that sensibility from Bob Beauregard. I am still learning from Bob's work.

Thank you to my family and friends for their support throughout this project. Asa and Sue have been champions of the cause. Susan has definitely been my best cheerleader. My love and thanks to Scott for his willingness to be game (to join me on a hike or to fix a computer glitch in the middle of the night).

Thank you also to New York, the city of my dreams.

Lastly, this book is dedicated to those that I meet in the forest and by the campfire.

Part 1

Understanding the rise of prepping in the global city of New York

1 "Ready.Gov" versus "Ready without Gov"

Prepping for disaster

Imagine this: America terrified by an advancing march of godless sub-humans, massacres at sacred places and grocery stores, planned explosions across the country, fears of government corruption and collapse, swaths of devastation caused by a hurricane and a visit by an alien probe.

A pitch for a new *Mad Max* movie or another apocalyptic blockbuster? No.

This scary synopsis is derived from America's headlines just before the 2018 Midterm Elections.

A snapshot of the national news during the pivotal time of Midterm Elections reveals that Americans were anxious about much more than congressional races. Threatened by a large caravan of Central American migrants walking to the US to seek refuge from violence and poverty, President Trump moved quickly to tighten Southern border controls and send Army troops to protect the country from what he termed an "onslaught" that included "criminals" and "Middle Easterners" (Davis and Gibbons-Neff, 2018). Shouting anti-Semitic slurs and brandishing an assault rifle, a gunman opened fire and killed eleven worshipers at a Pittsburgh synagogue (Robertson, Mele, and Tavernise, 2018). After forcibly attempting to enter a predominately black church, a man killed two black senior citizens at a Kroger store in Jefferson, KY (Zraick and Stevens, 2018). Thirteen pipe bombs were mailed across the nation to prominent Democrats and critics of President Trump (Wootson and Horton, 2018). Reports of voter suppression in Georgia (Fausset and Blinder, 2018) and Florida sparked national debate (Thrush and Peters, 2018). At the same time, suspicion continued to mount about the competency and trustworthiness of a White House whose operations were described as "a nervous breakdown of the executive power of the most powerful country in the world" (Woodward, 2018, p. xxii). In addition to these man-made crises, sections of the South were dealing with the aftermath of Hurricane Michael (Fausset, Mazzei, and Blinder, 2018). On Election Day, two Harvard astronomers increased national jitters by announcing the possibility that a mysterious flying interstellar object (a quarter-mile long and traveling at a speed of more than 196,000 miles per hour) sighted over Maui may have been a fully operational space probe (Molina, 2018). Was this strange national news cycle an anomaly? Hardly.[1]

Since the September 11th attacks, there has been an undercurrent of fear and anxiety in American culture, encompassing our politics, our media and our private lives. For the last seventeen years, 70% of Americans have worried about the possibility of a future terrorist attack.[2] According to Chapman University's Survey of American Fears (2018), corrupt government officials are the top American fear (73%), followed by fears about the environment (climate change and pollution), fears of bad things happening to loved ones (serious illness or death) and fears about financial security (not enough money for the future or high medical bills).[3] Furthermore, we are becoming more afraid; all top fears are now shared by more than half of Americans.

With no shortage of terrifying news, it is no wonder that, at the close of 2018, less than one-third of Americans believed that the country was headed in the right direction (Saad, 2018). This loss of faith in America's moral compass, however temporary, has been attributed to the culture of fear now omnipresent in our country (Altheide, 2017; Glassner, 2010). However, this consternation about America's future also stems from knowledge gained from a source far more significant than media cycles or the warnings of politicians: Experience. Americans, particularly New Yorkers, are becoming increasingly familiar with disaster and are thus learning to take matters into their own hands. We have come to understand that

> although the world has experienced major crises in the past, our time is unique in combining high levels of technical expertise with a continuing sense of extreme vulnerability. The more we learn about our world, the more we realize our existence is precarious.
>
> (Wuthnow, 2010, p. 3)

Given New York's stature as a global city, September 11th has come to symbolize an attack not just on our nation, but an attack on the Western world. However, it is also important to understand 9/11 from a localized perspective in order to determine its specific meaning and impact on New York residents. Taking the attack out of the local context prevents it from being situated within New York's recent history of disaster. In tracing New York's recent history of disaster, a different perspective starts to emerge on experiencing disaster or its threat at the local level post 9/11. While national memory may be stuck in 2001, New Yorkers have continued to contend with disaster. Since 2001, New York has endured many severe crises (or threats of disaster) including five terrorist attacks, natural disasters (including two hurricanes, two tornadoes and an earthquake), technological failures (such as two blackouts), fears of pandemics (COVID-19, the Swine Flu and the Ebola Virus) and economic or government instability (the longest recession since World War II) (See Table 1.1). In 2020, New York has now become the epicentre of the COVID-19 pandemic in the United States. As a result of this unpredictability, some New Yorkers are now looking beyond governmental assistance to protect their families. They are increasingly turning toward the practice of

Table 1.1 New York's disasters and disruptions (2001–17)

YEAR	DESCRIPTION	NATURAL DISASTER	TERRORIST ATTACK	PANDEMIC/EPIDEMIC THREAT	TECHNOLOGICAL FAILURE	GOVT OR ECONOMIC INSTABILITY
2017	Port Authority Terminal Bomb attack		X			
	West Side Bike Path Vehicular Attack		X			
	Flooding *	X				
	Winter Storm Stella *	X				
	Winter Storm Niko	X				
2016	Chelsea Bomb Attack		X			
	Flash Flood	X				
	East Harlem Metro North Train Fire				X	
	Coastal Flooding	X				
	Zika Virus Threat			X		
2015	Legionnaires Disease Outbreak			X		
	East Village Gas Explosion				X	
	Blizzard - Juno	X				
	Measles Threat			X		
	Hepatitis A Threat			X		

(Continued)

Table 1.1 (Cont.)

YEAR	DESCRIPTION	NATURAL DISASTER	TERRORIST ATTACK	PANDEMIC/EPI-DEMIC THREAT	TECHNOLOGI-CAL FAILURE	GOVT OR ECONOMIC INSTABILITY
2014	Ebola Virus Threat			X		
2012	Hurricane Sandy *	X				
	Hurricane Sandy *	X				
	Tornado, Waterspout	X				
2011	Hurricane Irene *					
	Hurricane Irene *					
	Earthquake	X				
2010	Time Square Bomb Attack		X			
2009	The Great Recession					X
2008	The Great Recession					X
2007	The Great Recession					X
	Steam Pipe Explosion				X	
2006	Queens Blackout				X	
2005	Hurricane Katrina *	X				
	Severe Storms and Flooding *	X				

Year	Event	(1)	(2)	(3)
2004	Tropical Depression Ivan *	X		
	Severe Storms and Flooding *	X		
	Severe Storms and Flooding *	X		
	Snow *	X		
2003	Power Outage	X		X
	Severe Storms, Tornadoes and Flooding *	X		
2002	Earthquake *	X		
2001	Snowstorm *	X		
	World Trade Center Attack *		X	
	Severe Storm, Winter Storm *	X		

NYC Emergency Management Natural Hazard Mitigation Plans (2009–2016)

* Disaster declared

prepping—developing skills and strategies to minimize physical and economic harm to themselves and their families in the event of disaster.

As Jason Charles, the leader of the NYC Prepper's Network (NYCPN) explained,

> Zombies aren't real. Neither are aliens. This isn't about science fiction stuff. Preparedness is about preparing for real things. Real things like what we've already been through, like 9/11 and Sandy. New Yorkers need to be educated about preparedness skills.

In speaking about the government's ineffectiveness in responding to disaster, another NYCPN member, Marlon, observed that:

> 9/11 told us that, Hurricane Katrina told us that. There is no cavalry coming. The world has grown too fast, where there are simply not enough resources. Manpower, military, everything. You can go to a town and there may be 50,000 people. That's not Manhattan. In New York, there is 8 million. Where do you put 8 million people in a disaster? So, you have to fend for yourself—and to fend for yourself, you have got to learn these things.

With strategies ranging from moderate to obsessive, prepping is the practice adopted by individuals who prepare and plan to independently survive disaster (and sustain themselves) in a context of scarce food, dwindling supplies and without government assistance (Mills, 2018; Perry, 2006; Reinhardt, 2017). This book aims to explore the city dweller's unique approach to prepping. Given the density and diversity of New York, urban prepping culture promotes strategies for learning diverse skills and knowledge (unrelated to city life) as well as forming strong social networks to aid survival in a crisis situation. The architecture, infrastructure and resources of New York impact how one preps to survive disaster. As one former gang member and prepper stated, "We are about showing people how New Yorkers prep. That this isn't about rednecks and monster trucks." What defines Doomsday for these urban dwellers? What skill sets and supplies constitute being "prepared" for disaster in the city? How are preppers' expectations of government and individuals defined by class, race and gender? For example, within the city, prepping strategies seem to be heavily influenced by income and locale. Wealthy NYC preppers prepare by building bunkers, while middle-class NYC preppers plan to leave the city in the event of a disaster. Exposing the stark contrast between wealthy and less affluent preppers adds a dynamic layer to the debate about the divided city and class disparity (van Kempen, 2007).

Disaster scholarship has an extensive history of complex and sometimes competing definitions of disaster that has been shaped by conceptualization processes, new knowledges and discipline paradigms (Perry, 2018). This research project supports Quarantelli's (2000, p. 682) consensus definition of disasters as "relatively sudden occasions when … the routines of collective social units are seriously disrupted and when unplanned courses of action" must be taken and that "disasters are social and that they are [to be] understood in human interactions" (Perry, 2006, p. 12). Within the field of disaster research, disasters are also viewed as distinct from emergencies and catastrophes (Alexander, 2014; Perry and Lindell, 2007) and extreme disruptions from conflict situations (Peek and Sutton, 2003; Quarantelli, 2005). However, a central research question remains regarding the influence of culture and who has the power to define disaster and frame a crisis as disaster (Webb, 2018). In the effort to acknowledge the significance of the term's assigned meaning with a culture, this qualitative study defines disaster broadly to reflect the wide range of scenarios referred to within the prepping community, including natural disasters, pandemics, terrorist attacks, nuclear and technological disasters, as well as the collapse of the global economy and national governments. (For prepper examples of disaster, see Charles, 2014; Edwards, 2009).[4]

While many disaster scenarios have been firsthand experiences for New Yorkers, these scenarios also echo the real or predicted disasters that have been frequently featured in American media. Mills' study (2018) argues that the American phenomenon of prepping is a response to uncertain anxieties around disaster risks that are driven by the consumption of disaster-based news reported in mainstream media rather than any singular fixation on an impending apocalypse. Mills' finding is significant because it breaks free from the earlier limited contention that prepping is driven by the fear of a final and complete collapse of civilization (Foster, 2014) rather than a reflection of disaster-based media and uncertainties about our current world.[5]

Therefore, this research addresses a popular misconception that preppers plan to protect their families against one particular type of disaster—the apocalypse. Derived from the ancient Greek word "apokalupsis," which means to uncover or reveal, the apocalypse refers to the complete final destruction of the world as described in the biblical book of Revelation (Oxford Dictionaries, 2019). In the Book of Revelation, the Four Horsemen of Apocalypse symbolize Conquest, War, Famine and Death, all grave dangers that signal the end of days (See Revelations 6: 1–8);[6] no longer only literary devices used in the Bible to reinforce compliance to church doctrine by instilling fear about the last judgement. The chaos and pain supposedly brought forth by the Four Horsemen might now be considered part of the American news cycle. In prepper jargon, references to the apocalypse are numerous. For example, TEOTWAWKI (The End of the World as We Know It) and WTSHTF (When the Shit Hits the Fan) are two popular acronyms used as shorthand to indicate any number of disasters (with temporary or long-term effects). If unfamiliar with this discourse, a researcher may risk incorrectly determining that the use of these terms reflects a prepper's strong belief in an impending final and complete destruction of the world. However, as Annette, a NYCPN member explained, "We are *not* crazy people. People need to understand that we are not preparing for doomsday and the end of the world. *We are prepping for tomorrow. Tomorrow.*"

Annette's need to make people understand that preppers are not awaiting the apocalypse is significant. It is a reminder that preppers face a bias, as American discourse has already categorized their activities as fringe or extreme behaviors (Huddleston, 2016). Preppers have been grouped with survivalists and other fringe groups such as militias and white supremacists even though their respective goals are quite different. Survivalist groups and other extremist groups have seized apocalyptical myths (religious or secular) and the traditions of American individualism and exceptionalism to promote their distorted views of the world and its demise (Lamy, 1997; 1996). In these narratives, after Armageddon, the new world order will be determined by the most deserving; the strongest who fought for our survival (identified as their particular group.) Yet, as Mitchell (2002) explains, survivalism is not centered on "practical readiness for coming uncertainties" (p. 214) but rather on apocalyptic "storytelling." Such storytelling "is primarily resistance to rationalization, to fixed meanings and predictable process, an encompassing game of make-believe" (p. 215). Conversely, preppers are committed to practicality and self-sufficiency.

The drive to protect one's family from disaster has launched a tremendous prepping economy that expands well beyond the sales of traditional survivalist goods. Beyond survival guides and manuals, the prepping economy now includes popular entertainment, outdoor recreation and wellness, as well as military equipment. In popular entertainment, apocalyptic storylines and prepper characters allow viewers to engage in the creative process of the destruction and rebirth of both society and self. While preppers still purchase knives and guns (for both hunting and protection), the outdoor market also appeals to preppers through its diverse array of camping gear (often repackaged as survival items), nature courses and adventure retreats. Given their interest in natural resources, preppers often practice sustainability by producing or purchasing organic and local foods. In the wellness market, preppers become certified in first aid, learn about natural remedies, and practice mindfulness and situational awareness techniques to increase their resilience in a disaster.

To better understand the prepping phenomenon, this book explores the origins and practices of the urban prepper subculture in New York City in the 21st century—an era of intense public anxiety about government and economic instability, environmental catastrophes, pandemics and technological collapse (Beck, 2009). Concerns about all levels of security (ranging from national to personal) drive both public policy and personal decision making. Rather than relying on the promise of aid by government agencies in disasters, Americans have turned to self-protection strategies to ensure their safety. Urban prepping's reliance on self and social bonds rather than on government assistance during disaster is a pragmatic move that harnesses local resource networks and community building to minimize harm. As a participant-observer, I studied the social structure of the NYCPN (NYC Prepper's Network), the city's only publicly-known prepping group, to analyze how their organization, rituals and language demonstrate their commitment to self-reliance and the weakened belief in the bond between government and citizen in a time of crisis.

My study draws on symbolic interaction theory to explore how NYCPN's membership practices work to have a long-term impact on behavior. Based on extensive fieldwork completed in 2017–18 and 43 in-depth interviews I conducted (with NYCPN members, independent preppers, prepping consultants and prepping suppliers), my exploratory research compares the NYCPN's social solidarity (Collins, 2004) and its prepping strategies with the strategies of independent preppers. Independent preppers are not members of a formal prepping group. While they may sometimes attend classes or events related to prepping, independent preppers engage in prepping practices alone and do not train with a group. In the event of a disaster, independent preppers do not plan to survive with or gain assistance from anyone beyond their close circle of family and/or close friends. Independent preppers have a wide range of incomes—from extremely wealthy to modest.

In 2010, NYCPN was established to serve as a group for city dwellers to learn and to share knowledge about prepping. Their mission is based on three principals: learning, commitment and trust. As explained on the NYCPN Meetup page (2019),

> NYC Preppers Network is an Emergency Preparedness and Wilderness group for city dwellers that are concerned with preparing for disasters. Some of us don't live in a home, have garages, wells, basements or attics to store our survival gear in. Most of us live in apartments. City occupants face a different set of challenges. Space, Food Storage, Water, Security, Sanitation, Evacuation Routes and many other issues are of a great concern for city dwellers.

To work on overcoming these numerous challenges, the NYCPN engages in activities ranging from lectures to weekend excursions at various skill levels. Therefore, my field research has encompassed sites ranging from a church meeting room in Washington Heights to a remote snowy mountainside in the Catskills. Regardless of the physical location, field research has meant "the small scale, the here-and-now of face-to-face interaction … the scene of action and the site of social actors" (Collins, 2004, p. 23).

The NYCPN's (2019)

> primary goal is to create a community network of like-minded individuals who share their knowledge of all things related to self-sufficiency … to establish a network of folks to share ideas with, learn from and eventually hope to trust should the need arise.

In 2019, the number of members was 459. However, most meetings and excursions attract between 20–30 members. The majority of group members are people of color. Group members are located across the boroughs with most living in Manhattan, the Bronx, Queens and Brooklyn. Some members also live on Long Island or in New Jersey, but they still participate in the group. Most group members are middle-aged and have families. NYCPN members are in the age range of responsibility; they have people and property to protect. The members also hold jobs in diverse economic sectors such as emergency response, law, retail, security, technology, tourism and education.

In 2012, National Geographic's hit reality television series, *Doomsday Preppers*, introduced America to the prepper stereotype: a camouflage-wearing and gun-toting white male fixated on protecting himself and his loved ones against a dangerous unknown. The series profiled (and sometimes mocked) preppers who stockpiled supplies, weapons and other items to prepare for the apocalypse. Through staged performances of masculine labor and manly rituals, this show cast prepping as a predominately white masculine activity (Kelly, 2016) with few preppers of color or female preppers shown. The enormous popularity of *Doomsday Preppers* gave rise to other reality television shows such as *Apocalypse Preppers, Doomsday Castles* and *Meet the Preppers*. In addition to television shows, popular American movies (such as *Mad Max: Fury Road*) were also cashing in on our fear of the apocalypse, offering "a glimpse of what the end might be like—thought experiments that provoke us to think about the unthinkable, dress rehearsals for a show we hope will never open" (Biskind, 2018, p. 25).

Hollywood depictions of preppers reflect an exaggerated expression of American individualism, a core theme in preparedness. Given the popularity of apocalyptic storylines and the extreme characterization of preppers, Foster (2014) refers to this genre as "apocotainment": the apocalypse as entertainment for the masses. In analyzing reality television shows on prepping, Kelly (2016) argues that male performances of disaster preparedness promote hegemonic masculinity by staging scenarios that require stereotypically "manly" skills for survival. Disaster scenarios, such as widespread chaos and destruction, are perceived to require a militaristic outlook to prevail in the imaginary post-apocalyptic world (Christian, 2016). After studying the representations of women preppers in the reality television series *Doomsday Preppers*, Christian (2016) finds that the show's depictions of female preppers are framed only to reinforce the recuperation of wounded hegemonic masculinity rather than recognizing the women's respective prepping abilities. As the televised preppers engage in intense labor and invent novel ways to escape disaster, their actions encourage viewers to tap into the collective belief in the power of the fierce white male hero, full of bravado and might, that has a starring role in the popular American imagination.

This stereotype of the American prepper depicted in the media disappears in the context of New York. New York preppers are not exclusively white males who exhibit traits of hegemonic masculinity. The majority of the NYCPN are people of color. Preppers are African American. Preppers are Puerto Rican. Preppers are Mexican. Preppers are Asian. Many preppers are also women. These are the people left out of the "prepper as hero" narrative.

This is particularly surprising, considering that Jason Charles, the leader of the NYCPN, a rugged African American firefighter (described as "calendar-worthy"), actually appeared on the *Doomsday Prepper* televised series. In reflecting on the white male stereotype of preppers, Inshirah, a female, African American member of the NYCPN, explained:

> That cowboy idea doesn't apply to everyone in prepping. Preppers aren't necessarily those white guys in the backwoods or the guys wearing tactical gear. This isn't about being an individual, the lone wolf. This involves mothers and families. This is about the city. That's not who we are and what we are about.

I believe that she is right.

Furthermore, New York's white preppers also do not fit easily into the low to middle income economic stereotype portrayed by the media. The New York prepping world also includes America's extremely wealthy whites—multi-millionaires and billionaires. For these white elites, prepping has little to do with independently surviving disaster in difficult conditions. For this prepping set, disaster preparedness requires staff, involves escaping to a private hideaway in a distant exotic locale or tucking oneself away in a posh safe room to nosh on treats prepared by the chef.

My research in studying New York preppers revealed to me that analyzing this phenomenon solely according to the national political context and its links to individualism is misguided. Instead, I argue that urban preparedness is not really about the national. Preparedness is about the local, where the work happens. It is about place. It is about self. It is about tribe. It is about connection. Therefore, I argue that the goal of urban preparedness is more closely connected to other philosophical underpinnings such as Stanley Cavell's (2004, p. 326) concept of "moral perfectionism," in that being triggered by crisis causes one "to seek to know what you are made of". In keeping with Emerson (1841), urban preparedness is about self-reliance as an aversion to conformity, casting off one way of knowing the world and embracing the challenge that "character teaches above our wills" (p. 184). By stepping outside of the identity of a typical city dweller, urban preppers break free from their way of knowing the world and expand their respective self-identities to include new roles and ways of engaging in life as New Yorkers. One NYCPN member explained, "We are about getting you comfortable in the discomfort, pushing you past your normal way of life."

Within New York's prepping subculture, prepping is a practice of strengthening one's mental acuity as well as one's skills. The focus is on improving one's self to make a greater contribution to the group. In this regard, prepping seems to require more than just stuffing a big bag with emergency supplies. When adapting to tremendous pressure or adjusting quickly to harsh surroundings, responding to disaster requires a presence of mind that reminds one that "nothing is at last sacred but the integrity of your own mind" (Emerson, 1841, p. 178). This moment calls for self-reliance, Emerson's interior turn; the demand of silence and attention to the inner self as it asserts knowledge. In such an instance, one engages in the project of moral perfectionism by moving toward one's further self. Perfectionism in this sense is not about striving for superior achievement in all aspects of life, but determining what makes a life good by exploring how to fulfill our duties to one another given our limitations (Levine, 2011).

Urban life offers the chance to pursue perfectionism by promising a rich and authentic experience that is based on risk; the risk to know oneself and the attempt to know "the other" (Holden, 2017). For city dwellers, this opportunity for exploration and connection is what makes a life good. Cities have always been at the intersection of the strange and the risky. As Jane Jacobs (1961) notes, "Great cities are not like towns, only larger. They are not like suburbs, only denser. They differ from towns and suburbs in basic ways, and one of these is that cities are, by definitions, full of strangers" (p. 30). To maintain order in a sea of strangers, New Yorkers have always had to rely on a discrete code to assure and assess safety. As Sennett (1992) observes,

> ... the rituals by strangers on crowded streets give each other little clues of reassurance which leave each person in isolation at the same time; you drop your eyes rather than stare at a stranger as a way of reassuring him you are safe; you engage in the pedestrian ballet of moving out of each other's way ...
>
> (p. 299)

This etiquette of reservation and formality serves as a buffer. In addition to introducing a level of civility, it also reinforces a sense of distance from one another.[7] Through this figurative distance, we are able to remain tolerant of unacceptable behavior while simultaneously assessing our safety. Moving beyond a city made of a "world of strangers" (Lofland, 1973) to a city made for democratic progress (and the individual pursuit of perfectionism) requires the public realm.

The public realm is "the city's quintessential social territory" (Lofland, 1998, p. 9). The public realm encompasses treasured parochial and public spaces in urban life such as Washington Square's dog runs and political protests like the 2017 Women's March. In our common spaces, through our varied and daily interactions with one another, we practice local democracy. For the public realm to function successfully, so that it may reflect both the pleasures and tensions of city life, the expression of a shared set of social values among strangers—a sense of urban citizenship—is required. Urban citizenship is based on the influence of civil society on citizenship (Holston, 1999), and consists of five clusters of rights and responsibilities: safety, political engagement, tolerance, recognition and freedom (Beauregard and Bounds, 2000).

Urban prepping should be considered as an extension of this form of localized citizenship. First, urban prepping takes place in the public realm; prepping meetings are held in public spaces like Central Park and in parochial spaces such as church meeting rooms. Second, safety is a responsibility shared by both the state and citizens. However, New York's recent history of disasters has demonstrated the government's limitations in protecting its citizens. As a result, some citizens have sought to protect themselves by learning and practicing prepping strategies. Huddleston's (2016) participant observation study of a Midwestern prepping group indicates that the micro-resilience of these groups enhances larger local systems and may improve a community's ability to withstand disaster. Therefore, urban prepping may prove to be a vital measure in closing a perceived gap in our emergency response system.

A specific example of closing the perceived gap in New York's emergency response system is a coordinated response among neighborhood groups in the aftermath of Hurricane Sandy. As explained by one former gang member and prepper from the Lower East Side:

> The first night of the blackout, there was a gunshot and cops all around. We figured we'd better drop colors or we'd be wearing a noose instead. The OG's from all the gangs figured it out. Figured out which gang had more trucking licenses so we could get stuff in and out of our neighbors for our people. So, that's what we did. The women were incredible in finding out whatever we needed and the trucks brought it all in. We'd dropped colors until it was over.

Joining an urban prepper group or even connecting periodically with other preppers could also be interpreted as a form of political engagement. Rather than remaining unknown and alienated, urban preppers are banding together to form networks and to learn skills that are useful in helping others, not just themselves, in crises. Given their interest in preparedness, preppers might serve as community advocates to ensure that the local government meets its safety responsibilities such as conducting building and fire code inspections. Through studying online prepping communities, Kabel and Chmidling (2014) found that these preppers made health-related decisions such as changing lifestyle choices (such as dietary improvements and exercising) to reduce future health risks to improve their chances of survival after disaster, and sharing information regarding treatment for both emergencies and long-term health care needs in the absence of medical professionals. Beyond information sharing, urban preppers might also take on the role of advocating for better access to neighborhood health resources.

Given the popularity of apocalyptic storylines and the extreme characterization of preppers, one might expect New York preppers to be viewed negatively or with some suspicion. However, city life requires that we refrain from preventing non-violent activities or forms of expression that may run counter to our beliefs. Therefore, New York preppers benefit from the tolerance exercised by other city dwellers. In exchange, preppers must also recognize that other people may not share their same commitment to preparing for disaster. This right and responsibility allows us to inhabit the same space with one another.

Urban prepping may also be considered an expression of the right to recognition. For people of color who believe that their communities may have been underserved during previous disasters, prepping represents agency and a demand for recognition to address inequalities in the distribution of resources and aid. In this regard, urban prepping makes an important break with misperceptions about preppers' motivation to prepare against disaster and a lack of trust in the government. As depicted in the mass media, a stereotypical prepper's drive to stockpile and prepare for disaster is spurred by conspiracy theories such as a fear of the sudden loss of First Amendment rights. In short, a stereotypical prepper seems to be motivated by the fear that "the government is coming for me." Conversely, after observing media coverage of communities of color and poor communities receiving little emergency support during disasters such as Hurricane Katrina (Dyson, 2006), an urban prepper may believe that one should prepare themselves for disaster. Therefore, an urban prepper may be driven by the fear that "the government isn't coming for me." Finally, urban prepping also underscores the importance of freedom in city culture. New Yorker preppers are developing new social relations and make new claims for their interests and needs in city life. In other words, urban prepping provides a meaningful outlet for exploring a deeper understanding of one's self and one's responsibilities to others. However, urban prepping also demonstrates the danger of freedom, specifically the freedom to opt out of civil society. By retreating to secret locations or hiding in safe rooms, powerful elites choose isolation over democracy.

In keeping with Mills (2018) and Huddleston (2016), my exploratory research contributes to scholarship on prepping by using original empirical data to analyze the motivations for and practices of prepping in New York. Based on data gathered from field research as well as in-depth interviews, my work aims to provide a detailed and comprehensive analysis of New York prepping as understood by members of this subculture. This book is divided into four sections that provide a comprehensive approach for analyzing the rise and practice of prepping in New York.

Part I: Understanding the rise of prepping in the global city of New York

Following Chapter 1's overview of the study, Chapter 2 provides a profile of New York as a global city, outlining both its tremendous appeal and its tremendous dangers. As one prepper consultant explained, "Living in New York is like living on the X." Given New York's power and prestige as a global capital, it is an attractive target for terrorist attacks. For New Yorkers, the advantages of city life seem to outweigh the risks represented by the city's recent history of disasters and potential threats. However, in the wake of these crises, many New Yorkers have now sought to make preparations to protect themselves against disaster. Since 2001, New York has experienced several crises (or threats of disaster) that reflect the major categories of "Doomsday" scenarios including: terrorists attacks, natural disasters, pandemics, technological failures and economic or governmental collapse. Each type of disaster (or its threat) has placed an unusual set of stressors on New Yorkers. Next, the NYC prepper economy is examined to learn how urban preppers utilize markets such as the city's local foods network and outdoor recreation retailers as well as prepping consultants and suppliers. The chapter closes with a discussion of my participant-observation research method and my subject position as a New Yorker studying this particular (and peculiar) topic. My experience as a New Yorker who has endured each of these disasters provides me with a unique sociological lens for studying prepping. Therefore, my reflexive approach encompasses a practice of participant-observation, in-depth interviewing, fieldwork (attending events such as meetings, retreats, conferences and lectures) and archival research (reviewing prepper literature and discussions of prepping in the popular press).

Chapter 3 explores current representations of the apocalypse and prepping throughout popular entertainment. These representations hold meaning for both mainstream audiences and preppers. In popular entertainment (television, movie and books), apocalyptic storylines allow audiences to engage in the creative process of the destruction and rebirth of both society and self. These narratives reinforce collective anxiety about the future and the importance of self-reliance and agency. This chapter also examines the influence of popular culture on preppers. movies and books that are significant to New Yorker preppers are discussed. The NYCPN has also been widely covered in the popular press. Members have sometimes viewed this coverage as negative or demeaning. To combat such coverage, group members have become media savvy to promote a more positive image of prepping.

Part II: Prepping in New York: Going it alone or going together

Chapter 4 studies the prepping strategy of sheltering in place (Bugging In) that is practiced by both the extremely wealthy and the middle class. Based on their economic position and location, extremely wealthy New Yorkers sometimes construct safe rooms (often smaller interior apartments within their apartments) as places of refuge during disaster. Given their higher income, these posh preppers are also able to purchase expensive prepping equipment in response to reports of disasters in other areas or in the early stages of potential disasters in New York. Middle-class New Yorkers have more modest preparations for sheltering in place. Given that safe rooms are unaffordable to them, this segment of the population stores supplies in "prepper closets" (designated areas of their homes, which are often small apartments). These preppers have also developed strategies to protect their homes and apartments from certain disasters.

Chapter 5 discusses the prepping strategy of leaving an area to escape disaster (Bugging Out) that is practiced by both the extremely wealthy and the middle class. For the extremely wealthy, bugging out practices include purchasing secret strategic relocation destinations (homes in exclusive and remote areas) as well as purchasing curated luxury bug out bags that contain state-of-the-art survival equipment. Middle-class New York preppers also seek to escape disaster through more modest means such as leaving the city on foot to reach safe locations in the Tri-State Area and preparing their own bug out bags with more reasonably priced equipment.

Part III: Urban prepping and symbolic interaction

Chapters 6–8 provide a narrative and analysis of my experience as a participant-observer in the NYCPN. Unlike independent preppers who rely only on their individual skills without support, this group learns and practices prepping together in the hope of bolstering their success in surviving (and sustaining themselves throughout) a disaster. Throughout these chapters, symbolic interaction theory is used to study the NYCPN as a social structure and its valuable use of symbols, rituals and language to reinforce prepping behavior. After discussing the NYCPN's history and organizational structure, the narrative then recounts and analyzes my experience at different types of group events (retreats, excursions, workshops and meetings) as well as relevant non-group prepping events.

Part IV: Urban prepping as a new reflection of citizenship

Chapter 9 concludes by suggesting that prepping is a meaningful lens for examining both the anxiety about and promise of 21stcentury America. In the Cold War era, Americans were concerned about civil defense against an ideological enemy. In our current period, we are confronted by many potential enemies—political, economic, environmental and technological. Urban prepping is a reflection of how we depend on community (and self), not solely government, in moments of crisis. The qualities and challenges of urban prepping are discussed in comparison to preppers in rural and suburban areas. New directions for research on urban prepping groups are introduced. For example, the social structure and interactions of an urban prepper group that plans to survive together must be analyzed to understand how the recognition of future dependency impacts its agenda and practices. The social structure and interactions within female-led prepping groups (or all-female groups) should also be investigated to learn if and how their agendas and practices might differ from male-led groups (or predominately male groups). In future research on urban prepping groups, symbolic interactionism remains a critical tool for analysis.

Notes

1 News of the election results were quickly replaced by the continued coverage of events such as the deadly California wildfires (Fuller et al., 2018) and allegations of voter suppression and ballot fraud (Gardner et al., 2018).

2 My analysis of Gallup's yearly polling on Terrorism (2002–18) indicates that every year roughly 42% of Americans worry a great deal about a future attack while roughly 28% of Americans indicate that they worry a fair amount.

3 According to the Chapman University Survey of American Fears, the top fears for 2018 were: Corrupt government officials (73.6%); Pollution of oceans, rivers and lakes (61.6%); Pollution of drinking water (60.7%); Not having enough money for the future (57%); People I love becoming seriously ill (56.5%); People I love dying (56.4%); Air pollution (55.1%); Extinction of plant and animal species (54.1%); Global warming and climate change (53.2%); and high medical bills (52.9%).

4 In this regard, the definition acknowledges how preppers conceptualize disaster as a result of both experience and fear (imagining the consequences of a disaster type that has yet to occur in the United States such as a large nuclear strike).

5 However, this argument should now be reexamined in response to the rise of "Brexit Preppers," Britons who fear crisis after Britain's withdrawal from the European Union (Castle, 2018).

6 In American culture, references to the deadly power and evil of the Four Horsemen remain a constant. As a child half-listening to Sunday sermons, any strange scripture about the Four Horseman only made me daydream even more about the conquests in *King Arthur and the Knights of the Roundtable*, my favorite book series. I could only be terrified by the mesmerizing power and deadly evil of The Four Horsemen of Mid-Atlantic Championship Wrestling (Ric Flair, Arn Anderson, Ole Anderson and Tully Blanchard).

7 An older New York Guidebook makes this assertion more humorously and definitely more cynically in observing, "Perhaps more than in any other city, a sense of nervy self-preservation is rife here: people make studied efforts to avoid eye contact, and any unusual behavior clears a space immediately: the atmosphere of impending violence is sometimes sniffable" (Dunford and Holland, 2002).

References

Alexander, D. A. (2014). Emergency and disaster planning. In M. Fordham, A. Lopez-Carresi, B. Wisner, I. Kelman, Jc. Gaillard (Eds.), *Disaster management: International lessons in risk reduction, response and recovery* (pp. 125–141). London: Routledge.

Altheide, D. L. (2017). *Terrorism and the politics of fear* (2nd ed.). Lanham: Rowman and Littlefield.

Beauregard, R. A., and Bounds, A. (2000). Urban citizenship. In E. F. Isin (Ed.), *Democracy, citizenship and the global city* (pp. 243–256). London: Routledge.

Beck, U. (2009). *World at risk*. Cambridge: Polity Press.

Berger, P. L. (1963). *Invitation to sociology: A humanistic perspective*. Garden City, NY: Anchor Books.

Biskind, P. (2018). *The sky is falling: How vampires, zombies, androids, and superheroes made America great for extremism*. New York: The New Press.

Castle, S. (2018, October 16). British hoarders stock up on supplies, preparing for Brexit. *The New York Times*. Retrieved from https://www.nytimes.com/2018/10/16/world/europe/brexit-preppers-united-kingdom.html.

Cavell, S. (2004). *Cities of words: Pedagogical letters on a register of the moral life*. Cambridge: Belknap Press of Harvard University Press.

Charles, J. (2014). *Emergency bag essentials: Everything you need to bug out*. New York: Potter Style.

Christian, T. A. (2016). The recuperation of wounded hegemonic masculinity on doomsday preppers. In L. A. Clark, A. Firestone, and M. F. Pharr (Eds.), *The last midnight essays on apocalyptic narratives in millennial media* (pp. 48–59). Jefferson, NC: McFarland.

Collins, R. (2004). *Interaction ritual chains*. Princeton, NJ: Princeton University Press.

Davis, J. H., and Gibbons-Neff, T. (2018, October 25). Trump considers closing southern border to migrants. *The New York Times*. Retrieved from https://www.nytimes.com/2018/10/25/us/politics/trump-army-border-mexico.html.

Dunford, M., and Holland, J. (2002). *The rough guide to New York City*. London: Rough Guides.

Dyson, M. E. (2006). *Come hell or high water: Hurricane Katrina and the color of disaster*. New York: Basic Civitas.

Edwards, A. (2009). *Preparedness now!: An emergency survival guide*. Port Townsend, WA: Process.

Emerson, R. W. (2001). Self-Reliance (1841). In *Nature and selected essays*. New York: Penguin Classics.

Fausset, R., Mazzei, P., and Blinder, A. (2018, October 11). Search and rescue begins amid ruins of Florida coast. *The New York Times*. Retrieved from https://www.nytimes.com/2018/10/11/us/hurricane-michael-live-updates-florida.html.

Foster, G. A. (2014). *Hoarders, doomsday preppers, and the culture of apocalypse*. New York: Palgrave Macmillan.

Fuller, T., Medina, J., and Real, J. A. D. (2018, November 9). 'The whole world was on fire': Infernos choke California, piling on the grief. *The New York Times*. Retrieved from https://www.nytimes.com/2018/11/09/us/california-fires.html.

Gallop. (2017, November 4). *Terrorism*. Retrieved from http://news.gallup.com/poll/4909/terrorism-united-states.aspx.

Gardner, A., Reinhard, B., and Rozsa, L. (2018, November 9). Prospect of another recount in Florida sparks partisan showdown. *The Washington Post*. Retrieved from https://www.washingtonpost.com/politics/prospect-of-another-recount-in-florida-provoke s-partisan-battle/2018/11/09/b513aa12-e447-11e8-b759-3d88a5ce9e19_story.html.

Glassner, B. (2010). *The culture of fear: Why Americans are afraid of the wrong things: Crime, drugs, minorities, teen moms, killer kids, mutant microbes, plane crashes, road rage, and so much more*. New York: Basic Books.

Holden, M. (2017). *Pragmatic justifications for the sustainable city: Acting in the common place*. New York: Routledge.

Holston, J. (1999). *Cities and citizenship*. Durham: Duke University Press.

Huddleston, C. (2016). "Prepper" as resilient citizen: What preppers can teach us about surviving disasters. In M. Companion and M. S. Chaiken (Eds.), *Responses to disasters and climate change: Understanding vulnerability and fostering resilience* (pp. 239–248). Boca Raton: CRC Press.

Jacobs, J. (1961). *The death and life of great American cities*. New York: Random House.

Kabel, A., and Chmidling, C. (2014). Disaster prepper: Health, identity, and American survivalist culture. *Human Organization*, 73(3), 258–266.

Kelly, C. R. (2016). The man-pocalpyse: Doomsday preppers and the rituals of apocalyptic manhood. *Text and Performance Quarterly*, 36, 95–114.

Lamy, P. (1996). *Millennium rage: Survivalists, white supremacists, and the doomsday prophecy*. New York: Plenum Press.

Lamy, P. (1997). Secularizing the millennium: Survivalists, militias, and the new world order. In T. Robbins and S. J. Palmer (Eds.), *Millennium, messiahs, and mayhem: contemporary apocalyptic movements*. New York: Routledge.

Levine, P. (2011, October 26). *The importance of the inner life to moral philosophy*. Retrieved from http://peterlevine.ws/?p=7326.

Lofland, L. H. (1973). *A world of strangers: Order and action in urban public space*. New York: Basic Books.

Lofland, L. H. (1998). *The public realm: Exploring the city's quintessential social territory*. Hawthorne, New York: Aldine de Gruyter.

Lurie, A. (1967). *Imaginary friends*. London: Heinemann.

Mills, M. F. (2018). Preparing for the unknown... unknowns: 'Doomsday' prepping and disaster risk anxiety in the United States. *Journal of Risk Research*, 1–13.

Mitchell, R. G. (2002). *Dancing at Armageddon: Survivalism and chaos in modern times*. Chicago: University of Chicago Press.

Molina, B. (2018, November 6). Mysterious interstellar object floating in space might be alien, say Harvard researchers. *USA Today*. Retrieved from https://www.usatoda y.com/story/news/nation-now/2018/11/06/mysterious-oumuamua-object-space-a lien-probe-harvard/1900213002/.

New York City Prepper's Network (APN Chapter). (2019). Retrieved from https:// www.meetup.com/NYC-Preppers-Network/.

Oxford Dictionaries. (2019). *Apokalupsis*. Retrieved from https://en.oxforddictionaries. com/definition/us/apocalypse.

Peek, L. A., and Sutton, J. N. (2003). An exploratory comparison of disasters, riots and terrorist acts. *Disasters*, 27(4), 319–335. doi:10.1111/j.0361-3666.2003.00236.x.

Perry, R. W. (2006). What is a disaster? In E. L. Quarantelli, H. Rodriguez, and R. R. Dynes (Eds.), *Handbook of disaster research* (pp. 1–15). New York: Springer.

Perry, R. W. (2018). Defining disaster. In H. Rodríguez, W. Donner, and J.E. Trainor, (Eds.), *Handbook of disaster research* (2nd ed.) (pp. 3–22). Cham, Switzerland: Springer.

Perry, R.W. and Lindell, M. K. (2007). *Emergency Planning*. Hoboken, New Jersey: Wiley.

Quarantelli, E. L. (2000). Disaster research. In E. F. Borgatta and R. J. V. Montgomery (Eds.), *Encyclopedia of sociology* (pp. 682–688). New York, NY: Macmillan.

Quarantelli, E. L. (2005). A social science research agenda for the disasters of the 21st century. In R. W. Perry and E. L. Quarantelli (Eds.), *What is a disaster? New answers to old questions* (pp. 325–396). Philadelphia: Xlibris.

Reinhardt, G. Y. (2017). Imagining worse than reality: Comparing beliefs and intentions between disaster evacuees and survey respondents. *Journal of Risk Research*, 20 (2), 169–194.

Revelation: Chapter 6: 1–8. Retrieved from https://www.kingjamesbibleonline.org/ Revelation-Chapter-6/.

Robertson, C., Mele, C., and Tavernise, S. (2018, October 27). 11 killed in synagogue massacre; Suspect charged with 29 counts. *The New York Times*. Retrieved from https://www. nytimes.com/2018/10/27/us/active-shooter-pittsburgh-synagogue-shooting.html.

Saad, L. (2018, December 28). U.S. mood remains mixed at end of 2018. *Gallup*. Retrieved from https://news.gallup.com/poll/245639/mood-remains-mixed-end-2018. aspx.

Sennett, R. (1992). *The uses of disorder: Personal identity and city life* (2nd ed.). New York: Vintage Books.

Thrush, G., and Peters, J. W. (2018, November 18). Charges of vote stealing in Florida portend more distrust in system for 2020. Retrieved from https://www.nytimes.com/2018/11/18/us/politics/florida-recount-voter-fraud.html.

van Kempen, R. (2007). Divided cities in the 21st century: Challenging the importance of globalisation. *Journal of Housing and the Built Environment*, 22(1), 13–31. Retrieved from http://www.jstor.org/stable/41107366.

Webb, G. R. (2018). *The cultural turn in disaster research: Understanding resilience and vulnerability through the lens of culture*. In H. Rodríguez, W. Donner, and J. E. Trainor (Eds.), *Handbook of disaster research* (pp. 109–121). Cham, Switzerland: Springer.

Wilkinson College of Arts, Humanities and Social Sciences. (2018, October 16). America's top fears 2018: Chapman University survey of American fears. Retrieved from https://blogs.chapman.edu/wilkinson/2018/10/16/americas-top-fears-2018/.

Woodward, B. (2018). *Fear: Trump in the White House*. New York: Simon and Schuster.

Wootson Jr., C. R., and Horton, A. (2018, October 26). What we know about the 13 pipe bombs sent to prominent democrats and Trump critics. *The Washington Post*. Retrieved from https://www.washingtonpost.com/nation/2018/10/25/bomb-timeline-list-people-targeted-with-packages-devices.

Wuthnow, R. (2010). *Be very afraid: The cultural response to terror, pandemics, environmental devastation, nuclear annihilation, and other threats*. New York: Oxford University Press.

Zraick, K., and Stevens, M. (2018, October 25). Kroger shooting suspect tried to enter black church before killing 2 in Kentucky, police say. *The New York Times*. Retrieved from https://www.nytimes.com/2018/10/25/us/louisville-kroger-shooting.html.

2 New York marks the spot
Living on the X

Since its beginnings as New Amsterdam, countless images of New York have been collected. The New York City Municipal Archives preserves over 200,000 cubic feet of original documents, photographs, ledgers, maps, architectural renderings, manuscripts and moving images about the city (http://www.archives.nyc). The Municipal Archives also maintains a vast public database of more than 870,000 photos from its collection of over 2.2 million images of New York City throughout the 20th century.[1] Like the city itself, the collection's subject areas are expansive and complex, with categories including construction, business, crime, the arts and daily life. However, official archives are no longer our top resources for viewing the multi-faceted life of New Yorkers. Now, through social media, New Yorkers and the city's visitors curate and share their own personal archives of New York. As of 2019, on Instagram (one of the most popular social media platforms), 241 million photos of life in New York are shared under the hashtags (categories) of #nyc, #newyork, #newyorkcity. This staggering number reveals that New York's image as a global financial and creative capital remains steadfast. Yet, the city's image as a place of great risk is increasing, making E.B. White's observation that, "In the mind of whatever perverted dreamer might loose the lightning, New York must hold a steady, irresistible charm" (1949, p. 54) even sharper. The city's intoxicating, often clashing appeal of greed and beauty, power and pleasure, continues to make it a prime target. As Joel Smernoff, the chairman of Black Umbrella, a luxe prepping company, explained to me, "Living in Manhattan is like living on the X." His comment made me think of a familiar image of New York that I see daily, outside my kitchen window overlooking Broadway: a large NYC Department of Emergency Management poster with a rendering of an apocalyptic, nearly submerged city street, reminding people about the importance of preparing for disaster with the slogan: "Disasters Don't Plan Ahead but You Can." For me, there is no forgetting that I live on the X.

X marks the spot—the location of the treasure or target. New York City offers a compelling mix of both. Therefore, this chapter first discusses New York City as a unique locale for prepping. As a global city driven by capital and competition, New York has earned its position as the "X". With its tremendous wealth and its cultural cache, New York offers an embarrassment of riches, but the sharp class division between its classes reminds us that only a select few have access to high levels of wealth. Still, many New Yorkers benefit from the rich culture and social networks to be found in city life. Beyond its profile as a thriving urban center, New York's recent history of terrorist attacks and natural disasters provides an important context for understanding the rising interest in prepping. Furthermore, the city's geography and population size, (particularly Manhattan), poses great challenges to all facets of prepping. Prepping for disaster seems to clash against Manhattan's culture of immediate gratification, yet prepping is also supported by some New Yorkers' interest in sustainability and homesteading. Lastly, this chapter explores my approach to researching New York's prepping culture.

Reflecting on New York's culture in 1895, Mark Twain wrote, "In Boston they ask, how much does he know? In New York, how much is he worth? In Philadelphia, who were his parents?" (p. 48).[2] One hundred and twenty-four years later, Twain's characterization of New York as driven by wealth maintains its currency. With its status as a world banking center and an international tourist destination, as well as a media force that captivates a worldwide audience, New York is a global city (Sassen, 2001, Sassen and Roost, 1999, Castells, 1989). As a global city, New York is a financial and cultural center for the US and the world. New York's position is reinforced by its powerful economy, with worldwide connections that draws on its dominant share of lucrative industries relative to other American cities and benefits from their high levels of employment (Gladstone and Fainstein, 2013). In 2019, New York's powerhouse service economy sectors of finance and real estate, services, tourism industries and media comprised nearly seventy percent of the city's 4.635 million jobs (NYC Economic Development Corporation, 2019).[3] New York is also forecasted to become the largest urban economy in the world by 2035 with the largest finance and business services sector (Adams, 2019).[4] Despite its diverse economy and diverse population, New York is also counted among the most unequal cities in one of the most unequal countries in the world (Halle and Beveridge, 2013). According to the Organisation for Economic Co-operation and Development's (2016) review of developed countries, income inequality in the United States is outranked only by Russia, Turkey, Indonesia, Mexico, Chile, Brazil and South Africa, respectively. For US cities, New York has one of the highest rates of income inequality within the country (Brookings Institute, 2018).

With a diverse population of 8,560,072, New York is the largest city in the US (American Community Survey, 2017). The city's population in 2017 was estimated to be 42.8% white (32.1% non-Hispanic white), 24.3% black (22% non-Hispanic black), 14.1% Asian, 0.4% Native American, with Hispanics of any race represented in 29.1% of the population. (American Community Survey, 2017). New York's racial and ethnic composition is changing due to factors such as the rise in Latino and Asian populations as well as slower rates of white migration to the suburbs (Beveridge and Beveridge, 2013).

New York City is comprised of five boroughs. Brooklyn has the largest population (2.58 million), followed by Queens (2.28 million), Manhattan (1.63 million), the Bronx (1.43 million) and Staten Island (476,179) (NYC Department of City Planning, 2018). Taking into account the city's five boroughs, New York's top five percent of households earn incomes at least 14 times higher than the bottom twenty percent of households (Brookings Institute, 2018). However, the highest income inequality is found within Manhattan, the city's financial and cultural nexus. Manhattan's top 1 percent earned an average of $8.98 million in 2015, 113 times more than the average $79,528 income earned by the bottom 99 percent of Manhattan residents (Economic Policy Institute, 2018). Given the power and wealth enjoyed by the top 1 percent of its residents (or, at least, the illusion of it for the city's other residents), Manhattan offers the pleasures of immediate gratification and self-indulgence. Manhattan may even mark the precise production point [genesis] for what Roberts (2014) describes as The Impulse Society, a socio-economic system that functions to meet our personal desires rather than our collective needs.

However, the adage that "Money can't buy happiness" might actually be true. Since the start of the 21st century, New York has experienced significant crises (or threats of crises) that represent the range of disaster scenarios that are of primary concern for preppers: terrorist attacks, natural disasters, pandemics, technological failure and governmental or economic collapse. Starting with the September 11th terrorist attack on the World Trade Center, New York has experienced five terrorist attacks, all occurring in Manhattan: World Trade Center Attack (2001), Failed Car Bombing of Times Square (2010)[5], Chelsea Bomb Explosion (2016)[6], Truck Driven into People on West Side Bike Path (2017)[7] and the Times Square Port Authority Subway Bomb Partial-Detonation (2017)[8]. Not all attacks were successful; however, each attack was attempted in a public space with the expectation that it would result in significant loss of life and property damage. Manhattan residents also feared a gas attack when a mysterious maple odor wafted through the city once every year from 2005–09. The odor was ultimately determined to be harmless, but went without explanation until 2009 when a city investigation reported that the smell resulted from the processing of the fenugreek plant at a fragrance factory in New Jersey (Barbaro and Schwebber, 2009).

Technological failures have also contributed to the state of unease in the city. In 2003, the Northeastern Blackout left 50 million people without power in eight Northeastern states and parts of Canada (Barron, 2003). Just two years after the September 11th attack, this blackout left New Yorkers without power for nearly two days. While some neighborhoods held block parties and had barbeques on the street, thousands were without mass transit and were forced to walk home or sleep on the street. For New York, the blackout caused a 28% increase in deaths due to accidents, cardiovascular conditions and respiratory problems (Anderson and Bell, 2012). Occasional explosions have also created chaos. Two noteworthy examples include malfunctions of a steam pipe and a gas line. An underground steam pipe (installed in 1924) exploded and shot up a geyser of hot steam and debris from a crater near Grand Central Station in 2007 (Barron, 2007). The geyser lasted for nearly two hours, killing one person (a heart attack) and injuring at least thirty others. In the second example, three buildings in the East Village were destroyed in a gas line explosion due to an illegal tap into a gas line, killing two and injuring nineteen (McKinley, Jr. and Santora, 2016). To obtain quicker profits from high rents, the landlord had an illegal tap put into the main gas line. After being ordered to shut off the first illegal tap, the landlord installed a second hidden tap, which caused the explosion. These technological failures were initially feared to be terrorist attacks by some New Yorkers. In their initial responses to these incidents while in office, both Mayor Bloomberg and Mayor de Blasio reassured the public that the events were in no way related to terrorism.

Beyond periodic severe storms and snow, New York has also been affected by natural disasters. Hurricane Sandy (2012), with its massive size and high winds, stands alone as the worst storm in New York history. Sandy's devastation of the city was tremendous, resulting in the destruction of neighborhoods, 43 deaths, two million residents without power and $19 billion in damages (NYC Special Initiative for Rebuilding and Resiliency, 2013). However, Sandy is not the only storm in New York's recent battle with the effects of climate change. Several tropical storms, hurricanes and tornados have threatened the city—even slight earthquakes. For example, in 2011, just days before Hurricane Irene, an earthquake that originated in Virginia was actually felt in the city (NYC Emergency Management, 2011).[9] In advance of Hurricane Irene, the city government evacuated 370,000 people, shut down mass-transit, and sandbagged storefronts. However, the storm's major impact was on the suburbs, with no storm-related fatalities in the city (Dolnick, 2011). In late 2010, tornados struck the Bronx, Brooklyn and Queens. According to the National Weather Service (2010), the Bronx tornado was only the second tornado to hit the borough since its first recorded tornado in 1974. With winds averaging 100 miles per hour, the brief Bronx tornado caused damage to property and injuries to seven people. During that same year, the separate Brooklyn and Queens tornados caused extensive property damage (including thousands of fallen trees, crushed cars and downed power lines) and one driver was killed when a tree fell on her car (Rivera and Roston, 2010). Brooklyn and Queens were again struck by tornadoes in 2012. While there were no fatalities, a waterspout was reported, as well as some minor damage (Santora and Magg, 2012). In 2018, a tornado whipped through College Point, Queens, knocking down trees and tearing the siding off of homes (Wilson, 2018).

Hurricane Sandy also served as a unique warning for urban preppers about relying only on government support in the aftermath of a disaster. Because NYC is an international tourist destination and host of mega sporting events, the city government may risk privileging visitors over residents in allocating resources in the aftermath of a disaster. The city government's initial decision to hold the 2012 New York City Marathon in the wake of Hurricane Sandy sparked concerns about such a possibility. A furious public debate surrounded Mayor Bloomberg's decision to have the marathon despite extensive damage to neighborhoods along the race route (in particular, areas in Staten Island). Initially, it was assumed that New Yorkers would support the Mayor's decision, because hosting the annual Marathon would boost the city's morale and its tourism revenue. However, the Mayor was forced to cancel the race due to public backlash and resistance to the event as the competition for resources grew between residents and race participants.

Since 1970, the NYC Marathon has been organized by the New York Road Runners (NYRR), a city runners' organization. The NYC marathon is an annual, 26.2 miles long race that courses through all five boroughs. Supported by the NYRR, the city government, and corporate sponsors, the race promotes running and raises money for charities (https://www.nyrr.org/). In 2011, the year before Hurricane Sandy, the NYC marathon had 47,000 runners, 2 million spectators, and a television audience of about 315 million (Macur and Belson, October 13, 2012).

City residents are usually important stakeholders in the planning and hosting of mega sporting events (Sautter and Leisen, 1999). At mega sporting events, residents often provide local color by serving as volunteers and interacting with event participants (Smith et al., 2014). However, in the wake of Hurricane Sandy, many New Yorkers failed to support the race because they believed that the city officials and race organizers had prioritized the interests of tourists over residents. It was feared that while many New Yorkers would be without power, water and shelter, these same provisions would be supplied to the race and its participants. However, among the general public, there was some confusion over the ownership and distribution of generators and other supplies. Many residents were concerned that the generators would be used to supply power to the race, and not to help those in need. Media reports only reinforced this fear, by broadcasting images of generators on television and in the newspaper, suggesting that the city government was supporting a sporting event to generate tourism revenue rather than helping its citizens. These assumptions were not entirely accurate, as it is important to note that these generators were owned by the Road Runners organization, not publicly owned generators that needed to be installed in hard-hit areas. The water, food, clothing and medical supplies for the Marathon would have also been provided by the Road Runners. However, a significant number of already overburdened police officers (roughly 1,000) would have been stationed throughout the race rather than working in areas devasted by the hurricane and monitoring gas stations.

Overall, residents perceived that the costs of holding the 2012 NYC Marathon outweighed any benefits. In addition, race officials felt that holding the race would have damaged the image of the Marathon and the Road Runners, and jeopardized the ability of future races to raise money for charities. The debate and subsequent cancellation of the race occurred in a very short, roughly three-day, period. On Tuesday, it was announced that the race would be held. By Friday afternoon, the race was cancelled. The controversy seemed to serve as a warning to preppers; the confusion about the distribution of water and power reminded preppers of the possibility of unfair allocation of resources by the government during disasters. Even after learning that the water and power generators were private resources owned by the NYRR, preppers still may have been wary of the city government's interest or ability to aid hurricane victims because it was still redistributing an important resource to the Marathon—police security. Without police security, some neighborhoods and people attempting to get fuel would have been more vulnerable.

Beyond natural disasters, New Yorkers must also contend with the possible threat of pandemics and epidemics. Given that the city is a gateway to the world, there is a higher risk for the spread of diseases that could be contracted from international travel or exposure to infected people who had recently returned from travel. In 2016, New Yorkers faced the possibility of the rapid spread of the Zika virus which causes severe birth defects in newborns whose mothers were infected while pregnant. According to the New York City Department of Health (2019), the city had 987 cases of Zika in 2016, with all of those linked to travel to a Zika-affected area. Although the number of cases has declined significantly since 2016, individuals must still be cautious about traveling to areas with Zika outbreaks because a vaccine has still not been discovered (Jacobs, 2019). New York was also at risk for exposure to the highly fatal Ebola virus at the height of the epidemic in West Africa during 2014. According to the Center for Disease Control (2014), New York's status as a popular port of entry for travelers from West Africa, as well as its sizable community of West African immigrants who travel back to their home countries, and healthcare workers who travel to West Africa to treat Ebola patients, heightened the possibility that an infected person could arrive in the city.

In 2014, Craig Spencer, a New York doctor who treated Ebola patients in Guinea, contracted the virus upon his return to the city (Santora, 2014). After being isolated and treated for nineteen days, the doctor recovered. In discussing his experience as an Ebola patient in New York, Spencer (2015) argued that the city government and media wasted valuable time fueling public fear about the virus rather than explaining how it is spread:

> People fear the unknown, and fear in measured doses can be therapeutic and inform rational responses, but in excess, it fosters poor decision making that can be harmful. After my diagnosis, the media and politicians could have educated the public about Ebola. Instead, they spent hours retracing my steps through New York and debating whether Ebola can be transmitted through a bowling ball.
>
> (p. 1091)

During that same year, the nation also experienced its first documented outbreak of EV-D68, a virus associated with severe respiratory illness sometimes resulting in death. Almost all of the 1,395 confirmed cases in 2014 were children, many of whom had a history of respiratory problems such as asthma or wheezing (Center for Disease Control, 2018). The city also endured an outbreak of the H1N1 influenza (Swine Flu) epidemic in 2009. To prevent the rapid spread of the influenza within New York's public school system, fifteen schools were closed throughout Queens and Brooklyn (Hartocollis, 2009). H1N1 caused the death of twelve New Yorkers, including a Queens middle school principal, and an estimated 550,000 became sick (Hartocollis, 2009).

City neighborhood conditions and cultural factors increased the spread of two disease outbreaks. From October 2018 through April 2019, orthodox Jewish communities in Brooklyn experienced a measles outbreak of at least 483 cases (Kilgannon, 2019). In response to this public health emergency, Mayor de Blasio required mandatory measles vaccinations for unvaccinated individuals living in Williamsburg, Brooklyn, and Governor Cuomo removed religious exemptions for the vaccination (McKinley, 2019). A 2015 outbreak of Legionnaires' disease in the Bronx caused by a contaminated cooling tower, resulted in twelve deaths and 120 people becoming ill (Hu, 2015). The outbreak prompted a city government action requiring building owners to conduct quarterly inspections of their cooling towers. In 2019, two residents in the NYCHA's Bronx River Houses contracted Legionnaires' disease due to a contamination in their water system (Hicks, 2019). Outbreaks of this disease are common in low-income neighborhoods due to the lack of maintenance on building cooling systems and the weakened health of many poor residents (Farnham, et al., 2014).

Lasting over eighteen months (from December 2007 until June 2009), The Great Recession was the longest of any recession since World War II (National Bureau of Economic Research, 2010). The economic downturn was fueled by the financial crisis of 2007–09 and the related subprime mortgage crisis which originated from the power and practices of Wall Street (Sorkin, 2009; Rajan, 2011). Almost immediately, all of New York, not just wary preppers, could see the effects of the recession, such as job losses, a decrease in the lucrative tourist market and mortgage loan defaults that affected entire neighborhoods in the outer boroughs. These realities sparked anxiety about American's economic stability and the strength of New York's position as a global city. Yet, in all phases of the financial crisis, Wall Street prevailed through its successful lobbying to deregulate the financial sector, its quick turnover of risky mortgage loans and its bailout by the national government (Halle and Beveridge, 2013).

In Fall 2011, the Occupy Wall Street political movement attempted to usurp the power of capital by protesting (and camping out) for roughly three months in New York's financial district. With their slogan: "We are the 99%," Occupy Wall Street protesters rallied against the income and wealth inequality between America's richest 1% and the rest of the nation. The protest called attention to the reality that "income inequality was grinding down the middle class, increasing the ranks of poor, and creating a permanent underclass of able, willing but jobless people" (New York Times Editorial, 2011). While the movement did not gain much leverage against Wall Street, it did gain the support of some New Yorkers who struggle to make ends meet. For NYC preppers, the Occupy Wall Street movement served as a reminder of the dangers of financial collapse and social unrest. High-net-worth preppers took to constructing safe rooms or buying safe havens in exotic locations while middle class preppers increased their stockpiles and tried to tuck more money away in their savings.

In the event of disaster, it will likely prove difficult for most New Yorkers to leave the city without advance warning or access to air travel. As one NYC prepper observed, "It is like a hall of mirrors. It looks like there are so many ways out but there really aren't. It's an illusion. The city has geographical limitations if you plan to leave by a car or to walk." While New York has an extensive mass transit system, it is structured for travel between boroughs. The city's roads and expressways are also likely to be heavily congested. A disaster may render the city's rail and bus system inoperable, or it may be overwhelmed by demand as riders try to get closer to exit points. Three of the five boroughs have direct exits out of the city via car or foot: the Bronx, Staten Island and Manhattan. If one is located in the Bronx when disaster strikes, one may be able to leave the city more quickly by fleeing to Westchester County. If one is in Staten Island when disaster strikes, one may be able to leave the city more quickly by crossing over to New Jersey, respectively. If one is located in Brooklyn, one can leave the city through Staten Island or Manhattan. If one is located in Queens, one must first pass through Manhattan or Brooklyn to leave the city.[10] Manhattan's residential population is over 1 million; however, on weekdays, its population swells to over 3 million with the addition of commuters (NYC Department of City Planning, 2019). Furthermore, Manhattan has twenty-one bridges and four tunnels leaving the borough, but only one bridge, the George Washington Bridge, goes to New Jersey. The other twenty bridges lead back into the city. Only two tunnels exit the city to New Jersey, the Holland and Lincoln Tunnels. Traffic congestion may therefore make driving out of Manhattan impossible. If one chooses to walk out of Manhattan and away from the city, one is faced with about a mile walk across a high bridge jammed with other panicky New Yorkers or a walk through either the Holland or Lincoln Tunnels, which may be blocked with cars, leaving very limited space for pedestrians. Therefore, attempting to leave the city through Manhattan will be extremely difficult. Other escape routes include flying or sailing out of Manhattan. However, securing helicopters and boats during emergencies are beyond the economic and logistical reach of most New Yorkers.

For city dwellers, prepping is also closely connected to the philosophy of urban homesteading. As Coyne and Knutzen (2018) explain in their primer on urban homesteading,

Though we have fantasies about one day moving to the country, the city holds things that are more important to us than any parcel of open land. We have friends, and family here, great neighbors, and all the cultural amenities and stimulation of a city. It made more sense for us to become self-reliant in our urban environment.

(p. 14)

For city dwellers who are not interested in relocating to a rural area, homesteading involves practicing sustainable living strategies and striving for self-sufficiency. Urban homesteading practices include reducing resource dependency (such as bicycling), repairing and upcycling goods (refashioning items for alternative uses), growing produce or buying locally produced food, composting, urban foraging and even raising animals. Through such activities, city dwellers practice self-sufficiency and demonstrate their willingness to break with societal norms by learning diverse skills beyond those traditionally associated with city life (Seymour, 2009). In New York, residents embrace these ideals by shopping at green markets, growing gardens, keeping bees, as well as raising chickens and rabbits (Kaysen, 2014).

In conjunction with homesteading, prepping can also be understood in the context of New Yorkers' rising interest in consuming local foods and supporting urban agriculture. To be healthful and to improve self-sufficiency, many preppers try to purchase locally produced food or grow their own. Local food movements are valuable because they connect food producers and food consumers in the same geographic area as a strategy for creating self-reliant and resilient food networks, improving community health and environment as well as strengthening the local economy (Feensta, 2002). To promote the sale of local fresh food, New York hosts over fifty-one greenmarkets across the five boroughs, with twenty-three markets open year-round and several open on multiple days per week (GrowNyc, 2019). Farmers and food producers at the green market are from upstate New York, New Jersey and Pennsylvania. Goods are diverse, ranging from items such as produce, meat and fish, baked goods, condiments and plants. Of special interest to preppers, some farmers even sell plants and plant-based goods that can be used for medicinal purposes. Some enterprising family farmers have also sidestepped selling at greenmarkets and stores to grow and supply food directly to New York families (Applebome, 2010). For example, some city dwellers sign up for regular produce and meat deliveries. These subscription services enable buyers to pick up food at a designated location or to receive deliveries at home.

Surprisingly, New York's agricultural system has about 900 food-producing farms and gardens (Bauer and Fletcher, 2014).[11] Institutional farms and gardens (school and residential facilities), community gardens, commercial farms and community farms are the four types of urban agriculture found in the city. While food production is not the primary focus of institutional farms and gardens, some programs do grow edible produce. Out of 286 public school gardens, 117 grow food (GrowNyc, 2019). GreenThumb,

New York's collection of community gardens, is the nation's largest gardening program with over 600 gardens and about 20,000 volunteer gardeners throughout the city (NYC Parks Department, 2019). The GreenThumb program provides programming, technical assistance and supplies to support the gardens. These gardens are important community resources with diverse uses including recreation and farming. They are also important resources for immigrants seeking to continue agrarian traditions and for immigrants longing for fresh fruits and vegetables in food deserts such as the South Bronx (Hu, 2017).

New York's small network of communal farms and commercial farms is expanding to include indoor agriculture. Communal farms are operated by nonprofits that serve the nearby communities through food production and programming (information sessions and events). Commercial farms focus on maximizing profitability while also helping to shape urban agricultural goals (Bauer and Fletcher, 2012). Both types of farming include both traditional farms as well as rooftop farms. New York's innovative agricultural system is growing to incorporate both hydroponic and aeroponic farming. Plants grown in a hydroponic environment require only water and temperature control with no natural light,[12] whilst in aeroponic farming, plants are misted with water and nutrients typically found in soil.[13] Both farming systems require little room, as plants can be grown on vertical shelving units. In the NY region, vertical farms are produced in Brooklyn, Queens and New Jersey, with the largest farm in Newark (Frazier, 2017).

While support of the city's food-producing system might be increasing, it is important to note that New York's overall food network is vulnerable, and it may be jeopardized during a disaster. Hunts Point, located in the Bronx, is the city's largest food distribution facility, as it supplies produce and meats to nearly half of the city's restaurants. Sections of the sixty-acre facility, such as its meat market, are in low-lying areas and may be prone to flooding during heavy storms, while other sections on higher ground might be subject to power outages (Hester, 2017). Concerns about the scarcity of food during disaster have also influenced preppers to learn food preservation techniques. In addition to buying local foods and attempting to grow some produce, preppers practice canning, freezing and drying methods for storing food.

"Urban foraging" refers to two distinct practices: harvesting wild edible plants and neglected fruits, or searching for food in trash receptacles (Coyne and Knutzen, 2010). Within cities, edible plants can be found growing in parks, along sidewalks and in any patch of green. Successfully harvesting wild edibles requires extensive knowledge to correctly identify plants and to avoid consuming poisonous plants. Opportunities for exploring New York's plant life are endless because the city has more than 1,700 diverse parks and playgrounds throughout its five boroughs (https://www.nycgovparks.org/). Naturalists have always periodically foraged in the city's parks. For example, in Central Park, popular plants to forage include Poor Man's Pepper, Sassafras and wild berries. However, an increased popularity in foraging within city parks has been attributed to factors such as the rising costs of city living and to an increase in curious gourmands (Foderaro, 2011). This growing trend in urban foraging has sparked controversy. Park officials argue that removing plant life is illegal and ruinous because it destroys the natural habitats of city parks and their wildlife. Foragers dismiss this claim by arguing that they support sustainability by only removing invasive plants or non-native plants (See Meredith and Katz, 2010). Foraging in New York City parks is subject to a fine; however, fines are rarely issued.

Steve Brill, naturalist and vegan, is the city's best-known forager. Brill has led foraging tours in the city's parks for over thirty years. In addition, Brill has created a smartphone app for identifying edible plants. He has been featured in the popular press and gained some notoriety after being arrested for foraging in the 1980s. In an appearance on David Letterman after his arrest, Brill stated that he was released because he "had eaten all of the evidence" (Zeldovich, 2015). In 2019, I attended an urban foraging tour in Central Park with Steve Brill. His knowledge of plant life in Central Park was tremendous. As we toured the park, Brill identified and explained various edible plants. Safety permitting, we sampled the offerings of the plants or trees. For example, we smelled and tasted bark from Sassafras saplings and learned how a small amount of bark could brew a large quantity of tea. In addition to this foraging, Brill also provided samples of items such as homemade baked goods that were made with nuts or plants from Central Park. Halfway through the tour, Brill and our group were chased off by five NYC Park Enforcement officers. While Brill was not fined, the park officers ordered that he stop foraging and end the tour immediately. Brill apologized and then moved the tour to another section of the park. However, Brill is not alone in his scrappy approach to being a New York tour guide, as his dedication to educating people about plant life in the city's park and his disregard for park rules reflect a common ethos among NY specialty tour guides, who often see their tours as a way to capitalize on a hobby or existing skill set rather than performing a formal job with defined duties in the tourism sector (Wynn, 2017).

Not as appreciated as an unexpected lovely plant or wildflower, trash containers are all too present in cities. In New York, trash cans are usually located on streets and subway platforms. Waste containers are often stationed on streets, and mountains of garbage bags appear weekly outside of restaurants, offices and apartment buildings. New York's Department of Sanitation (DSNY) is the world's largest sanitation department. DSNY (2019) collects more than 10,500 tons of residential and institutional garbage as well as 1,760 tons of recyclables daily; the city's commercial sector also produces 9,000 tons of trash daily, which is collected by private waste management companies. Scavenging for food in trash containers, known as "waste reclamation," "food rescue," or "dumpster diving" is another rising trend in New York. Similar to foraging for edible plants, this type of urban foraging is attributed to attempts to offset the high cost of living in the city. However, "waste reclamation" is also part of a broader social movement called "freeganism" that aims to reject consumer culture and to break free from capitalism. Freegans argue that

> despite our society's sterotypes [sic] about garbage, the goods recovered by freegans are safe, useable, clean, and in perfect or near-perfect condition, a symptom of a throwaway culture that encourages us to constantly replace our older goods with newer ones, and where retailers plan high-volume product disposal as part of their economic model.
>
> (https://freegan.info/)

By recovering discarded food and consumer items, freegans seek to reduce waste and pollution. Freegan tours are even offered to introduce New Yorkers to the perils and pleasures of searching for food and goods in the trash. While "waste reclamation" would seem to be a valuable skill in a post-apocalyptic setting, urban preppers seem to mainly support plant-based foraging for now.

It is also important to note that this type of foraging, as described, seems to stem from the decision to move away from consumer culture (as well as reducing expenses). This motivation is very different from a homeless person searching for a meal in the garbage out of desperation. Foraging, whether it is an economic choice or an economic necessity, points to the cruelty of wealth inequality and gaps in social welfare measures within this global city. These stark economic realities fuel prepper anxieties about government and economic collapse, reinforcing their drive for self-sufficiency.

Urban preppers' interest in healthful eating and supporting local sustainability extends to the health and wellness market; they have adopted holistic medicine and mindful health practices as vital life-saving strategies in emergency situations. For example, essential oils are now widely used as alternative medical treatments (with few side effects) to heal ailments and injuries. Essential oils are also lauded for their flavoring and aromatic qualities for cooking and disinfectant properties for cleaning. As consumer interest in multi-purpose natural and organic products has increased, the demand for essential oils has skyrocketed. The US essential oil market is expected to reach 7.34 billion by 2024 (Grand View Research, 2017). An essential oils kit is considered a valuable survival kit in a bug out bag and stored in a prepper closest. Urban preppers often create their own kits by selecting oils to treat common ailments or injuries. Peppermint is often included to treat digestive issues. Lavender oil is often also carried because it is multi-purpose; it can be used to treat insect bites, ease sore muscles and promote calmness. Helichrysum is thought to stop bleeding; therefore, it is often packed to treat wounds. Beyond their treatment properties, essential oils are also used by urban preppers because they are purported to have a long shelf life. However, the shelf life of each essential oil is different—their effectiveness is affected by exposure to light, heat and oxygen.

Some NYC preppers also practice mindfulness exercises like meditation to improve their situational awareness and cognition. Broadly speaking, mindfulness is defined as present-centered attention and awareness (Brown and Ryan, 2003). By studying centering techniques, urban preppers learn to remain calm and focused in stressful situations. Mindfulness training improves core centers of human functioning: attention, cognition, emotion, behavior and physiology (Good et al., 2016). Therefore, in dire circumstances, improved situational awareness can help preppers more accurately access and respond to situations rather than panicking or freezing with fear.

My experience as a New Yorker who has endured several of the city's recent crises provides me with a unique sociological lens for studying prepping. Conducted from late 2017 through 2018, my ethnographic study encompassed a practice of participant-observation, in-depth interviewing, and archival research.[14] My participant-observation focused on attending the meetings of the New York City Prepper's Network (NYCPN) as a member and academic researcher. Based in Manhattan, NYCPN is a group of urban preppers that studies and practices preparedness strategies together. The membership roll contains over 459 New Yorkers; however, events are typically attended by between 20–30 participants. My fieldwork allowed me to learn from immersion. As an NYCPN member, I attended meetings, workshops and weekend excursions in the woods. Outside of the group, I also completed select classes and activities to familiarize myself with basic prepping skills (such as an urban prepping class or foraging tour). On my own, I also took short hikes to improve my ability to walk with my bug out bag and to practice my prepping skills. Given the intense nature of practicing survivalism, my fieldwork required a significant commitment of time, expense and energy. Making this commitment involves striking the balance between an engaged group member (an insider) and an objective outsider (Gill and Temple, 2014). This project demanded my full participation, and for the safety of the group members, as well as myself, it was important that I learn the proper techniques for dangerous tasks such as fire building and cutting with a large knife. However, I gave careful and realistic consideration to signing up for tough excursions to avoid becoming a burden on other group members.

To develop a comprehensive view of prepping in New York, I conducted in-depth interviews with New York Prepper's Network's leaders and active members as well as independent preppers. Furthermore, to understand how class influences approaches to prepping, I studied both independent preppers with middle class income levels and high-net-worth (HNW) preppers whose wealth is in the multimillions. I conducted 43 in-depth interviews and numerous short interviews. Interviews focused on motivations for prepping, prepping skills, networks and perceptions of post-apocalyptic life. My personal experiences with different New York crises including Hurricane Irene and Hurricane Sandy as well as three terrorist attacks, allowed me to empathize with the interviewees. In keeping with Symbolic Interactionism, I sought to uncover the unique perspectives of these New York preppers during interviews. My goal was to engage in the interpretative process by allowing myself to experience my response to their stories rather than remaining aloof (Blumer, 1969). To explore and process my feelings regarding particular narratives or informants, I often wrote in a field journal to clarify my thoughts and to re-focus my research agenda. Journaling provided a mechanism for acknowledging and releasing fearful or sad emotions. For example, listening to recounts of the September 11th attacks sometimes triggered my own anxieties about that day. Journaling also reinforced the focus on my project by helping me to avoid the pitfall of adopting the concerns of participants as my own concerns (Kleinman and Kolb, 2011). By spending a significant amount of time learning from and talking with participants, I ran the risk of adopting their mission of educating New Yorkers about the importance of prepping, rather than remaining committed to providing a "thick" description (Geertz, 1973) of the city's prepping culture. Journaling about the relationship between my research goal and my conversations with and observations of preppers kept me on target. These reflections provided me with an outlet to use "self-awareness [as] a tool for sociological analysis of data" (Kleinman and Kolb, 2011, p. 438).

To further understand which skills and resources are important to prepping, I interviewed prepper consultants and teachers of survival classes. To develop a better understanding of the prepper market, I interviewed businesses owners that supply prepper goods (such as popular prepping gear websites and supply stores). I also spoke with consultants responsible for constructing and outfitting safe rooms for HNW preppers. These interviews focused on their understanding of the needs of preppers (types of disasters feared by preppers and the equipment selected to protect themselves).

Archival research involved collecting primary texts that provided insight into the context of New York prepping and its representation in the media. Historical records and government documents about disasters in New York were compiled to develop a context for exploring the city's recent experience with hazardous events and its level of risk. These documents were varied, ranging from press clippings to publications supplied by New York City's Department of Emergency Management. Prepper literature was also reviewed to discover popular topics and equipment. This literature included: magazines, books, training manuals, handouts and website materials (Facebook, YouTube channels and blogs, for example). Media coverage consisted of relevant articles and features in the popular press as well as social media content. American movies and television shows were also screened to study the depictions of both preppers and post-apocalyptic life.

As a personal journey, much of this research has been about pushing beyond the boundaries of my comfort zone. My usual "trail map" of the city might now be considered too safe (but entirely age appropriate). My city discoveries often result from tips gleaned from art and movie reviews as well as recommendations about dining and shows from friends. This project forced me to abandon these conveniences and to study the city in a new and eerie light. How could I survive in the city without any creature comforts or indulgences? How could I make sure that I had something in a crisis that could leave me with nothing? My view of my apartment immediately changed. Sacred closet space reserved for shoes and purses was sacrificed to store basic food and supplies needed in an emergency. My view of my Greenwich Village neighborhood also changed. My strolls through Washington Square moved beyond carefree people watching to activities like inspecting tree bark for its quality as tinder, and examining plant life to see if it was edible. After charting walking routes to leave the city, I recognized that my home's far proximity from a bridge or tunnel added significant travel time to any escape plan. However, it is also important to note that I am now not fearful of any particular scenario. As a result of this project, I remain a reasonable person who is now better prepared and equipped to deal with any emergency. I would like to write that I gave up that desire for immediate gratification found in city life, but that statement would be dishonest. However, I will say that after living without any indulgences for short periods of time, I certainly appreciate them much more. I am grateful for my life and, yes, this project has made me realize its fragility and its privilege.

Learning prepping skills also led me to scrutinize the myths that I have created about myself. I am not the brave feminist in great shape. My physical strength needs improvement. As hiking with the prepper group and carrying my bug out bag has made me realize, there is a big difference between having a gym membership and actually using your gym membership. My patience and confidence were also strained, as it sometimes took me longer to learn new skills. At these points, as a researcher, I struggled with seeing "me" revealed through the looking-glass, when I imagined how the preppers viewed me (Cooley, 1902). However, the group members were always encouraging and supportive of individuals new to the rigors of prepping. As the following chapters will illustrate, experienced preppers made things look so easy.

That clearly was not the case.

Notes

1 In 2018, the Archives even held an exhibit titled "Unlike Historians: Materials Collected by the NYPD Surveillance Teams, 1960–1975." The exhibition explored the images of surveillance photographs of civil rights, anti-war, and feminist protestors (Targets included the Communist Party, the Black Panthers, the Nation of Islam, the American Renaissance Party and Youths Against War and Fascism).

2 The quote was not originally attributed to Mark Twain. It was first stated by Paul Bourget (1852–1935), a French novelist and critic, in his commentary on American culture. His critique of American culture was first published as a series of articles in US newspapers and then later became the book *Outre-Mer: Impressions of America* (1895). Twain used the quotation in the first line of his satirical essay which is a response to Bourget's reflections. Although not well-remembered, Bourget had a remarkable literary career in which he was nominated for the Nobel Prize for Literature five times.

3 Services is the largest employer at fifty-eight percent of all jobs in the city. However, this category is quite broad, encompassing not just professional and business services but media and tourism jobs as well.

4 The top four cities are forecasted to be New York, Tokyo, Los Angeles, with Shanghai and London tied for fourth place.
5 A Nissan Pathfinder filled with smoke but did not fully detonate (Baker and Rashbaum, 2010).
6 A pressure cooker bomb exploded on West 23rd Street, injuring thirty-one people; a second bomb was discovered on West 27th Street. Another bomb also exploded on the Jersey Shore but did not injury anyone (Workman, Rosenberg, and Mele, 2016).
7 A driver plowed a pickup truck down the bike path along the West Side Highway, killing eight people and injuring eleven (Mueller, Rashbaum, and Baker, 2017).
8 A would-be suicide attacker detonated a pipe bomb strapped to his chest; however, the bomb failed to fully detonate and seriously injured the attacker (Nir and Rosenbaum, 2017).
9 New York also experienced slight earthquakes in 2002 (FEMA Disaster Report, 2002) and in 2019 (Hignett, 2019).
10 If in Queens, one may also go to Long Island. However, as an island, this area provides limited resources and no possible option for moving farther out by car or foot.
11 A variety of local organizations also support other agrarian interests. For example, the New York City Beekeepers Association (NYCBA) promotes sharing best practices and interest in beekeeping in an urban environment. The NYCBA (2018) reported in 2018 that there were roughly 550 beehives kept by New Yorkers throughout the city with the majority of hives located in Manhattan and Brooklyn.
12 Commercial hydroponic farms now supplies rare herbs to New York's top restaurants (Krueger, 2017).
13 For a compelling discussion of vertical farming, see Despommier (2010).
14 I completed a pilot study in 2013. In 2017–18, I returned to the field to conduct a revised and expanded full study. In the interim period, I focused on my teaching responsibilities and worked on other research projects.

References

Adams, S. (2019). *Global cities outlook*. Retrieved from http://resources.oxfordeconom ics.com/global-cities-2035-nov-2019?source=recent-releases.

Anderson, G. B., and Bell, M. L. (2012). Lights out. *Epidemiology*, 23(2), 189–193. doi:10.1097/ede.0b013e318245c61c.

Applebome, P. (2010, October 17). Keeping agriculture alive near New York City (yes, really). *The New York Times*. Retrieved from https://www.nytimes.com/2010/10/18/nyregion/18towns.html.

Baker, A., and Rashbaum, W. K. (2010, May 1). Police find car bomb in Times Square. *The New York Times*. Retrieved from https://www.nytimes.com/2010/05/02/nyregion/02timessquare.html.

Barbaro, M., and Schweber, N. (2009, February 5). Aromatic mystery in New York City is solved. *The New York Times*. Retrieved from https://www.nytimes.com/2009/02/06/nyregion/06smell.html.

Barron, J. (2007, July 19). Steam blast jolts midtown, killing one. *The New York Times*. Retrieved from https://www.nytimes.com/2007/07/19/nyregion/19explode.html.

Barron, J. (2003, August 15). The blackout of 2003: The overview; power surge blacks out Northeast, hitting cities in 8 states and Canada; midday shutdowns disrupt millions. *The New York Times*. Retrieved from https://www.nytimes.com/2003/08/15/nyregion/blackout-2003-overview-power-surge-blacks-northeast-hitting-cities-8-states.html.

Bauer, C. and Fletcher, R., (Eds). (2014). *Five borough farm phase II: Growing the benefits of urban agriculture in New York City*. New York: Vanguard Direct.

Berube, A. (2018, February 5). *City and metropolitan income inequality data reveal ups and downs through 2016*. The Brookings Institution. Retrieved from https://www.brookings. edu/research/city-and-metropolitan-income-inequality-data-reveal-ups-and-downs-thro ugh-2016/.

Beveridge, A., and Beveridge, S. (2013). The big picture: Demographic and other changes. In D. Halle and A. A. Beveridge (Eds), *New York and Los Angeles: The uncertain future*. New York: Oxford University Press.

Blumer, H. (2009). *Symbolic interactionism: Perspective and method*. Berkeley: University of California Press.

Bourget, P. (2012). *Outre-mer: Impressions of America*. Sligo, Ireland: Hardpress Ltd.

Brown, K. W., and Ryan, R. M. (2003). The benefits of being present: Mindfulness and its role in psychological well-being. *Journal of Personality and Social Psychology*, 84(4), 822–848. doi:10.1037/0022-3514.84.4.822.

Castells, M. (1989). *The informational city: Information technology, economic restructuring, the urban-regional process*. Oxford: Basil Blackwell.

Center for Disease Control. (2014). *Morbidity and mortality weekly report: Surveillance and preparedness for ebola virus disease — New York City, 2014*. Retrieved from https:// www.cdc.gov/mmwr/preview/mmwrhtml/mm6341a5.htm.

Cooley, C. (1902). *Human nature and the social order*. New York: C. Scribner's Sons.

Coyne, K., and Knutzen, E. (2010). *The urban homestead: Your guide to self-sufficient living in the heart of the city*. Los Angeles: Process Media.

Davis, D. M., and Hayes, J. A. (2011). What are the benefits of mindfulness? A practice review of psychotherapy-related research. *Psychotherapy*, 48(2), 198–108. doi:10.1037/a0022062.

Despommier, D. D. (2010). *The vertical farm: Feeding the world in the 21st century*. (1st ed.) New York: Thomas Dunne Books.

Dolnick, S. (2011). Recovery is slower in New York suburbs. *The New York Times*. Retrieved from https://www.nytimes.com/2011/08/29/nyregion/wind-and-rain-from-hurricane-ire ne-lash-new-york.html

Farnham, A., Alleyne, L., Cimini, D., and Balter, S. (2014). Legionnaire's disease incidence and risk factors, New York. *Emerging Infectious Disease*, (11), 1795–1802. Retrieved from https://www.ncbi.nlm.nih.gov/pubmed/25513657?report=docsum Federal Federal

Federal Emergency Management Association. (2002). *Disasters*. Retrieved from https:// www.fema.gov/disasters?field_dv2_state_territory_tribal_value_selective=All&field_ dv2_incident_type_tid=All&field_dv2_declaration_type_value=All&field_dv2_ incident_begin_value%5Bvalue%5D%5Bmonth%5D=1&field_dv2_incident_begin_ value%5Bvalue%5D%5Byear%5D=2002&field_dv2_incident_end_value%5Bvalue %5D%5Bmonth%5D=12&field_dv2_incident_end_value%5Bvalue%5D%5Byear% 5D=2002.

Feenstra, G. (2002). Creating space for sustainable food systems: Lessons from the field. *Agriculture and Human Values*, 19(2), 99–106.

Foderaro, L. W. (2011, July 29). Enjoy park greenery, city says, but not as salad. *The New York Times*. Retrieved from https://www.nytimes.com/2011/07/30/nyregion/ new-york- moves-to-stop-foraging-in-citys-parks.html.

Frazier, I. (2017, January 1). The vertical farm. *The New Yorker*. Retrieved from http s://www.newyorker.com/magazine/2017/01/09/the-vertical-farm.

Geertz, C. (1973). Thick description: Toward an interpretive theory of culture. In Geertz, C. *The interpretation of cultures: Selected essays*. New York: Basic Books, (pp. 3–30).

Gill, P. R., and Temple, E. C. (2014). Walking the fine line between fieldwork success and failure: Advice for new ethnographers. *Journal of Research Practice*, 10(1), 1–13.

Gladstone, D., and Fainstein, S. (2013). The New York and Los Angeles economies from boom to crisis. In D. Halle and A. A. Beveridge (Eds), *New York and Los Angeles: The uncertain future*. New York: Oxford University Press.

Good, D., Lyddy, C., Glomb, T., Bono, J., Brown, K., Duffy, M., Baer, R., Brewer, J., & Lazar, S. (2016). Contemplating mindfulness at work: An integrative review. *Journal of Management*, 42.

Grand View Research. (2017, February). *U.S. essential oils market to reach $7.34 billion by 2024*. [Press Release]. Retrieved from https://www.grandviewresearch.com/p ress-release/us-essential-oil-market-analysis.

GrowNYC. (2019). *Our greenmarkets and youthmarkets*. Retrieved from https://www. grownyc.org/greenmarket/ourmarkets.

Halle, D., and Beveridge, A. A. (2013). New York and Los Angeles: The uncertain future. In D. Halle and A. A. Beveridge (Eds), *New York and Los Angeles: The uncertain future*. New York: Oxford University Press.

Hartocollis, A. (2009, May 17). New York reports its first Swine Flu death. *The New York Times*. Retrieved from https://www.nytimes.com/2009/05/18/nyregion/18swine.html.

Hartocollis, A. (2009, June 10). 12 flu victims have died, and ill may total 550,000. *The New York Times*. Retrieved from https://www.nytimes.com/2009/06/11/nyr egion/11flu.html.

Hester, J. L. (2017, October 27). The long tail of a storm. *CityLab*. Retrieved from https://www.citylab.com/environment/2017/10/sandy-5-years-later/544185/.

Hicks, N. (2019, February 20). Legionnaires' breakout from NYCHA water leaves 2 sick. *New York Post*. Retrieved from https://nypost.com/2019/02/20/legionnaires-breakout-from-nycha-water-leaves-2-sick/.

Hignett, K. (2019, June 26). Was there an earthquake in New York City last night? Yes–but you almost definitely didn't feel it. *Newsweek*. Retrieved from https://www. newsweek.com/new-york-city-earthquake-magnitude-intensity- damage-1445969.

Hu, W. (2017, July 30). Food from around the world, homegrown in New York. *The New York Times*. Retrieved from https://www.nytimes.com/2017/07/30/nyregion/ food-from-around-the-world-homegrown-in-new-york.html.

Hu, W. (2015, August 20). Bronx Legionnaires' outbreak is over, health officials say. *The New York Times*. Retrieved from https://www.nytimes.com/2015/08/21/nyr egion/health-officials-declare-end-of-legionnaires-outbreak-in-the-bronx.html.

Jacobs, A. (2019, July 2). The zika virus is still a threat. Here's what the experts know. *The New York Times*. Retrieved from https://www.nytimes.com/2019/07/02/ health/zika-virus.html.

Kaysen, R. (2014, July 25). Heard on the street: E-i-e-i-o. *The New York Times*. Retrieved from https://www.nytimes.com/2014/07/27/realestate/new-york-city-ba ckyards-welcome-chickens-and-bees.html.

Kilgannon, C. (2019, May 2). *What we know about the measles outbreak in N.Y.* Retrieved from https://www.nytimes.com/2019/05/02/nyregion/newyorktoday/nyc-news-measles-outbreak.html.

Kleinman, S., and Kolb, K. H. (2011). Traps on the path of analysis. *Symbolic Interaction*, 34(4), 425–446. doi:10.1525/si.2011.34.4.425.

Krueger, A. (2017, December 6). Herbs from the underground. *The New York Times*. Retrieved from https://www.nytimes.com/2017/12/06/nyregion/herbs-from-the-underground.html.

Macur, J., and Belson, K. (2012, November 2). Wittenberg's actions met head on by critics. *The New York Times*. Retrieved from https://www.nytimes.com/2012/11/03/sports/marathon-starts-to-divide-not-unite-new-york-city.html.

McKinley, J. (2019, June 13). Measles outbreak: N.Y. eliminates religious exemptions for vaccinations. *The New York Times*. Retrieved from https://www.nytimes.com/2019/06/13/nyregion/measles-vaccinations-new-york.html.

McKinley, J. C. M., and Santora, M. (2016, February 11). 5 arrested in connection with East Village gas explosion. *The New York Times*. Retrieved from https://www.nytimes.com/2016/02/12/nyregion/5-arrested-in-connection-with-east-village-gas-explosion.html.

Meredith, L., and Katz, S. E. (2010). *The locavore's handbook: The busy person's guide to eating local on a budget*. Guilford, CT: Lyons Press.

Mueller, B., Rashbaum, W. K., and Baker, A. (2017, October 31). Terror attack kills 8 and injures 11 in Manhattan. *The New York Times*. Retrieved from https://www.nytimes.com/2017/10/31/nyregion/police-shooting-lower-manhattan.html.

National Bureau of Economic Research. (2010, September 20). *Business cycle dating committee report*. Retrieved from https://www.nber.org/cycles/sept2010.html.

National Weather Service. (2010, July 27). *Bronx Tornado Report*. Retrieved from https://www.webcitation.org/5rZ13kunl?url=http://forecast.weather.gov/product.php?site=NWSandissuedby=OKXandproduct=PNSandformat=CIandversion=1andglossary=0.

New York City Beekeepers Association. (2019). *Welcome to the hive for Gotham city beekeepers*. Retrieved from http://www.bees.nyc/.

New York City Department of City Planning. (2019). *The ins and outs of NYC commuting*. https://www1.nyc.gov/assets/planning/download/pdf/planning-level/housing-economy/nyc-ins-and-out-of-commuting.pdf.

New York City Department of City Planning. (2019). *Population - current and projected populations*. Retrieved from https://www1.nyc.gov/site/planning/planning-level/nyc-population/current-future-populations.page.

New York City Department of Emergency Management. (2011). *OEM 2010/2011 biennial report*. Retrieved from https://www1.nyc.gov/assets/em/biennial2011/index.html.

New York City Department of Health. (2019). *Zika virus*. Retrieved from https://www1.nyc.gov/site/doh/health/health-topics/zika-virus.page.

New York City Department of Parks and Recreation. (2019). *Frequently Asked Questions*. Retrieved from https://www.nycgovparks.org/about/faq.

New York City Department of Parks and Recreation. (2019). *GreenThumb New York City*. Retrieved from https://greenthumb.nycgovparks.org/about.html.

New York City Department of Parks and Recreation. (2019). *History of the community garden movement*. Retrieved from https://www.nycgovparks.org/about/history/community-gardens/movement.

New York City Department of Sanitation. (2019). *About DSNY*. Retrieved from https://www1.nyc.gov/assets/dsny/site/about.

New York City Economic Development Corporation. (2019). *Economic snapshot: A summary of New York City's economy*. Retrieved from https://www.nycedc.com.

New York City Special Initiative for Rebuilding and Resiliency. (2013). *Plan NYC: A stronger, more resilient New York*. [PDF file]. Retrieved from http://smedia.nyc.gov/a gencies/sirr/SIRR_singles_Lo_res.pdf.

Nir, S. M., and Rashbaum, W. K. (2017, December 11). Bomber strikes near Times Square, disrupting city but killing none. *The New York Times*. Retrieved from https://www.nytimes.com/2017/12/11/nyregion/explosion-times-square.html.

Organisation for Economic Co-operation and Development. (2016). *OECD factbook 2015–2016: Economic, environmental and social statistics*. Retrieved from doi:10.1787/factbook-2015-en.

Protesters against Wall Street. (2011, October 8). *The New York Times*. Retrieved from https://www.nytimes.com/2011/10/09/opinion/sunday/protesters-against-wall-street.html.

Rajan, R. G. (2011). *Fault lines: How hidden fractures still threaten the world economy*. Princeton: Princeton University Press.

Rivera, R., and Roston, M. (2010, September 16). New York City battered by fierce storm. *The New York Times*. Retrieved from https://www.nytimes.com/2010/09/17/nyregion/17storm.html.

Roberts, P. (2015). *The impulse society: America in the age of instant gratification*. New York: Bloomsbury USA.

Santora, M. (2014). First patient quarantined under strict new policy tests negative for ebola. *The New York Times*. Retrieved from https://www.nytimes.com/2014/10/25/nyregion/new-york-ebola-case-craig-spencer.html?searchResultPosition=3.

Santora, M., and Maag, C. (2012, September 8). Tornadoes touch down in Brooklyn and Queens. *The New York Times*. Retrieved from https://www.nytimes.com/2012/09/09/nyregion/tornado-causes-damage-along-a-beach-in-queens.html.

Sassen, S. (2001). *The global city*. Princeton, NJ: Princeton University Press.

Sassen, S., and Roost, F. (1999). The city: Strategic site for the global entertainment industry. In *The tourist city*. New Haven, CT: Yale University Press.

Sautter, E. T., and Leisen, B. (1999). Managing stakeholders a tourism planning model. *Annals of Tourism Research*, 26(2), 312–328. doi: doi:10.1016/S0160-7383 (98)97–98.

Seymour, J. (2009). *The new complete book of self-sufficiency*. London: DK Publishing.

Smith, K. A., Lockstone-Binney, L., Holmes, K., and Baum, T. (2014). Introduction to event volunteering. In K. A. Smith, L. Lockstone-Binney, K. Holmes, and T. Baum (Eds), *Event volunteering. International perspectives on the event volunteering experience*. London: Routledge.

Sorkin, A. R. (2018). *Too big to fail: The inside story of how Wall Street and Washington fought to save the financial system—and themselves*. New York: Penguin Books.

Spencer, C. (2015). Having and fighting Ebola — Public health lessons from a clinician turned patient. *The New England Journal of Medicine*, (372), 1089–1091. Retrieved from doi:10.1056/NEJMp1501355.

Twain, M. (1895, January). What Paul Bourget thinks of us. *The North American Review*. 160(458), pp. 48–63.

United States Census Bureau. (2017). American Community Survey Data Releases. *U. S. Department of Commerce*. Retrieved from https://aka.ms/AA6qxap.

White, E. B. (1949). *Here is New York* (1st ed.). New York: Harper.

Wilson, M. (2018, August 3). A tornado took on New York. The tornado didn't last long. *The New York Times*. Retrieved from https://www.nytimes.com/2018/08/03/nyregion/tornado-warning-nyc-twitter-response.html.

Workman, K., Rosenberg, E., and Mele, C. (2016, September 18). Chelsea bombing: What we know and don't know. *The New York Times*. Retrieved from https://www.nytimes.com/2016/09/19/nyregion/chelsea-explosion-what-we-know-and-dont-know.html.

Wynn, J. R. (2011). *The tour guide: Walking and talking New York*. Chicago: University of Chicago Press.

Zeldovich, L. (2015, February 16). Foraging through Central Park. *NY Press*. Retrieved from http://www.nypress.com/news/foraging-through-central-parkNBNP 1020120509305099983.

3 Popular entertainment

Preppers as characters and as consumers

The tropes of self-reliance and individualism portrayed in the US popular media are important reference points for examining the emergence of prepping in American culture. Such hints represent a "structure of feeling" in that they are part of an emergent social process that rises in the gap between a dominant ideology and popular responses (Williams and Orrom, 1954). These clues can be spotted quickly in ordinary objects like a board game. Monopoly, to be exact. Not the old version of Monopoly with the chubby top-hatted old white guy wearing tails, but the recent version based on the hit television series *The Walking Dead*. In this game, the curtain is pulled back to reveal the tension wrought by a new notion of self-reliance in American culture that moves beyond the egotism of financial success.[1] Capital turned on its head.

In a reflection of these anxious times, *The Walking Dead* version of Monopoly is no longer singularly focused on securing expensive properties in order to charge exorbitant rent. Gone are the prized properties of Boardwalk and Park Avenue. In this Monopoly's apocalyptic world, those luxury addresses have been replaced by costly properties that provide protection against the deadly unknown. Hotels are valueless. Guard towers and prison cells are now the sought-after architectural prizes designed to protect their owners and fortunate tenants against zombies (the stand-in for all disasters) and evil-doers battling to survive. Gone are the classic game tokens that symbolize industry or wealth such as the thimble and the racing car. Game tokens instead represent and reflect a violent sense of power, with icons like a revolver and a baseball bat covered with barbed wire. This new game reflects the perception that success in American culture is no longer measured only in economic terms. Instead, given America's rising fears about threats such as natural disasters, terrorist attacks, pandemics, technological failures and economic collapse, the calculus of success now includes the desperate need to protect oneself and one's family against a wide range of catastrophes. After all, most Americans are already too familiar with fears about their own financial collapse. Life for many American households is best described as a cycle of disaster and recovery with families moving from one financial crisis to the next in a context where work is now less secure (with pensions and employer-provided insurances nearly relics) and incomes unpredictable (Cohen, 2017).

American popular entertainment has always been an outlet for expressing our collective anxieties. As Biskind (2018) observes:

> Far from mere escapism, movies and TV reflect the arguments that agitate the waters of our political life. Unlike the rhetoric of speechifying politicians and bloviating intellectuals that puts people to sleep, telling stories affects them directly, touching their hearts and engaging their minds.
>
> (p. 6)

Consider the Cold War era. During the early years of the standoff, American television shows and movies reflected the country's unease about the threat of nuclear war (Rose, 2001; May, 2017). Locked in a nuclear showdown with the Soviets, Americans feared a mutual Armageddon. In 1952, the US detonated the world's first hydrogen bomb in the South Pacific, demonstrating an explosive force roughly 450 times greater than the US bomb exploded over Nagasaki, Japan. The Soviet Union countered quickly with the detonation of their own hydrogen bomb in 1953. In 1956, the US again tested a hydrogen bomb with a force of 15 million tons of dynamite. A week after the explosion, Ed Sullivan, on his popular television show, aired a short anti-nuclear cartoon about the terror of a nuclear attack to 14 million frightened viewers. May (2017) notes how, in this period: "Americans learned to be fearful for their personal safety and came to understand that they were responsible for their own protection against external and internal enemies" (p. 9).

"The Shelter," a 1961 episode of *The Twilight Zone,* provided a Cold War era parable for Americans (May, 2017). "The Shelter" cautioned viewers about how fear in a time of crisis causes people to lose civility and revert to their base natures. In this episode, a neighborhood party is disrupted by news of a UFO approaching and ready to attack. The party quickly ends as all return home to protect themselves. The party host and his family immediately retreat and lock themselves in their bomb shelter, the only one in the neighborhood. Fearful about their lack of preparation, the neighbors return and beg to be let in the shelter. Their pleas are rejected because, as explained by the host, the small shelter only has enough air and provisions for their family of three. Spewing racism and bigotry, the neighbors begin to turn on one another until a few men decide to break down the shelter door even if it places those inside at risk. In that moment, the group of neighbors becomes a mob. Just as the angry neighbors smash through the entrance with a makeshift battering ram, a radio broadcast announces that the UFO report was a false alarm. However, it is too late. The neighborhood has already destroyed itself, as the sense of community and trust has been broken. While embarrassed and stunned neighbors stumble through the wreckage of the once lovely home, the episode's closing narration cautions viewers with a powerful observation: "No moral, no message, no prophetic tract, just a simple statement of fact: for civilization to survive, the human race has to remain civilized."

Our understanding of the apocalypse has shifted as we transitioned into the 21st century. Now our collective anxieties have expanded beyond the continued threat of nuclear destruction to encompass a much wider fearscape that includes new economic crises, increasing environmental catastrophes, global health emergencies and technological failures. The emergence of these new fears has resulted in a transformation of the meaning of the "apocalypse" in American popular culture. As Wojcik (1997) argues:

> ... the end of the world has been interpreted as a meaningful, transformative, and supernatural event, involving the annihilation and renewal of the earth by deities or divine forces. During the last half of the twentieth century, however, widespread beliefs about a meaningless apocalypse have emerged and now compete with traditional religious apocalyptic world views.
>
> (p. 1)

The split between the two interpretations, centers on the distinction between the promise of order and restored faith and the promise of no redemption (Rosen, 2008). In the traditional Western biblical narrative, "the promise of the apocalypse is unequivocal: God has a plan, the disruption is part of it, and in the end all will be made right. Thus, is suffering made meaningful and hope restored to those who are traumatized or bewildered by historic events" (Rosen, 2008, p. 2). Conversely, the new narrative "holds out only the promise of undifferentiated punishment" (Rosen, 2008, p. 2).

According to Foster (2016, 2014), the collapsing together of two current social preoccupations: the sharply increasing economic inequity between classes and the emergence of an apocalyptic cultural mindset—fueled by factors such as paranoia, prepping, gated communities, the return of underground bunkers and increased gun sales—has resulted in a new genre of apocalyptically themed movies and television programs defined as "apocotainment". Foster (2016) argues that at the center of "apocotainment" is the merging of two groups, wealthy whites and preppers, as they share similar traits such as paranoia, a lack of empathy, a crisis of masculinity and a preoccupation with Doomsday scenarios. "Apocotainment's" exaggerated form of prepping depicts a darker version of the 1950s American nuclear family, turning wholesomeness into ruthless patriarchy accompanied by endless conspicuous consumption of survival gear that can be used to quickly kill off others and stored as essential provisions for the family. The movie *The Purge* (2013) and the reality-based television shows *Doomsday Preppers* (2012–14) and *Doomsday Castles* (2013) are key examples of the transformation of the home into "a theatre of war, presided over by a patriarch who acts as a drill sergeant over his family—as if it were a military unit at war with the world itself" (Foster, 2016, p. 286). Recognizing the skewed depictions of preppers found in "apocotainment" is important, because these exaggerations are revealing expressions of a culture of fear and a heightened sense of risk. Furthermore, extreme characterizations of preppers as paranoid and obsessive on television and in movie, underscore why some preppers are reluctant to discuss their practices for fear of being stereotyped.

Therefore, this chapter examines apocalyptic narratives that find a middle ground between the extreme categories of religious constrictions and the futility and gloom of a hopeless final outcome. After all, the majority of popular apocalyptic stories draw on qualities from both ends of the spectrum (Ford and Mitchell, 2018). In keeping with a prepper ethos, these apocalyptic narratives are moral stories that allow ordinary people to harness their own strength and wits to face the new world (Renner, 2012). In this chapter, "apocalyptic narrative" is defined broadly to include apocalyptic stories, in which disaster is threatened but has not yet occurred, and post-apocalyptic stories, in which the catastrophe has already happened (Renner, 2012). In popular entertainment, apocalyptic narratives are often an intermixture of both. (An apocalypse might occur at the start of a movie only to segue into a tale about living in the aftermath of destruction). Embedded in these apocalyptic narratives are harrowing messages for those who are contemplating their chances for survival in a postapocalyptic world and, sometimes, a far more complex characterization of preppers. This chapter explores these two themes in popular movies, television programs and one bestselling novel. While databases were utilized to determine the popularity of works within their genres, the works reviewed were recommended by specific NYC preppers as noteworthy for understanding prepping.[2] Noteworthy works are described as having shaped a prepper thinking about important topics such as the genesis and spread of a global catastrophe, what a post-apocalyptic world might be like, what strategies are crucial for survival in a post-apocalyptic world and the practice of social relations in a time of grave crisis. In the realm of popular culture, preppers are both characters within texts as well as consumers of texts. In addition, some urban preppers also see themselves as creators of popular culture, intent on changing their image through media-savvy techniques.

When Ben, a NYCPN member, and I first started to discuss movies and television shows that are noteworthy to him as a prepper, he replied with an understatement: "Some things pique my interest and made me think a little about stuff." Ben immediately named *The Day After Tomorrow* (2004) as a noteworthy movie. With box-office earnings of nearly $187 million, *The Day After Tomorrow* is ranked as the ninth highest-grossing disaster movie in the US market since 1979 (Box Office Mojo, 2019).[3] Loosely based on climate change, the storyline involves a scientist's race to save his son in New York from a massive hail storm brought on by the sudden dawn of a new ice age. When I didn't respond quickly with a comment about the movie, Ben asked, "You know what movie I am talking about, right?" I was embarrassed to admit that I couldn't really remember very much and what I did remember classified me as a nerd. I could only recall the scene that involved a debate about which book should be brought into the new age. After being holed up in the New York Public Library's Research Branch at Bryant Park, the survivors decide to save a copy of the Bible as a priceless text. I clearly remembered being preoccupied with figuring out my two book selections after seeing the movie (Yes, I granted myself an additional book). I chose the Bible and the collected works of Shakespeare while my friend, who I'd seen the movie with, chose *The Physician's Desk Reference* and *Physics for Dummies*. We came to the conclusion that I would die enlightened and he would die informed—and after me. Ben, of course, was more concerned about the movie's broader message about the dangers of ignoring important warnings from scientists about the potential of global disaster. He explained to me: "Yeah, it could happen like that, a scientist knows something and people don't really listen. I could see it. It just starts off somewhere and keeps getting bigger. It makes you think about what you need to be ready for."

I have since thought a lot about how powerful and timely Ben's remark is. At the time of writing this, it is January 30, 2019. With temperatures reported to be lower than in Antarctica, the Midwest is facing the brunt of a polar vortex (Bosman and Davey, 2019). It's negative 18°F in Chicago. O'Hare airport is closed. The Metra tracks were set on fire to keep them from cracking. It's negative 22°F in Minneapolis. Negative 20°F in Des Moines. Instagram photos show sea smoke rising from Minnesota's lakes and the Iowa sun has an eerie halo caused by ice crystals. A University of Iowa student has been found frozen behind a building. A Milwaukee man has been found frozen in his garage. Like most people, I feel even sadder because I know that we will hear about more fatalities tomorrow.[4] Power and gas companies are asking people to lower their thermostats. I am relieved that it is a relatively cozy 5°F degrees in New York. These apocalyptic events aren't from a fictional movie. This is real. It is climate change. According to the Fourth National Climate Assessment Report (United States Global Change Research Program, 2018), "More frequent and intense extreme weather and climate-related events, as well as changes in average climate conditions, are expected to continue to damage infrastructure, ecosystems, and social systems that provide essential benefits to communities." Ben is right. Climate change has already started, and it is just getting worse. Urban preppers like Ben might be better equipped (both literally and figuratively) to contend with extreme weather like a polar vortex, but for how long?

For Ben, (and for most viewers), movies offer the chance for deeper reflections on our connections with one another. Ben also found *The Book of Eli* (2010) particularly compelling. Grossing almost $95 million, the movie is ranked number fifteen in the "Post-apocalyptic" genre of movies (Box Office Mojo, 2019). More in the tradition of religion-based narratives, this post-apocalyptic movie traces a lone man's brutal quest to protect a sacred book that contains the knowledge to save humankind. Ben noted,

> Of course, it is a cool movie, great entertainment, but it made me think about a lot of questions. Denzel Washington plays the lone wolf guy who is supposedly ordered by God to do this. But it really isn't about the lone

guy. The story made me think about how groups are formed. What makes people follow bad guys. How people who are psychotic could persuade people and become leaders. Would it be like this? What would happen? It's about group formation. Think about it. That's what we are doing in our group, right? We're learning things together, we're helping each other, and we're making alliances, right?

Into the Forest (2016) reinforces the importance of forming a strong alliance in its story of two sisters learning to survive in their remote Pacific Northwestern home after a massive power outage. Jason recommended the movie to the group while conducting a homesteading demonstration on making your own detergent. During the middle of the presentation, Jason stopped and said, "Listen, it's all about homesteading, learning how to do these kinds of things." He thought for a moment more: "To get this, you need really to watch that movie ... What was it? ... *Into the Forest* ... it's about those two girls." He stopped for a moment and shook his head when recalling their perseverance. "All those things they had to do. Those girls. Like killing and skinning that boar. That movie, that's what got me thinking about homesteading." Truth be told, I avoided watching the movie for quite some time despite my research project. It sounded dreadful. I have a fear of canning and other Martha Stewart-ish activities. I got a D in Home Economics. There. It's out. Eventually, I ran out of reasons for not watching it. I believe Jason may have undersold the movie. Its subdued nature is quietly riveting, with its depiction of the girls' gradual (and sometimes jarring) slide away from modernity into an earlier moment. Each victory is hard-won as the girls study old botany guidebooks to start foraging or try hunting to sustain themselves. As weeks turn into months, their attempts at taking on new challenges often arise from their desire to care for one another. Their success is found in letting go of their dependency on technology in order to learn a new mindset—the life of the forest. For preppers, the movie emphasizes that real understanding is gained through a series of small steps. One lesson builds on another. As Jason later observed: "The movie hits all the points. They are learning as they go along." At the close of the movie, we are assured of the sisters' survival because they have made a sincere investment of time and patience in learning to adapt, not because we sense some suggestion of a rescue or the return to modernity.

In contrast, *Contagion* (2011) is a less uplifting story about the battle between two selfish and relentless enemies, a deadly virus that mercilessly moves from host to host to stay alive, and the Center for Disease Control and Prevention (CDC) as it ceaselessly pursues the virus to guarantee its extinction. In this movie, the CDC is depicted as a nimble and flexible agent in discovering a vaccine to end the epidemic (Biskind, 2018). Ranked number nineteen in the "Disaster" genre, earning about $76 million, the movie depicts the near-collapse of the world in the wake of a pandemic (Box Office Mojo, 2019). As Roger Ebert (2011) notes:

> *Contagion* is a realistic, unsensational movie about a global epidemic ... This scenario is already familiar to us ... through the apparently annual outbreaks of influenza ... The news chronology is always the same: alarmist maps, global roundups, the struggle to produce a vaccine at the Center for Disease Control in Atlanta, the manufacture and distribution of supplies of this year's 'flu shot.'

The movie depicts with eerie accuracy the possibility that a deadly virus can be spread so quickly and in such an ordinary fashion. For Brian, an independent prepper, the movie seems to reinforce the idea that the global risks are now part of daily life:

> *Contagion* made me think about how we live in such a small world, that something could spread that fast and so easily. It freaked me out because I watched it on a plane. I fly all the time for work. When the super flu was in high swing, I wore an antiviral face mask on the plane from here to LA. I was the only one. I didn't care. I always bring my own hand sanitizer and a face mask. Just prepper thinking. I stay updated on all my flu shots.

After a moment, he laughed and added:

> Hey, but we live in New York, so we really just need to lick the subway pole to stay healthy. It's like Desus and Mero say, 'Lick the subway pole to keep your immunities up.' It's the herd. It's about what immunities our local herd doesn't have.[5]

After thinking over the respective interpretations of these two preppers, I decided to carry out my own "thought experiment" by attempting to watch an apocalyptical movie from a prepper perspective. Beyond critiquing characters' survival techniques, what other prepping lessons could I draw from the movie? For my viewing as a rookie prepper, I chose a zombie apocalypse movie with minimal gore. I selected *Cargo* (2018) based on its movie festival buzz. *Cargo* was reviewed as a

> very strong, at times stirring achievement: a zombie movie with soul and pathos. The living dead are frightening again, not because of jump scares, surprise attacks or haunted house-style shenanigans, but because they remind us of truly terrifying things: losing ourselves, and our loved ones.
>
> (Buckmaster, 2017)

This review seemed to promise a movie that might offer a glimpse into what I imagine to be the ordinary and piecemeal horrors of a post-apocalyptic life.

Set in the Australian Outback, *Cargo* (2018) is the story of a father's struggles to find a safe home for his baby after a zombie apocalypse. In contrast to other movies that depict the apocalypse's aftermath as a frenzied bloodbath between good and evil forces, *Cargo* quietly emphasizes the unpredictability caused by an everyman's survival choices and chance encounters with other flawed humans. A little Aboriginal girl foreshadows his search: "I gotta find the clever man. He is a magic man. If you are sick, he can give you good medicine. And if someone steals your soul, he can put it back again." For preppers, *Cargo* could offer a complex message regarding approaches to prepping independently or prepping with a group. At first, the character's plight seems to reinforce the importance of prepping and one's resourcefulness and self-reliance under pressure. Throughout the movie, hungry families scavenge for food as they live in makeshift quarters. These scenes might remind preppers that stockpiling supplies and hiding away in a secret location would have decreased these hazards (or at least staved them off for a time). However, as the movie unfolds, one discovers that individual might, and the possession of supplies do not really matter very much. Instead, community is the key survival skill. In the movie's climax, the dying father relies on his resourcefulness to reach out to an Aboriginal group to save his baby. Perhaps for some preppers, he has become the clever man. The father has realized that his daughter's survival is only possible through community.

Inshirah, (another NYCPN member), selected a noteworthy movie for preppers that made me blush about the naiveté and sentimentality of *Cargo*. While I still argue that the movie has value, I must admit that, despite intermittent zombie attacks and the occasional bad human, the movie's quiet nature glossed over the possible harshness and cruelty of a post-apocalyptic life. The division between our movie selections reminded me of my role as participant-observer and her position as seasoned prepper. *The Survivalist* (2016) is an award-winning Irish independent movie that depicts life in a post-apocalyptic world of starvation and isolation. Set in the deep woods, a lone male carves out a meager existence on a tiny farm until the arrival of two women—an older mother and her young daughter—threatens his chance for survival. The movie is riveting, shocking and mainly silent. In such a stark and brutal world, the characters have no need for the eloquence of words. As a movie review explains:

> Sex can be traded for food and shelter, but trust has no price; and as relationships shift and outside perils multiply, the movie's real tension is cooked in the constantly adjusting space that separates these three characters. To survive, three must become two.
>
> (Catsoulis, 2017)

With winter nearing, the daughter discovers that she is pregnant with the man's child. To ensure her baby's survival, she poisons her mother. The remaining couple attempts to survive together; however, their farm is raided by other survivors with grisly intentions. At the close of the movie, the expectant mother escapes while the starving marauders roast the father.

After the movie ended, I took a walk around the block to try to shake off the movie's disturbing nature. It does not depict the flashy CGI post-apocalyptic fantasy of movies such as *Mad Max: Fury Road* (2015).[6] Instead, its minimalism was disturbing, a lonely forest inhabited by desperate and starving strangers who happen to have a few weapons and supplies. Inshirah contended:

> That is how it is going to be. No tough guy. It is a small-framed guy trying to survive. The juxtaposition of characters. There is always going to be sexual friction between men and women. There is nothing that we can do about it. For women, it's going to be a double-edged sword. You have power but it exposes you to danger. It's better to have a relationship built on loyalty or trust or recognition of need with a known devil. A rival male comes, you are gonna need your male. Also, when it comes to resources and generational issues, you are choosing between the past and the future. Are you willing to expend limited resources on the past? That's a tough question.

Our conversation expanded to a more general discussion of the economics of a post-apocalyptic world. Inshirah asked: "I'm a lawyer! What am I gonna do? You are a Ph.D. What are you gonna do?" She then shared a list of surprising post-apocalyptic entrepreneurial ideas that she requested not be disclosed. We both laughed as she observed, "Here we are thinking about the market after the apocalypse." Sex and money. Drivers in any setting.

Unlike the survivalists studied in Mitchell (2002), urban preppers are not seeking to abandon the skills that they have mastered as city dwellers in favor of a simpler form of life. As urbanites and workers in the service economy, many of these preppers are accomplished in their professions. However, as their interest in disaster preparedness has increased, urban preppers have discovered that they have a critical weakness. They lack the right skill set for the job of surviving disaster. As a result, their interest in learning prepping skills represent a familiar business survival strategy for urbanites: gaining a competitive edge. For example, in the typical New York spirit, Inshirah and Al, both NYCPN members, have moved beyond learning how to build fire to learning how to build generators.

Inshirah's insightfulness about post-apocalyptic realities brought to mind the flawed representations of both men and women in reality-based television shows. In analyzing reality television shows on prepping, Kelly (2016) argues that male performances of disaster preparedness in these series reenact hegemonic masculinity by staging scenarios that require manly skills for survival.[7] In reality, this perspective is not reinforced by most NYC preppers as they are a diverse group that includes women with expert survival training. Still, many NYC preppers did find the National Geographic *Doomsday Preppers* series to be noteworthy. The series provided them with evidence that prepping was not exclusively the domain of wealthy whites or white rural survivalists (Foster, 2016). Instead, the show depicted preppers from a range of economic backgrounds and ethnicities, like Jason Charles (a middle-class NYC African-American firefighter and prepper). The series also revealed that prepping was not confined to the suburbs and rural areas, but was practiced in urban areas as well. As Jason often explains to the press: "Everyone and anyone can be a prepper. Preppers come from all walks of life." With his brawn and matter-of-factness, Jason gave a face to New York prepping as a diverse culture of city dwellers. Al explained:

> I've been a prepper since I was 15. I didn't know there was even a name for what I was doing. I saw Jason. I mean, he was a New Yorker. I thought, he's like me so I reached out to him. I can't remember if it was on Facebook or LinkedIn.

Marlon, another member, made the same comment: "I saw Jason on the show. He was like me. So, I got in touch with him." Jason's appearance on *Doomsday Preppers* was a conduit for those who do not fit the prepper stereotype to develop their interest in prepping. With nearly one million internet search hits, Jason is an ambassador for bringing prepping into the mainstream.

Through promoting their interest in prepping, Jason and other group members also participate in the production of popular culture. Jason is an effective spokesperson for urban prepping. On camera and in print, his appeal is genuine and thoughtful as he shares the ins-and-outs of prepping. His stature and his composure communicate reassurance. Jason might even be considered to be cultivating his own brand. Under the name of "The Angry Prepper," he operates a YouTube channel, a podcast, an Instagram account and a Facebook page. He has also written a primer for creating a bug out bag (Charles, 2014) which has been sold on websites ranging from Amazon to One Kings Lane.

Inshirah also has a YouTube channel called "Mrs. Vital Survival." She offers "practical advice and intelligent discussion" about prepping from the perspective of a "mom who is black, urban, and nonpolitical." Her channel's broad purpose is to generate dialogue with other preppers and to eventually create a network of prepper-subscribers. For Inshirah, her videos are conversation starters intended to foster an exchange of ideas and to engage in problem-solving for issues such as coping with emotional trauma or sleep deprivation during bug out situations (leaving your home to escape danger and to reach a safe destination). She views establishing a successful YouTube channel as a platform for launching other prepping ventures such as the development of a survival skill camp which is now in its conceptualization stage. As a female prepper, Inshirah's expertise and her interest in creating a media presence counters the misrepresentation of female preppers in reality-based television shows. For example, Christian (2016) finds that the show's depictions of women preppers are framed only to project a dependency on the survival skills of their male partner rather than recognizing the women's respective prepping abilities.

Members of the NYCPN are particularly media savvy and seek to protect their image. Media coverage of the group is fairly common, so members are familiar with the press; it is business as usual when reporters and camera crews accompany them on excursions. Group members are interested in demystifying prepping and breaking stereotypes. Therefore, they are willing to be movied engaging in various activities such as fire building or first aid training. As the group's leader and primary spokesperson, Jason screens media requests. To support a particular story's focus, he will refer reporters to specific group members to be interviewed if needed. For example, an interview request for a story with a focus on women preppers would be referred to a female prepper. Group members have learned to be particularly careful during interviews as statements may be taken out of context in order to convey extremism or even something humorous. In discussing perceived misrepresentations of the NYCPN in the press, Annette, a member, often referred to a PBS News Hour story (2013) as both a funny and somewhat embarrassing depiction of the group. The segment is a witty and mostly positive discussion of the group that emphasizes its sense of community as well as its imperfections. At the start of the televised segment, Jason arrives late to begin movieing and he is shown explaining that he had to buy dog food before leaving for the trip. Another member is gently made fun of for their expensive taste, bringing Italian fish filets in olive oil rather than regular canned tuna. However, the audience is then reminded that one might prefer to eat what they enjoy during a disaster rather than unappetizing and unfamiliar foods. A seasoned prepper is also jokingly no longer considered a survivor because he developed stomach flu on the trip. The segment ends by reviewing the group's training activities and complimenting its commitment to embracing community as the key to survival. The segment also closely notes the NYCPN's unique position as a diverse group of city dwellers dedicated to learning prepping. For Annette, the segment is a humorous reminder about the need to always remain professional and to understand that any events that occur during a visit from the press could be misconstrued for effect.

While the NYCPN moves forward with breaking stereotypes about preppers, television programming has also shifted to present survivalism from a new angle. Instead of imaginary struggles, these survivalist shows present real-life tests of human will and perseverance. Now there is no need to imagine the cruelty of a post-apocalyptic world, as viewers are given the chance to see real people suffer through harsh conditions with few or no supplies— and sometimes without any clothing. Nominated for three Emmy awards, *Naked and Afraid* (2015–) pairs two naked strangers with varying levels of survival skills to survive in the wilderness for twenty-one days. Given one tool per person, the pair is challenged to work together to sustain themselves by finding food and water, creating a shelter and battling nature. Brian, an independent NYC prepper, argued that this series was of no interest to him as a prepper. "It didn't really interest me because it wasn't a real challenge. They knew that they only had to last twenty-one days. They didn't have to be good at it. You could go fetal or whatever. You can just make a shelter and hold out until the twenty-one days are up. It's a finite period."

In the TV series *Alone* (2015–), contestants with varying levels of survival skills attempt to survive alone for as long as possible for a cash prize. Stationed alone in remote areas such as Vancouver Island, Mongolia, or Patagonia, each contestant must try to survive by securing water, hunting for food, building a shelter and frequently fending off animals who have discovered the survivalist's food or who have discovered the survivalist as food. While neither series was mentioned as noteworthy, *Alone* came up in casual conversations on NYC prepper outings. Preppers occasionally discussed the quality of bushcraft techniques, or the impact of mistakes made by contestants. For example, one prepper expressed surprise when commenting on a contestant's decision to withdraw from the game after losing his fire tool: "Yeah, that guy lost his fire starter and that was it for him. He lost it! He couldn't think of what else to do." In response, other preppers offered possible strategies for starting a fire. As *Alone* contestants seemed to be more knowledgeable and actually had tools, I chose to watch this series to see if I could gain some understanding of what it would be like to try to survive for an extended period of time. Most winners, it should be noted, last over thirty days.

However, despite any bushcraft tips that I may have learned, or however fervently I may have rooted for a particular contestant, I ultimately turned away from the show because its quest for discovering the sense of will and fortitude was replaced by a sharp focus on fragility and futility. In Season Three, the mental agility of a lead contestant starts to slip away as he begins to deliberately starve himself. With winter approaching, the man becomes obsessed with smoking fish to preserve it for the impending cold. Standing in the interior of his shelter with strips of dried fish hanging on all the walls, he obsesses over his fear about a lack of protein in the weeks ahead. Emaciated and surrounded by food, he shares the flawed logic behind his decision to stop eating in order to stockpile as much fish as possible. Eventually, he was removed from the competition to prevent further damage to his health from continued starvation. This series reflects Tietge's (2018) argument that

> there is a disturbing pessimism running through our culture that seems to embrace the dark and the unpleasant … to map this collective fetish onto nature programs seems off, to say the least, but perhaps the most important question is, what does it do to the public perception about nature when it is portrayed as a battleground, or on a more personal level, a sentient fiend bent on human destruction?
>
> (p. 9)

The popularity of the television series *The Walking Dead* (2010–) cannot be overstated. *The Walking Dead* holds the second-highest total viewership in cable television history, slightly trailing *Game of Thrones* (Rowles, 2017). Based on a comic book written by Robert Kirkman, the series portrays life after the zombie apocalypse as it follows a group of survivors led by a former sheriff. The comic book has sold over 50 million copies globally and has been translated into over thirty languages (Fear, 2016). Kirkman explains his show's appeal:

> It's the global economic crisis, income inequality, the post-9/11 world. Everyone is scared shitless. It's not the worst time ever to be alive, but you know, it's tough out there. I feel like if you worry every day about the world around you and then you go home and watch a guy get chased by zombies — it's like, well, could be *a lot worse*.
>
> (Fear, 2016)

However, despite a post-apocalyptic narrative in which people rely on their skills and instincts to stay alive, *The Walking Dead* has not been identified by preppers as important for understanding prepping or even talked about in any observed casual conversation regarding survival strategies. The reason for this omission is simple. As explained by Jason, "Zombies are not real. Zombies are not a threat or a danger. Therefore, there is no need to prepare for a zombie apocalypse." According to Brian:

> *The Walking Dead* is awesome. It's scary and great for laughs. But I don't relate it to prepping. It was about relationships and now it's about warring factions. Rick is a lousy leader and they always make bad decisions to drive the plot.

When asked about this show, Inshirah said:

> It's fun but I don't watch it regularly. How realistic is it? Zombies running around. And, it is always summer. How accurate is that? Atlanta gets snow and ice. On YouTube, some people do a good job of using it as a springboard to talk about subjects. In prepping, zombies are your neighbors who aren't prepared and come to take your food. People need to think about that kind of zombie.

Inshirah's comments are apt as she reveals the potential for conflict in a severe crisis. As both a post-apocalyptic and a zombie narrative, *The Walking Dead* serves as a keen lens for examining our social and political landscapes.[8] Duren (2016) argues that the zombie's single focus on consuming and moving forward might just be a metaphor for life in the 21st century. As Duren (2016) observes:

> Survival depends on mobility, adaptability, and an understanding of what seems safe and permanent today will likely disappear tomorrow … All that was is no more; there are enemies within and monsters without. The only hope for survival is, you guessed it, to eat and keep moving.
>
> (p. 12)

Given their definition of zombies as unprepared neighbors and their philosophy of self-reliance, preppers may have already learned this lesson.

Beyond movies and television, novels have also been influential in shaping the mindset of NYC preppers. Written by William R. Forstchen (2009), *One Second After* is a popular post-apocalyptic novel that traces the struggles of a history professor and former colonel as he battles to protect his family and his town in the aftermath of an electromagnetic pulse (EMP) attack on America, that has short-circuited all electronic devices, rendering modern technology useless. Released in March 2009, the novel was listed as number eleven on *The New York Times* Bestseller list by May that year, and then released in paperback in November. The novel's scenario was given legitimacy with a foreword written by the author's friend and former Republican House Speaker Newt Gingrich. In his foreword, Gingrich (2009) suggests that the novel should be considered as a "'future history' that should be thought-provoking and even terrifying for all of us" (p. 11). The danger of an electromagnetic pulse was discovered in 1962 when the American military detonated a hydrogen bomb over the Pacific, causing the streets of Hawaii to immediately go dark. Throughout his presidential bid, in conference speeches and on the campaign trail, Gingrich argued that an EMP was an overlooked threat and that America needed to develop a response or perhaps even make a preemptive strike on rogue nations such as Iran or North Korea[9] (Broad, 2011). President Trump has taken a similar position. In 2019, President Trump issued "Executive Order on Coordinating National Resilience to Electromagnetic Pulses" in an effort to assess the risks of such an attack to critical US infrastructure (Cohen, 2019).

While Gingrich's endorsement was valuable, the success of *One Second After* is most likely attributable to Forstchen's ability to transform Black Mountain, NC from a college town into one of America's last fortresses. In *One Second After*, the main character and the town slide toward oblivion—minor inconveniences such as the lack of a hot cup of coffee and a decent smoke, quickly segue into loss of life due to the lack of medicine such as insulin, then starvation and battles with gangs of cannibals. Five NYC preppers referenced the book as noteworthy to their thinking. For example, Jason explained to me that *One Second After* strongly influenced his interest in prepping. He said:

> That book, I'll never forget it. The book is all about stuff that the guy could have done to help his family before things happened. All the stuff he could have done and the ways that he could have protected them, but he didn't think to do any of it. It made me think about what I could be doing for my family. Things that I could be doing in advance of something happening.

After I read the novel, I must admit that it has given me new worries. Not worries about an EMP strike. Worries about a prolonged power outage. My college-age niece is insulin-dependent. My sister passed away, so I have the honor of caring for my niece. She does have extra insulin, but "extra" and "enough" are two very different things. My dad is on oxygen and I refuse to think about that. I have also thought about my vices, stupid things like secret sips of Diet Coke and nibbling on Golden Oreos. But prepping excursions have toughened me up, no doubt. When you are in the woods, the conditions make you forget about those things. That is why, for me, *One Second After*, is so intriguing. There is no forgetting the comforts of home; expectations are ingrained. The book generates fear because it illustrates the erasure of the everyday until catastrophe becomes the everyday.

As a future history, *One Second After* doesn't bode well for cities. Reflecting the populist suspicion of city dwellers as rich elitists, the college town survives but New York doesn't.[10] At the novel's conclusion, a general report states that:

> They say in all of New York City there's not much more than twenty-five thousand people now and those are either savages or people hiding and living off scraps of garbage ... Cholera broke out last fall and the government decided to abandon the city ... A friend of mine stationed there on duty said it was like the Dark Ages.
>
> (Forstchen, 2009, p. 338)

This imaginary outcome speaks to the debate among New Yorkers about planning to stay in the city (bugging in) or leaving the city (bugging out) in the event of a catastrophe, which is explored in the following chapters of this book.

In studying the apocalyptic turn in America's movie and television during the 21st century, Ford and Mitchell (2018) observe that

> the suffocating ethos of fear impels us to replay stories about the dangerous terrain we traverse, about the disasters that befall us from within and without, about those who might save or enlighten us, about the end-of-days preparations we might make, and about the ways in which the whole might be darkly funny, or teetering on the edge of exhaustion.
>
> (p. 21)

Through their imaginary worlds of chaos and danger, the texts discussed in this chapter also represent such an ethos. However, in these prepper-selected stories, there is still a glimmer of hope, however dim, in the resilience of the ordinary person. In each story, the day is saved—or at least salvaged—by an everyday man or woman. This message has clearly been received by urban preppers as consumers of popular culture. From their perspective, these texts help one to think through both the origins of disaster and strategize about possible means for survival. For urban preppers, there is an important distinction. While these texts critique modern society, all urban preppers are not necessarily nostalgic for an earlier period in which people engaged in craft and could create or repair things for themselves. Instead, developing prepping skills enhances the knowledge base of these city dwellers. With disaster preparedness, NYC urban preppers are seeking to ensure that they can survive in any world.

Notes

1 For an analysis of social organization and action attribution as revealed through interactions of manipulation in competitive board game play, see Hofstetter and Robles (2019).
2 Current movie databases do not include an "apocalyptic" category for movies. Apocalyptic movies are scattered across genres (including categories such as science fiction, horror, disaster, and super-hero action). Furthermore, the use of the words "apocalyptic" or "post-apocalyptic" in storylines is sometimes misleading as both terms are invoked to capture interest rather than to serve as an accurate description. Also, some apocalyptic movies are really superhero movies in which a famous comic book character must use his or her strength to save the world from ruin. For example, in Wonder Woman (2017), the superhero aids mortals by killing Ares, a god who is set on destroying humankind.
3 *Titanic* is ranked number one by earning $659 million in US box-office ticket receipts. The Boxmojo.com database contains information on box-office grosses from the 1979 to the present day.
4 On January 31, The New York Times reported twenty-one deaths due to the polar vortex (Smith, Bosman, and Davey, 2019).
5 Desus and Mero is a popular American late-night talk show on Showtime. Known as Desus and Mero, the New York comedy duo of Daniel Baker, a Jamaican-American, and Joel Martinez, a Dominican-American, has attracted large audiences across different media platforms. Their humor and witty interactions draw on their experiences as Bronx natives and their observations about American culture and politics. Their previous successes include their popular "Bodega Boys" podcast and hosting Viceland's first daily late-night talk show.
6 For an interesting discussion of Mad Max: Fury Road (2015) and similar movies, see Ford and Mitchell, 2018.
7 Disaster scenarios, such as widespread chaos and destruction, are perceived to require a militaristic outlook that allows hegemonic masculinities to prevail in the imaginary post-apocalyptic world (Christian 2016).
8 Simpson and Mallard (2017) accurately and amusingly observe that the volume of scholarship across disciplines on the television series has launched the field of Walking Dead studies. For anthologies, see (Simpson and Mallard, eds., 2017); (Langley, ed., 2015); (Keetley, ed., 2014); (Robichaud, 2012); (Yuen, 2012); and (Lowder, 2011).
9 At the American Israel Public Affairs Committee's annual policy conference, Gingrich discussed Forstchen's novel and advocated for an American EMP strategic plan. He argued: "It's based on fact, it is accurate, and it's horrifying, and we have zero national strategy to respond to it today." He laid out a scenario in which three small nuclear weapons detonated at the right altitude would eliminate all electricity production in the United States. Which is why, he concluded, "I favor taking out Iranian and North Korean missiles on their sites" (Crowley, 2009).
10 This novel does not address the reality that New York's extremely wealthy were probably doing quite well in their luxury bunkers.

References

Albrecht, R. (Producer). (2013, June/July). The jungle curse [Television series episode]. In *Naked and afraid*. Discovery.

Alpert, D., Darabont, F., and Eglee, C. H. (Executive producers), Nicotero, G. (Director.) The walking dead 2010. United States: American Movie Classics.

Anderson, B. (Director and Executive producer). (2015). *Dirty rotten survival*. United States: National Geographic.

Behr, Z. (Producer). (2015, June/July). And so it begins [Television series episode]. In *Alone*. United States: Leftfield Pictures.

Behr, Z., Kahler, G., Mandle, B., George, D., Palek, G., Pender, R., and Witt, S. (Executive producers). (2015). *Alone*. United States: Leftfield Pictures.

Biskind, P. (2018). *The sky is falling: How vampires, zombies, androids, and superheroes made America great for extremism*. New York: The New Press.

Blum, J., M. Bay, A. Form, B. Fuller, and S. K. Lemercier (Producers), DeMonaco, J. (Director). (2013). *The purge*. United States: Platinum Dunes, Blumhouse Productions, Why Not Productions.

Bosman, J., and Davey, M. (2019, January 30). A merciless cold lingers in the midwest. *The New York Times*. Retrieved from https://www.nytimes.com/2019/01/30/us/extreme-cold-weather.html.

Brilliant, Z., Dawson, I., Deeker, C., Grady, F., Harrison, J., Hunt, P., Kirk, I. and Ross, C. (Producers), Howling, B., and Ramke, Y. (Writers). (2017). *Cargo*. Australia: Umbrella Entertainment, Addictive Pictures, Causeway movies, Head Gear movies.

Broad, W. J. (2011, December 11). Among Gingrich's passions, a doomsday vision. *The New York Times*. Retrieved from https://www.nytimes.com/2011/12/12/us/politics/gingrichs-electromagnetic-pulse-warning-has-skeptics.html.

Box Office Mojo. (2019). *Top gross earnings by genre*. Retrieved from https://www.boxofficemojo.com/genres/chart/?id=disaster.html.

Buckmaster, L. (2017, October 7). The living dead have us spooked, but in a painful way. [Review of the motion picture *Cargo*, 2017], *The Guardian*. Retrieved from https://www.theguardian.com/movie/2017/oct/07/cargo-review-the-living-dead-have-us-spooked-but-in-a-painful-way.

Catsoulis, J. (2017, May 11). Three must become two in 'The survivalist.' [Review of the Television series *The survivalist*]. *The New York Times*. Retrieved from https://www.nytimes.com/2017/05/17/movies/the-survivalist-review.html.

Charles, J. (2014). *Emergency bag essentials: Everything you need to bug out*. New York: Potter Style.

Christian, T. A. (2016). The recuperation of wounded hegemonic masculinity on *Doomsday Preppers*. In L. A. Clark, A. Firestone, and M. F. Pharr (Eds.), *The last midnight: Essays on apocalyptic narratives in millennial media* (pp. 48–59). Jefferson, NC: McFarland.

Cohen, A. (2019, April 5). *Trump moves to protect America from electromagnetic pulse attack*. Forbes. Retrieved from https://www.forbes.com/sites/arielcohen/2019/04/05/whitehouse-prepares-to-face-emp-threat/#7010ff86e7e2.

Cohen, J. N. (2017). *Financial crisis in American households: The basic expenses that bankrupt the middle class*. Santa Barbara, CA: Praeger.

Crowley, M. (2009, June 3). The Newt bomb. *The New Republic*. Retrieved from https://newrepublic.com/article/64755/the-newt-bomb.

Duren, B. L. (2016). Zombies 'r' us. In P. L. Simpson and M. Mallard (Eds.) *The walking dead live! Essays on the television show* (pp. 4–18). London: Rowman and Littlefield.

Ebert, R. (2011, September 27). *Contagion. {Review of the motion picture Contagion,* 2011]. Retrieved from https://www.rogerebert.com/reviews/contagion-2011.

Emmerich, R. and Gordon, M. (Producers), Emmerich, R. (Director). (2004). *The day after tomorrow.* United States: Centropolis Entertainment, Lionsgate movies, Mark Gordon Company.

Fear, D. (2016, May 31). *Robert Kirkman: Inside 'walking dead' creator's twisted mind,* new show. Retrieved from https://www.rollingstone.com/tv/tv-news/robert-kirkman-insi de-walking-dead-creators-twisted-mind-new-show-51826/.

Fichman, N. (Producer), and Rozema, P. (Director). (2015). *Into the forest.* United States: Elevation Pictures.

Ford, E. A., and Mitchell, D. C. (2018). *Apocalyptic visions in 21st century movies.* Jefferson: McFarland.

Forstchen, W. R. (2009). *One second after.* New York, NY: Tom Doherty Associates Book.

Foster, G. A. (2014). *Hoarders, doomsday preppers, and the culture of apocalypse.* New York, NY: Palgrave Macmillan.

Foster, G. A. (2016). Consuming the apocalypse, marketing bunker materiality. *Quarterly Review of movie and Video,* 33(4), 285–302.

Gilbery, D., Godfrey, W. M., and Jones, R. (Producers), Fingleton, S. (Director). (2015). *The survivalist.* United Kingdom: The Fyzz Facility.

Gingrich, N. (2009). Foreword. In W. R. Forstchen (Ed.), *One second after* (pp. 11–12). New York, NY: Tom Doherty Associates Book.

Hofstetter, E., and Robles, J. (2018). Manipulation in board game interactions: Being a sporting player. *Symbolic Interaction,* 42(2), 301–320.

Johnson, L. (Director). (1961). *The shelter.* [Television series episode] In B. Houghton, (Executive producer), *The twilight zone.* United States: Cayuga Productions.

Keetley, D. (Ed.) (2014). *"We're all infected": Essays on AMC's the walking dead and the fate of the human.* Jefferson: McFarland.

Kelly, C. R. (2016). The man-pocalpyse: Doomsday preppers and the rituals of apocalyptic manhood. *Text and Performance Quarterly,* 36, 95–114.

Langley, T. (Ed.) (2015). *The walking dead psychology: Psych of the living dead.* New York: Sterling.

Lowder, J. (Ed.) (2011). *Triumph of the walking dead: Robert Kirkman's zombie epic on page and screen.* Dallas: Smart Pop/BenBella Books.

Madison, A. (Director and Executive Producer). (2011). *Doomsday preppers.* United States: Sharp Entertainment.

Doyle, R. (Director). (2013). *Before the flood.* In J. J. Mallari, (Executive producer), *Doomsday castle.* United States: Sharp Entertainment.

May, E. T. (2017). *Fortress America: How we embraced fear and abandoned democracy.* New York, NY: Basic Books.

Mitchell, D., Miller, G. and Voeten, P. (Producers), Miller, G. (Director). (2015). *Mad Max: Fury road.* Australia: Warner Bros. Pictures.

Mitchell, R. G. (2002). *Dancing at Armageddon: Survivalism and chaos in modern times.* Chicago, IL: University of Chicago Press.

PBS News Hour (2013, October 25). *NY survivors of Sandy ditch the city to 'bug out' in preparation for doomsday.* Retrieved from https://www.pbs.org/newshour/show/survi vors-of-sandy-ditch-n-y-to-prepare-for-doomsday.

Renner, K. J. (2012). The appeal of the apocalypse. *LIT Literature Interpretation Theory,* 23(3), 203–211.

Robichaud, C. (Ed.) (2012). *The walking dead and philosophy: Shotgun, machete, reason.* Hoboken: John Wiley and Sons.

Rose, K. D. (2001). *One nation underground: The fallout shelter in American culture.* New York, NY: New York University Press.

Rosen, E. K. (2008). *Apocalyptic transformation: Apocalypse and the postmodern imagination.* Plymouth: Lexington Books.

Rowles, D. (2017, July 18). Has 'game of thrones' surpassed 'the walking dead' as the highest rated show on cable? *UPROXX.* Retrieved from https://uproxx.com/tv/game-of-thrones-walking-dead-ratings/.

Silver, J., Downey, S., Kosove, A., Johnson, B. and Washington, D. (Producers), Hughes, A., and Hughes, A. (Writers). (2010). *The book of Eli.* United States: Alcon Entertainment, Silver Pictures.

Shamberg, M. Sher, S. and Jacobs, G. (Producers), Soderbergh, S. (Director). (2011). *Contagion.* United States: Participant Media, Image Nation Abu Dhabi.

Simpson, P. L., and Mallard, M. (Eds.). (2016). *The Walking dead live! Essays on the television show.* London: Rowman and Littlefield.

Smith, M., Bosman, J., and Davey, M. (2019, January 31). *Extreme cold weather spreads east.* Retrieved from https://www.nytimes.com/2019/01/31/us/weather-polar-vortex.html.

Tietge, D. J. (2018). Experiencing nature through cable television. In K. Rutten, S. Blancke, R. Soetaert, (Eds.), *Perspectives on science and culture.* Indiana: Purdue University Press.

United States Global Change Research Group. (2018). Impacts, risks, and adaptation in the United States: fourth national climate assessment, volume ii. *U.S. Global Change Research Program.* Retrieved from https://nca2018.globalchange.gov/.

Williams, B. (Producer), Oz, F. (Director). (1988). *Dirty rotten scoundrels.* United States: Orion Pictures.

Williams, R., and Orrom, M. (1954). *Preface to movie.* London: movie Drama.

Wójcik, D. (1997). *The end of the world as we know it: Faith, fatalism, and apocalypse in America.* New York: New York University Press.

Yuen, W. (Ed.) (2012). *The walking dead and philosophy: Zombie apocalypse now.* Chicago: Open Court.

Part 2

Prepping in New York: Going it alone or going together

4 "Bugging in"

Sheltering in place for the extremely wealthy and mere mortals

At the 1964 World's Fair held in Flushing Meadow Park in Queens, a Texas builder, Jay Swayze, introduced America's rich to the concept of surviving disaster in style. For a separate $1 admission fee, fair visitors were able to tour "The Underground Home," a luxury fallout shelter which was a 10-room, 5,600 square foot home complete with air conditioning, entertainment spaces and "outside" terraces that featured murals of panoramic landscapes backlit to mimic the natural light of the outside world, all encased in a twenty-inch concrete and steel shell (Carlson, 2017). The home was not a wildly popular exhibition as not all fair visitors could afford to spend extra money on a separate ticket. However, for the extremely wealthy, Swayze's project promised great hope. According to its brochure, a "few feet underground can give a man ... an island unto himself; a place where he controls his own world—a world of total ease and comfort, of security, safety, and, above all, privacy" (Carlson, 2017). This underground home promised that one could preserve the elements of a comfortable life in the event of disaster and during its aftermath. While Swayze was unsuccessful in selling even one underground home at the World's Fair, this exclusive option is now sought after by the extremely wealthy who have become interested in prepping to protect their families and their standard of life. Fifty-five years later, the concept of a luxury fallout shelter has been updated and is now envisioned as a luxury safe room (an interior mini-apartment) designed to both protect and pamper its residents. For the extremely wealthy, defined as multi-millionaires and billionaires, preparing for great disaster by any means necessary is a precaution just like protecting an investment portfolio. Both strategies are associated with evaluating risk and minimizing negative outcomes. In other words, prepping is an exercise in maintaining control. For New York's high-net-worth (HNW) preppers, preparing for catastrophe by investing in a safe room or hideaway destination is a form of "apocalypse insurance" (Osnos, 2017, p. 39).

For New York's everyday preppers, this level of "apocalypse insurance" is not available. Instead, these middle- and working-class preppers rely on their hands-on skills and resourcefulness to outfit their homes to protect against disaster. Although the majority of these preppers likely believe that they will probably have to leave their homes in the event of a severe and prolonged disaster, they still make plans for the possibility of remaining at home. Staying in your home (luxe or standard) during a disaster is known as "sheltering in place." As described by the Department of Homeland Security (DHS) (2019), "There may be situations, depending on your circumstances and the nature of the disaster, when it's simply best to stay where you are and avoid any uncertainty outside by 'sheltering in place.'" While one can shelter in place wherever you are, preppers commonly refer to "sheltering in place" as "bugging in," or staying in your home, hunkering down.

The history of New York's programs designed to support sheltering in place is an important context for analyzing different approaches to "bugging in." In 2018, I toured a multi-family, multi-story housing unit prototype designed to provide interim shelter for New York City families following disaster. Traditional trailers used for post-disaster housing are not suitable for use in urban areas because these units require too much horizontal space. In cities such as New York, wide swaths of horizontal space are virtually non-existent. Therefore, the New York City Department of Emergency Management and the New York City Department of Design and Construction, with the help of the US Army Corps of Engineers and FEMA, built and constructed a prototype of post-disaster housing based on a shipping container-style modular system. The housing system is intended as a temporary solution for families after emergency shelter and before they transition to housing that they can sustain without post-disaster aid (New York City Department of Emergency Management, 2018). If the prototype is realized, the units could be built on-demand following a disaster (with a production time of roughly three months). Located at Cadman Plaza in Brooklyn at the time of writing, the prototype is actually a series of micro-apartments that can be stacked on top of one another to build a low-scale but temporary apartment complex. On my tour, all visitors agreed that we would definitely enjoy living in such an apartment. Think a *Dwell* apartment, only tiny.

While this prototype represents dialogue about planning for post-disaster life of New Yorkers, the actual construction of housing units designed to protect families during disaster and its aftermath is now reserved only for extremely wealthy urbanites. Thanks to their economic positions and locations, New York elites sometimes construct and stock safe rooms (often smaller interior apartments within their residences) as places of refuge during disaster. These posh preppers are often able to purchase and install costly security and safety equipment in response to reports of disasters in other areas or in fear of potential disasters in New York.

While the construction of safe rooms in urban homes may seem like a novel response to potential crisis, protective structures have been a mainstay in urban architecture. Throughout the history of cities, the wealthy have often relied on the building of fortresses to protect themselves against physical harm and to preserve their riches. For example, as far back as ancient Rome, it was common for those with sufficient means to make special preparations for both man-made and natural disasters. Toner (2013) writes that risk was routinized and that the attitude toward disaster thus became one of acceptance and preparation when possible. To safeguard their belongs, these wealthy ancients built hidden storage rooms within their homes. Small safe rooms were even found in the ruins of the great homes of Pompeii. In particular, these wealthy ancients feared the loss of wealth caused by the social unrest spurred by disaster. For example, during the Great Fire of Nero's reign, night watchmen started new fires so they could join in looting wealthy homes, rather than continuing to protect Rome. Criminals and soldiers also often banded together to plunder Rome during other fires.[1] Throughout the medieval period, English royalty stored their treasures in strongholds, including in the bowels of Westminster Abbey and in obscure places within the Tower of London.

For this century's New York elite, safe rooms are larger, now designed to protect both families and property. As in earlier periods, the construction and location of these safe rooms is cloaked in secrecy. They are also an important status symbol. Possession of a safe room suggests that the individual is not only rich enough to afford—and require—such a refuge, but that the person is also powerful enough to maintain protection in any circumstance (Osnos, 2017). The phenomenon of safe rooms being built almost exclusively by the extremely wealthy in Manhattan (with a few in Brooklyn) certainly highlights class division in cities. Clearly, the construction of safe rooms by powerful and rich private citizens points to the potential advantages that this group may have in shielding their families from harm compared to those in lower-income brackets. These types of safe rooms suggest the possibility that, in the event of a great disaster, Manhattan really will become a place only for the rich—an ironic and final illustration of concerns raised by urbanists that the city is quickly becoming a place only for the wealthy.

As defined by FEMA (2006), safe rooms are standalone or internal shelters that are constructed to protect occupants from man-made threats and natural hazards. Man-made threats include terrorist attacks, technological accidents and malfunctions, assassinations, kidnappings, cyberattacks and CBRE attacks (the use of chemical, biological, radiological and explosive weapons). Natural hazards refer to threats such as hurricanes, blizzards and tornadoes. Dangerous weather patterns are fairly easy to predict based on meteorological research and historical data; however, forecasting specific man-made hazards is challenging given the scarcity of data and the variations in magnitude and recurrence of threats (FEMA, 2006).

According to a veteran real estate agent in the city's luxury residential market, the "interest in protecting one's family against disaster or social unrest is an unspoken but real concern for New York's high-end residential buyer." The clientele for safe rooms has expanded from industry leaders and celebrities to include international buyers who require advanced security in their home countries such as Saudi Arabia and Russia (Chaban, 2015). Known examples of Manhattan luxury homes that contain luxe safe rooms are billionaire Bruce

Kovner's historic townhouse, which contains a lead-lined room designed to shield occupants from threats such as a chemical attack or a dirty bomb as well as financial chief Alan Wilzig's expansive TriBeCa modern townhouse, which has a safe room hidden behind a bedroom closet (Gaffney, 2016). Celebrities Joan Rivers and Gwyneth Paltrow were reported to have safe rooms in their New York homes. (Chaban, 2015). No longer a rare novelty, the construction of safe rooms is now viewed as both urgent and fashionable for New York's extremely wealthy. According to one Upper East Side resident, investing in hideaway destinations and safe rooms

> becomes a competition at dinner parties. Who has what state-of-the-art hazmat suits, and kits where you can drink your own pee, etcetera … When I saw Showtime's *Billions*, I died laughing that they had millions in bearer bonds just as go money. People love to say how much go money they have.
>
> (Gaffney, 2016)

Bragging rights aside, Tom Gaffney, president of Gaffco Ballistics, a premier safe room builder for New York and global elites, contends that investing in a safe room stems from genuine concern about protection against terrorist attacks. While September 11th spurred initial interest in the building of safe rooms in Manhattan, the fear of "dirty bombs" drives contemporary construction. After the 2010 Times Square car bombing attempt, Gaffco Ballistics saw its biggest increase in safe room sales. As Gaffney explained to me, "9/11 was a game-changer for the industry. The first spike was after 9/11. The second spike was the car with explosives near Times Square. That reminded people of the reality of the situation." The United States Bomb Data Center's *Annual Explosive Incident Report* (2017) indicates that in 2017 there were 687 explosions, 335 of which were bombings. New York ranked fourth in the top eleven states with ten or more reported bombings, with California and Washington coming out on top. An explosive IED attack is the use of a "homemade" bomb or destructive device to destroy, incapacitate, harass or distract (Department of Homeland Security, 2018). IEDs that spread chemical, radiological or biological material are known as "dirty bombs."

Safe rooms have now transformed well beyond bare-bones separate chambers to become state-of-the-art rooms that make refuge both cozier and much more secure (Chaban, 2015). Bunkers of the Cold War years and the bleak prison-like cell depicted in the thriller *Panic Room* (2002) are no longer standards for safe room design. Now, modern safe rooms are designed as self-enclosed impenetrable rooms made of drill-resistant concrete that contain features such as biometric locks, air scrubbing systems and cutting-edge design. Therefore, prices for residential safe rooms range from the thousands to the millions depending on client needs. Real Estate agents usually address client interest in safe rooms by showing three possible dwelling types: new construction that features a safe room as a part of its design plan, an existing property that has a safe room or sufficient space for its construction, or an existing dwelling (a single-family home) that has been or could be retrofitted so that the entire dwelling functions as a safe house. In New York, Gaffney estimates that the initial cost of a safe room begins at $300,000 and increases depending on client needs. Custom-built and based upon client needs, safe rooms are designed to appear and function as a traditional room. Custom woodwork and fine architectural details promote everyday use and disguise the room's real purpose. Superior craftsmanship and outstanding security are both priorities in this approach. Only the owner would know that the room is actually a safe room. Furthermore, safe rooms also have a dual purpose. While built for use during disaster, safe rooms are also used to store valuable items (such as art or antiques) when clients are away from their homes. According to Gaffney,

> The very wealthy are viewing safe rooms as necessary features that now have applications in daily life. Dual-purpose rooms, usually the master bedroom or theater room, quality finishes, and a secondary use as a walk-in vault when owner is away, which is a great feature for a second home. It's a great selling point. The idea is that having a safe room is now low impact. It provides overall security.

To maintain their secrecy, safe rooms are constructed with great discretion (Brennan, 2013).[2] Extensive measures are taken to hide the existence of a safe room and property records rarely identify ownership of safe rooms. Public record of a safe room would undermine its integrity and purpose. Construction and legal documents are not usually filed under the property owner's name to avoid matching a name with a residence. To avoid official archiving, a safe room's design is generally omitted from the design plan/blueprint that is filed with the city government. Instead, the security overlay is hidden by being lodged separately from the architectural drawing. During construction, materials are disguised or shipped separately to prevent discovery. Safe room construction workers also work during limited hours in the middle of the day to remain unnoticed by neighbors. Lastly, contractors and household staff are often required to sign non-disclosure agreements. Therefore, the number of residential safe rooms in New York is difficult to determine. However, safe room builders indicate that these installations are only increasing as a response to fears about particular disasters. Gaffco Ballistics indicates that its New York business has significantly increased over the last decade. After September 11th, the company's safe room installations in New York increased from one-two per year to at least six rooms annually (Chaban, 2015). The company's safe room sales spiked, with the biggest jump occurring after the 2010 Times Square car bombing attempt. In 2017, Gaffco reported a 20% to 30% rise in inquiries spiked by fears about a nuclear attack from North Korea (Kutner, 2017). In our 2018 interview, Gaffney indicated that his company builds around thirty safe rooms per year in Manhattan and now builds safe rooms in Brooklyn.

Safe room ownership might now be viewed as a new necessity and status symbol for the extremely rich. However, in terms of access to this type of emergency shelter, the division between privileged and ordinary citizens is hardly a new development. Since the first threat of a nuclear strike on the US emerged, government elites have had access to bunkers while ordinary citizens have not been granted the same level of protection. Garrison (2006) argues that, since the 1950s, the US government, regardless of party affiliation, has promised to protect the American public through the creation of a civil defense policy while simultaneously reserving and stockpiling bunkers for politicians to preserve the continuity of government. Under President Truman, the federal government began to construct a series of large under-ground bunker complexes to support emergency operations and to ensure government the continuity after a nuclear attack; sites included Raven Rock Mountain, PA the Cheyanne Mountains, CO and the Blue Ridge Mountains, VA (Graff, 2017). Put plainly, bomb shelters were intended to protect designated elected officials, while the public was "simply encouraged to rely on 'self-help' and federal instructional materials" (Garrison, 2006, p. 178).

The history of New York's emergency shelters reflects the merits and shortcomings of civil defense policy. The faded signs still designating the location of long-forgotten bomb shelters on buildings throughout the city remind us of these abandoned policies. In the 1960s, the Cuban Missile Crisis and the Cold War prompted the creation of fallout shelters throughout the country. At the start of his presidency in 1961, President John F. Kennedy implemented a nationwide campaign for fallout shelters. New York's Gover-nor, Nelson Rockefeller, launched his own fallout shelter program based on his fear of a Soviet Attack (Smith, 2014). Rockefeller was so concerned about a potential attack that he had shelters installed under his Executive Mansion in Albany and his Fifth Avenue apartment (as well as under his homes in Pocantico Hills and Maine). By 1963, the Army Corps of Engineers identified 117,448 city buildings with shelter spaces that could house roughly 11.7 million New Yorkers (Vanderbilt, 2003). To qualify as a fallout shelter, existing buildings were inspected to determine if they could withstand a nuclear blast. After passing approval and receiving certification as fallout shelters, buildings were equipped with government-provided survival kits which included items such as medical supplies, toilet paper, appetite-sup-pressing hard candies and hard biscuits known as "Civil Defense Survival Rations." However, despite initial participation by landlords and building superintendents, the fallout shelter program became hard to maintain.

Funding for the city's fallout shelter program was difficult to secure. As a reflection of the federal government's declining commitment to cities and its rising interest in suburbia, there was no funding allocated to building shelters in cities. Instead, self-constructed backyard shelters were promoted. At the state level, Rockefeller also had trouble winning support for his program. His dramatic increase in state spending on other programs such as Medicaid fueled resistance in the state legislature (Peirce, 1972). In 1961, he passed a

$100 million shelter building program for homes and public buildings; however, the final authorization totaled only $15 million. Government support of the program was undermined by debates regarding its expense as well as the challenges of testing the structural resilience of buildings to withstand a nuclear blast.

Beyond the financial restrictions and concerns, enthusiasm for fallout shelters waned as concerns about a nuclear attack decreased. By the 1970s, New York's fallout shelters had become relics of an earlier time as international politics turned away from atomic warfare and nuclear threats. While Rockefeller's $3.5 million fallout shelter still existed in Albany, New York City's shelters had fallen into disarray, with no government efforts to keep them stocked or to maintain a careful accounting of available shelters. For example, if a building with a shelter was razed, no record was kept to indicate the loss of the shelter (Goldman, 1976). As explained by Casper M. Kasparian, then director of the New York field office of the Defense Civil Preparedness Agency, "What you have to realize is that the Government never built any special type of fallout shelter to be installed. We just made ordinary basements into ordinary building shelters" (Goldman, 1976, p. 2). As a result, the perils of ordinary life crept into the city fallout shelters. They reverted back to basements and storage areas with opened boxes of food rotting after being torn open by vandals and rodents. Much of the remaining and soon-to-expire medical supplies and nearly 4,000 tons of food were donated to needy countries through the CARE organization at the urging of then Representative Edward I. Koch ("Food in Fallout Shelters," 1975). Theft also occurred as drug addicts scoured survival kits to steal around $3 million worth of barbiturates (Cullen, 2017).

The reigniting of Cold War fears in the 1980s did not spark a return to transforming existing spaces within city buildings into bomb shelters. The bomb shelter plan was now defunct and a distant memory. Instead, the city's new emergency plan was based on FEMA's Crisis Relocation Planning (CRP) and Expedient Shelter programs. CRP involved the relocation of people from large cities and other risk areas in the event of a nuclear strike by the Soviets. CRP was envisioned as a collaborative planning effort between the federal government, state governments, and roughly 3,000 local governments. However, the collaboration was unsuccessful with state and local governments refusing to participate in planning or redirecting crisis relocation planners to work on other projects (May and Williams, 1986). If a Soviet nuclear attack seemed imminent, the CRP's primary strategy was to capitalize on US citizens' high rates of car ownership, by actively encouraging people to evacuate themselves in advance of crisis. (No evacuation plans were outlined for people without cars) (Homeland Security National Preparedness Task Force, 2006). The Soviets were also expected to evacuate their large cities before striking US cities, therefore, US intelligence would be able to monitor Soviets' evacuation first, and prepare to evacuate US cities in advance (Homeland Security National Preparedness Task Force, 2006).

Under the CRP plan, given a few days' notice, people would simply drive out of high-risk areas such as New York to small towns and rural areas. However, no alternative measures were put in place to deal with evacuation issues such as high traffic congestion, inclement weather, or people without cars. The small towns and rural areas were also poorly equipped to deal with an influx of evacuees as they did not have large shelters or extra provisions. To aid potential evacuees, FEMA also promoted the Expedient Shelter program which included teaching Americans to quickly construct shelters to help them survive the blast. The program provided written instructions on how to dig large holes to take cover during a nuclear attack. Once warned of an impending strike, a person was expected to dig a wide hole and then cover it with a parked car. If the trench was dug according to specifications, it would be large enough to house a family of four without provisions. Families were expected to stay in the holes for two weeks despite the lack of provisions. As might be expected, the programs were not well received.

In contrast to the hiding-in-a-hole strategy offered to the American public, the Federal Government determined that the bunker complexes constructed for government elites were no longer safe for public leaders as the sites had probably already been targeted by the Soviets. Furthermore, a small number of bunkers no longer seemed sufficient for the survival of America's top leaders. Therefore, in 1983, President Reagan signed National Security Decision Directive 55, "The Doomsday Project." The plan was to create a series of many new bunkers complete with assigned commando units and an elaborate communication and operations unit that included space satellites and lead-lined tractor-trailers with special transmitters (Weiner, 1994).

In 1994, eleven years later, the Pentagon announced that it was terminating the Doomsday Project (Weiner, 1994).[3] Nuclear tensions with the Soviets had de-escalated, resulting in a change in policy agendas, and the challenges of attempting to coordinate across the White House, the Pentagon, the Central Intelligence Agency and numerous highly classified programs, proved too great and too risky. The project also suffered a serious setback with the discovery that its lynchpin satellite communications network could not withstand a long nuclear war.

After the September 11th attack, the Bush administration once more focused on underground bunkers for government elites and promoting a familiar civil defense plan that encouraged Americans to store emergency supplies (Garrison, 2006). In 2019, New York City's emergency plans call for citizens to evacuate outside the city (NYC Emergency Management, 2019). For those who cannot evacuate, the city government will open disaster shelters in places such as schools and municipal buildings. These centers will provide basic food and water to evacuees, but people are reminded to bring their own "go bags" and necessary provisions such as medications, childcare items and sanitary supplies.

Unlike owners of luxe safe rooms, everyday preppers assume that they will probably have to leave their apartments in the event of a severe and prolonged disaster, as they have limited supplies despite their preparation. However, many preppers store provisions to "shelter in place" until they are able to evacuate the city. To ensure the safety of their families when "sheltering in place," NYC preppers typically engage in strategies similar to those recommended by the DHS (2019). The DHS's suggested guidelines address three main categories of protection: managing food and supplies, managing water and sealing one's shelter against containments if needed.

For managing food and supplies as well as storing water, many NYC preppers have dedicated spaces such as closets, cabinets or designated areas in their apartments that contain emergency supplies to help their families survive in dire circumstances. Such a storage area is referred to as a "prepper closet." A prepper closet contains essential items such as medical supplies, non-perishable food, large containers of water, flashlights and batteries, and waterproof matches.[4] Prepping closets are considered to be a viable alternative for New Yorkers who live in apartments with precious little space and who cannot afford the expense of constructing a safe room within their apartments. Prepping closets are also popular because they are viewed as a strategy for preparing for disaster regardless of home ownership. Renters can easily dedicate a closet or space without permission from their landlords.

The creation of the prepping closet is an expression of one's personal philosophy about prepping that involves contemplating not only what kind of disasters are likely to occur, but also considering what kind of disasters one would not want to survive. Ben, another NYCPN member also believes that one cannot protect oneself against all disasters and that one might not desire to do so. He argues that

> Certain things you can't prepare for. Technically, you could but why would you want to survive? I have tarps to protect against glass breaking. Imagine a nuclear blast and everything is contaminated, all that radiation, wouldn't you rather be dead? What's the point of it?

The specific products and tools chosen for a prepper closet are usually drawn from a common set of categories. However, prepper closets are also uniquely tailored to reflect an individual's preferences, needs and fears. Medical supplies may include traditional first aid supplies such as bandages and antibiotic ointment; however, the kit may also contain prescription pills needed for family members. Food stuffs may consist of freeze-dried meals and protein bars as well as favorite snack items such as special chocolate bars or even liquor. Games and books might also be stored. Preppers, like everyone else, agree that these treats and distractions are important tools for maintaining morale during difficult times, especially for children. Supplies (tarps, duct tape, plastic lining, etc.) to seal windows and doors are also stored to protect against flying glass and airborne contaminants. Families may also store gas masks personally fitted for each person to wear as an added layer of protection against airborne contaminants. A prepper closet and its supplies are expected to be "off-limits" to the family in ordinary situations. This approach ensures that the closet remains stocked and contains needed supplies for use during emergencies.

The type and quantity of provisions stockpiled is determined by the number of days that one expects to "shelter in place." When planning to "shelter in place," NYC Emergency Management recommends storing sufficient provisions for seven days (2019). However, some NYC Preppers store provisions for longer durations, from two weeks to up to a year (with the expectation that supplies could be stretched, if needed). For example, Jason Charles, the leader of the NYCPN, has an extensive prepper closet that consists of two separate spaces. He jokingly refers to it as his "end-of-the world" closet. Jason's plan is to prepare for any and all type of disasters. His prepping closet now comprises one traditional apartment closet and a 100 square foot storage unit. Ranging from freeze-dried and canned food to MREs (Meals Ready to Eat),[5] Jason has stored enough food to feed him and his family for a year. His equipment is varied, including everything from first aid supplies to an inflatable raft to a drone. Like some other preppers, Jason's prepping closet also contains weapons. Given the restrictions on owning a firearm in New York, Jason and other preppers store knives.

Preppers do not usually reveal their ownership of a prepper closet in order to protect its contents and to avoid scrutiny by those unfamiliar with prepping. A news article on Jason highlights the contrast between the interpretation of a prepping closet by preppers vs. non-preppers. The article, titled "Inside a prepper's 'end-of-the-world closet' that holds $10,000 worth of doomsday supplies" (Garfield, 2017) seems to stigmatize Jason as a hoarder. To those unfamiliar with prepping, storing emergency supplies in large quantities does indeed seem like hoarding. The storyline, accompanied by several photos, emphasizes peculiar items within his prepping closet with short descriptions and no explanations or context. The pictures also cast Jason in a somewhat unfavorable light because his prepping closet is not camera-ready. For example, one photo shows a pile of canned food heaped together in an uncovered jumbo plastic container. It looks jumbled and disorganized because the items are not neatly stacked in the bin. Yet, Jason's supplies are organized in a method that works for him.

In his prepping closet which is comprised of a 100 square-foot storage room and an apartment hall closet, Jason stores a collection of 100 knives. Taken out of context, this could be viewed as troubling, possible evidence that NYC preppers might be just another reiteration of an extremist survivalist group. However, as a group leader who demonstrates the use of equipment, Jason has a significant amount of prepping gear of various sizes. Furthermore, Jason's extensive knife collection is attributed to his interest in knife collecting and receiving knives as promotional items rather than amassing weapons for Armageddon. Based on his interest in bushcraft and survival skills, Jason tests knives and shares his reviews on his social media websites and among preppers. He also teaches knife skills workshops at group events (and displays different types of knives for review). A quick sensational story would not cover those important details. In the world of prepping, Jason is a curious researcher who is intent on investigating products and trying them out. He also stores equipment used for demonstrations to the group. His interest in preparing for all types of disaster also requires extensive equipment and numerous provisions. However, his is not the only approach to making a prepping closet.

My examination of four NYC prepper closets indicates that urban preppers are both highly inventive and highly organized in ways that reflected different prepping philosophies.[6] These preppers have enough supplies stored for periods ranging from two weeks to over a month. Given the tight quarters of New York apartments, Marie Kondo would be impressed with the ability of these New Yorkers to part with items to clear space for their emergency supplies. In a reinvention of the KonMari philosophy of decluttering,[7] these NYC preppers focus on the future joy that certain items will give them in the event of disaster. One Manhattan mother, Renee, created the more aesthetic version of Jason's purely functional storage technique. Her prepping closet looked like an HGTV showpiece. With little closet space, Renee created a prepping closet that ran the width of her living room. She simply placed three floor-to-ceiling industrial storage racks along the wall, and stacked them with supplies. Large items (like a portable power station, a jumbo first aid trauma kit, a radio and a stove system) were concealed in muted colored storage containers, while a tremendous variety of canned and boxed foods for both the family and their dog were neatly arranged on the shelves. Next to the food was a mini-pharmacy stocked with medicines for common ailments such as colds and stomach bugs. Five-gallon water containers also lined the bottom shelves. With enough supplies to last one month, the racks were hidden behind long flowing curtains that were hung from the ceiling. To me, it looked like a clever cross between The Container Store and a mini Costco. Renee stores emergency supplies because she fears relying on government support. She explained:

> I put this special pantry together so that we'll be OK if something happens. My family won't have to wait for help. I couldn't bear it. Another Sandy. Loss of power for several days? We're fine. Look at the news ... every hurricane, there's always a big delay between when people need help and when they get help. Or, sometimes, they don't ever get help. Our plans aren't to stay here. We have a home in [Deleted] and family in other areas. My prepping closet is for worst-case scenarios, when we are stuck and can't leave. It buys us time. I still think about 9/11. Our fighter pilots weren't even at their stations. How could they scramble? They were too busy playing cards.[8]

A Brooklyn mother, Leslie, used a series of cabinets in her laundry room as her family's prepper closet. Her decision to create a designated space for emergency supplies to "shelter in place" was motivated by her fear of climate change and by her sense of practicality with respect to prepping her family for disaster:

> I am worried about climate change. I've done a lot of reading and it scares me. No turning back the clock on this one. It has already started. Weather patterns are just going to become more brutal. Brooklyn, we have been pretty lucky. So, that's one layer of concern. The next layer is about my daily life. My husband travels frequently for work. If there is an emergency, there is a strong chance that it's just going to be me coping with everything. I cannot be two places at once, picking up our kids and rounding up everything we need—doing the milk, bread, toilet paper run. Impossible. My regular life has enough insanity. I didn't want the extra anxiety gnawing at me.

She showed me the contents of the cabinets with all of the supplies expected to last for a month. The cabinets were divided into sections which included a well-stocked pantry, medical supplies (including a few pairs of generic reading glasses in case one's prescription eyeglasses could not be located), flashlights, batteries, solar lights and a solar charger. On a high shelf, I spotted a bottle of Grey Goose Vodka and a few fancy bars of dark chocolate that had been tucked away. I smiled and shared that I store a flask of sipping tequila. She smirked at me said, "So much for you being a good lady prepper. Vodka's the best pick. Kids and husbands can't smell it."

In our conversations about prepper closets, Anne, a mother and NYCPN member from Queens, expressed that her prepping philosophy and her family responsibilities are intertwined:

> Mothers take on more of a sense of responsibility. My husband works in another borough. I am by myself with my child. I have to figure out how to take care of myself. The batteries, the food, the first aid. Not the head of household when it comes to making the money. Different responsibilities. Taking care of the house, making sure that we have everything that we need just in case. That's my job.

Anne also drew connections between her efforts to maintain a prepping closet and her family background:

> Some of us have been doing this since we were kids. People see it [prepping] on TV and they think that we are doing it because it is a cool thing to do because we saw it on TV. Having extra stuff? I've always done it. It's about being prepared. Cough syrup, aspirin. I have extra to be prepped, to be ready in case something happens. If you want it, you have it. If there is a torrential downpour, you don't wanna go out. If you have it, you don't have to go out. Look, I'm from an Old Italian family. My mom always had tons of pasta and tinned foods—tons of food,

emergency food in case we needed it. With children, you have extra diapers, why not have extra food? You don't think the baby will go pee three times and just bring three diapers. You bring extra. It's the same thing with food, water, and other needs. It's the same mindset. [Preppers] all have it.

Karlie, a female, single, independent prepper, added a prepping closet to her strategies when she moved to New York from the West Coast. At her Manhattan studio, she said:

> I moved here right after Hurricane Sandy from San Francisco. I used to keep a go bag at work there, you know, just in case. I didn't keep anything in my apartment. When I moved here, I knew that had to change. Way too unpredictable here. I'm good for about two weeks with my stuff.

Karlie then reached down to pull out her prepper closet; a pair of large roll-out drawers hidden underneath the bed (several one-gallon water containers were stacked in the kitchen area). Both orderly drawers were packed compactly with provisions. The first drawer was stacked with granola bars, bags of freeze-dried foods, trail mix, tuna salad packs (with mayonnaise and relish packets) and a large stash of individually wrapped Twizzlers. The second drawer contained other expected essential items such as a transistor radio, a first aid kit (put together by her), wipes, gloves, a few tarps for covering the windows, duct tape, a headlamp and flashlights, a knife, a multi-tool and a landline telephone. Next to the telephone was a box of condoms and a Plan B oral emergency contraceptive box. We spoke for a few minutes about the importance of having a landline even though we no longer use them on a daily basis. I nudged the conversation to the next set of items and commented that contraceptives were a good idea for a prepper closet. She tapped the birth control products and explained, "That's a lesson I learned from my sister and her husband. One year, there was a huge snowstorm where they live in PA so they were stuck inside for a few days. They accidentally made a snow baby! My nephew!" We both had a good laugh.

Birth control is probably not a provision that many preppers, or most people, consider when preparing for a disaster, but it is a logical and crucial choice. Most people do not think about the possibility of having sex in the aftermath of disaster. Catastrophes are not sexy. People think about suffering and turmoil, not romance and intimacy. However, sex relieves tension. Also, you might be isolated from everyone else with nothing to do. In the aftermath of disaster, individuals may choose to have sexual relations, or they may even be forced to do so. Therefore, birth control (condoms and emergency oral contraceptives) is a serious provision for protection against sexually transmitted diseases and for protecting against unwanted pregnancy. Perhaps some preppers do include such items, but the people I interviewed (besides Karlie) did not disclose this information. Based on my field research and interviews, male preppers do not seem to address these issues. Discussions of bug out bag contents (lectures or conversations) did not include advice regarding packing condoms and emergency oral contraceptives. My review of prepping literature also indicates these survival manuals and guidebooks focus on topics such as bushcraft (outdoor survival skills), first aid instruction, and self-defense tips. No discussions of protecting against sexually transmitted diseases or protecting against unwanted pregnancy were found. After meeting with Karlie, I asked a married male prepper and father of a daughter if he had thought about contraceptives as a provision. He was startled by the question. I discussed contraceptives as an important provision for both wanted and unwanted sex as well as the use of condoms to prevent sexually transmitted diseases. He said, "Great, Anna. Now, I have all these horrible pictures in my brain. What am I supposed to do about that? No, I haven't thought of it. Until now. Christ."

To protect their resources in the event of disaster (and to protect their identities as preppers), some NYC preppers hide their emergency supplies for sheltering in place throughout their apartments. A Brooklyn couple, (both independent preppers), had most of their supplies tucked discretely within their living room furniture. An ottoman and a pair of cube-shaped end tables contained most of their supplies. The ottoman stored food (about fifteen organic freeze-dried food packages, three cans of tuna, maybe ten packs of ramen noodles and two sandwich-sized plastic bags of locally made beef jerky) as well as a deck of cards and dominos. One end table contained medical supplies (including vitamins and essential oils) and the other held items such as two ham radios, a toolset and flashlights. While this table also stored a plastic covering that would need to be trimmed, I did note that no knives or box cutters were included. The couple indicated that they had supplies for a month. However, my quick estimate was that, excluding any supplements from their kitchen, they only had enough provisions for a lean two weeks. Therefore, given the absence of a cutting tool and the limited supplies, other provisions may have been elsewhere in the apartment, or the preppers may have been less knowledgeable than they indicated. My tactful questions about adequate food supplies were sidestepped. When I shared my experience covering my own windows to protect against flying glass during a hurricane, I mentioned my use of box cutters to trim the plastic. A prepper for two years, the husband politely changed the conversation, and asked if I thought REI's camping section was a good resource for preppers. I respected the hint. There may have been weapons or other materials that these preppers did not want to reveal. It is worth noting that, with the exception of a few knives, none of the prepping closets that I viewed had firearms. Weapons, legal or otherwise, may have been located in other areas of the homes or removed from the closets prior to my arrival. Furthermore, to maintain trust, my interviews focused on the prepping closets as presented.

Inshirah also distributed provisions throughout her home as a disguise tactic. She explained: "I camouflage my stuff by mixing it in with the everyday. I have provisions stretched out everywhere in my place ... Kitchen, closets, and in the cars." Recognizing the need for additional food stuffs in the kitchen is easy enough. However, finding a particular item might be confusing if only one family member knows its location. Therefore, this tactic is most effective when all family members know all provisions and their respective hiding places.

When I asked Inshirah about number of days she and her family were prepared for, her comments revealed the particular challenges of safe rooms and "sheltering in place." She thought quietly for a moment and then replied, "Depends on how many people I have to help. Few months. I think that we need more." "Sheltering in place" for a short-term emergency implies sheltering with the people that also occupy the home in daily life such as immediate family or roommates. However, in a long-term situation, that number might change because extended family or close friends might need help.

While sheltering in place for everyday preppers might include stretching provisions to additional people, sheltering in place for HNW preppers involves retreating to a safe room that immediately severs the connection with the outside world. It represents a turning away from everything and everyone. The possibility of that connection, that sense of responsibility to one another, is absent. It is opting out. However, many wealthy individuals already disengage with those whose life choices differ from their own. Education, healthcare, transportation and neighborhood choices are just a few such areas of divergence. As Nelson Schwartz (2016) notes, the increasing gap between classes has created another gilded age and generated "the velvet rope economy" that isolates the rich in a privileged and advantaged world that shields them from any unpleasantness caused by others' lack of money. Many of the rich, those who have abandoned civic life, are already living in safe rooms.

Although I am not a HNW individual, I experienced this kind of self-imposed isolation in my "sheltering in place" experiment To gain some insight into what "sheltering in place" would be like, I decided to stay alone in my apartment for a period of five days during the fall of 2018. My husband was scheduled to be away for the week so I thought that it would be the perfect time. I notified my mom, niece and a close friend. I live in a high-rise with thirty floors so it would be easy to disappear for a few days. However, sheltering in place alone was going to be tough. I am an extrovert. My spirit animal is a Westie. My ground rules were: All food and water must be taken from my prepper closet. No electricity. No gas stove. No showering. No tech (smartphone, computer, iPad, Surface, or landline). No ham radio. No bed (this made sense for some reason.). Toilet use permitted. No leaving apartment for any reason. Windows closed, shades down. Cooking only by JetBoil System. One flask limit. No books. No crying.

My own prepping closet is actually a large antique trunk. It contains basic supplies for "sheltering in place" like freeze-dried foods, peanut butter, protein and granola bars, jars of marina sauce as well as pasta. My favorite brands and organic, if available. Some people might call this splurging. Not me. Trying to survive in a disaster situation would be miserable enough without forcing myself to eat food that I can't stand. A safe room. *That's* splurging. On day one, the first morning and afternoon were uneventful. I woke up around 9:30 a.m. (My watch has no numbers). Had tea and some oatmeal. Immediately regretted making oatmeal as I needed hot water to clean the bowl. Straightened up a little but then left it alone because that seemed like extra punishment. Did some writing. Was grateful for my legal pad and my favorite pen. In the afternoon, I just sat and listened to the city for a bit. Thought about "Rhapsody in Blue." Gershwin was right. You can hear music in noise. Resisted turning on my transistor radio as I was worried about battery life. Also, one might need to stay quiet if "sheltering in place" to avoid detection. I made a lunch of a chicken and rice pouch. Made up a funny name for all of the freeze-dried and packaged foods—Pouch Cuisine. A little after 1:00 p.m., the doorman buzzed a few times. I ignored it. I read some back issues of *The New York Times* that I had not yet recycled. I wondered about what Trump was up to. My buzzer rang again around 3:50 p.m. I ignored it. Decided to organize my dresser drawers. Around 6:00 p.m., there was a knock at the door. I didn't answer, but the persistent and friendly knock continued. It was a porter. "Anna, are you OK in there? Anna? Everything all right?" I opened the door. He smiled and gave a package to me. I asked, "How did you know that I was home?" "You didn't leave today and haven't answered. Glad that you are all right." So much for being invisible in the big city. A lot of snacking and drinking boring water. Willed myself to sleep on the couch after the sun went down.

My experiment only lasted three days. After a cheerful morning on day two, I decided to spend some time reminiscing by going through my family photos. Unexpectedly, this idea led to a productive afternoon of grieving for my deceased sister and then transitioned to a useful review of my biggest regrets (otherwise known as my favorite line up). I quickly learned that "sheltering in place" was more complicated than I expected. I had plenty of supplies but no company and no distractions. For a busy and social person, this scenario is a disaster. In the early evening of day two, my neighbor from another floor popped over because I forgot about our morning date which was scheduled for the previous day. I did not meet her at our favorite breakfast spot, and I had not returned her text messages. She was concerned because she knew my husband was out of town. I peeked out and apologized for being ill. I was glad to see my friend if only for a moment. Saved on provisions. Didn't have much of an appetite. Listened to WCBS on low for a few minutes before I turned in.

On day three, I woke up and forced myself to snap out of it. After a breakfast of oatmeal and dried fruit, I read two journal articles and made some notes. I then organized my bathroom cabinets and my makeup case. As a reward, I treated myself to a cup of hot tea and peanut butter and jelly on crackers. Still motivated after my treat, I decided to tackle my kitchen cabinets. With most of the project nowhere near completed, I decided to take a nap. However, my close friend (the one who knew about the experiment) came over after work. She rang the bell repeatedly and jiggled the doorknob simultaneously. I snapped awake. She yelled through the door, "It's me. This is a rescue. I no longer think this is a good idea. This is weird." I waited for a minute before opening. She came in and checked things over. "The place looks clean but it's stuffy and you look a little dirty." I was a little dirty but, mostly, I was lonely. In terms of mastering "sheltering in place" techniques, my abbreviated training exercise was a failure. However, it had a valuable outcome. It reminded me of the differences between the social networks of men and women during a crisis. As Klinenberg (2015) discovered when studying the impact of a Chicago heatwave on poor, elderly men and women, women tend to live longer than men because they have stronger social networks. Overall, women are better connected socially; therefore, more people check on their well-being. Noticing my absence, my community kept reaching out to me.

The creation and purpose of prepper closets suggests the possibility that different approaches to prepping are based on traditional gender roles. Jason and Ben's prepper closets seem to function as all-purpose tools designed to meet a number of diverse emergencies. Their closets reflect their adoption of the role of "protector" of the household in any and all circumstances. Conversely, prepper closets created by women were narrower in purpose and were viewed as an extension of home management. Two mothers viewed storing emergency provisions as part of their roles as mothers. Another mother acknowledged that her prepper closet might also be needed to help others beyond her immediate family. In an important illustration of a prepping closet as a resource for personal health management, a female prepper packed two different types of birth control.

None of the everyday preppers I interviewed had tried sheltering in place for as extended a period as I did. My experience made me realize that they may not have been adequately planning for this scenario. Ample and useful supplies are crucial. However, there are other issues to contend with while sheltering in place. Isolation might be a real problem for city dwellers who are used to a high level of contact with other people on a daily basis. There is no rushing around that offers the experience of chance encounters or new discoveries. Being bored is also taxing. If I had settled into the process, my library would have been good company. However, popular entertainment recourses such as E-books, streaming platforms and video games, which offer welcome escapes from reality, would have been unavailable. Preparedness does not offer strategies for helping people to combat loneliness in the absence of media distractions.

Notes

1 See Dio's Account of the Great Fire and Herodian discussion of other fires.
2 My attempts at securing an interview with a New York safe room owner were unsuccessful. An interview with a former associate of a safe room owner (who was not required to sign an NDA) was informative. However, I did not include the information as its reliability could not be confirmed. Furthermore, disclosing any information about a safe room without the permission of the owner raises legal and ethical issues.
3 The scope of the project actually came to light during the Iran-Contra hearings in 1987 when it was briefly mentioned by Oliver North. Starting in 1982, North spearheaded the covert project that, along with other national security programs, consumed the majority of FEMA's funding for an eleven-year period (See Garrison, 2006). At Iran-Contra hearings, controversy arose when Representative Jack Brooks (Democrat of Texas) asked North if "'plans for the continuity of government' included a 'contingency plan in the event of an emergency that would suspend the American Constitution'" (Weiner, 1994; p. 1).
4 See ready.gov for a list of emergency supplies for sheltering in place.
5 Once issued to combat troops by the US military, MREs are ready to eat self-contained rations that are produced and sold to the public.
6 At the request of preppers, sometimes names (even pseudonyms) and neighborhoods are not provided to avoid disclosing their stockpile and to protect their safety in the event of catastrophe. However, I am permitted to disclose their gender, family status and borough location to facilitate an understanding of their approach to creating a prepping closet.
7 According to The New York Times bestseller, *The Life-Changing Magic of Tidying Up: The Japanese Art of Decluttering and Organizing* (Kondō, 2014), the KonMari method of decluttering is based on the principle of maximizing joy in one's home. People should only keep items that give them joy. All other items should be discarded.
8 Bamford (2004) attributes the failure to prevent the September 11th terrorist attack on the World Trade Center to a downsized military and weakened US intelligence. According to Bamford, on that day, only fourteen fighter jets were responsible for protecting the entire US mainland. Two F-15s were scrambled from the Otis Air National Guard Base in Falmouth, MA; however, they were too far away to intercept the highjacked planes. The closet fighters were located at the Air National Guard 177th Wing at the Atlantic City Airport. However, since 1998, the two fighters had been unarmed and used only training practices.

References

Bamford, J. (2004). *A pretext for war: 9/11, Iraq, and the abuse of America's intelligence agencies*. New York, NY: Doubleday.

Brennan, M. (2013, November 27). Billionaire bunkers: Beyond the panic room, home security goes sci-fi. *Forbes*. Retrieved from https://www.forbes.com/sites/morganbrenna n/2013/11/27/billionaire-bunkers-beyond-the-panic-room-home-security-goes-sci-fi/# 4e843a81463d.

Carlson, J. (2017, March 20). Is the 1960s world's fair underground home still there? An investigation. *Gothamist*. Retrieved from http://gothamist.com/2017/03/20/ underground_home_worlds_fair_revisited.php#photo-1.

Chaban, M. A. V. (2015, May 25). Still secret and secure, safe rooms now hide in plain sight. *The New York Times*. Retrieved from https://www.nytimes.com/2015/ 05/26/nyregion/still-secret-and-secure-safe-rooms-now-hide-in-plain-sight.html.

Chaffin, C., Hofflund, J., Koepp, D. and Polone, G. (Producers), Fincher, D. (Director). (2002). *Panic room*. United States: Columbia Pictures Corporation.

Cullen, T. (2017, August 10). New York is filled with thousands of abandoned bomb shelters from a time when a nuclear attack was almost certain. *New York Daily News*. Retrieved from https://www.nydailynews.com/new-york/new-york-filled-thou sands-abandoned-bomb-shelters-article-1.3399907.

Department of Homeland Security. (2018). *IED attack: Improvise explosive devices*. Retrieved from https://www.dhs.gov/xlibrary/assets/prep_ied_fact_sheet.pdf.

Department of Homeland Security. (2019). *Shelter*. Retrieved from https://www.ready. gov/shelter.

FEMA. (2006). *Safe rooms and shelters*. Washington, DC: FEMA.

Food in fallout shelters urged for poor. (1975, January 25). *The New York Times*. Retrieved from https://www.nytimes.com/1975/01/25/archives/food-in-fallout-shelters-urged-for-poor.html.

Gaffco Ballistics. (2018). *Transportable saferoom*. Retrieved from http://www.gaffco.com/safe-rooms/transportable-safe-rooms.

Gaffney, A. (2016, August 8). The latest high-end real estate amenity? The luxury safe room. *Town and Country Magazine*. Retrieved from https://www.townandcoun trymag.com/leisure/real-estate/a7282/luxury-safe-rooms/.

Garfield, L. (2017). Inside a prepper's 'end-of-the-world closet' that holds $10,000 worth of doomsday supplies. *Business Insider*. Retrieved from https://www.busi nessinsider.com/inside-doomsday-preppers- apartment-photos-2017-2.

Garrison, D. (2006). *Bracing for Armageddon: Why civil defense never worked*. New York, NY: Oxford University Press.

Goldman, K. L. (1976, November 21). Out of the past: Fallout shelters. *The New York Times*. Retrieved from https://www.nytimes.com/1976/11/21/archives/out-of-the-pa st-fallout-shelters-out-of-the-past-fallout-shelters.html.

Graff, G. M. (2017). *Raven Rock: The story of the U.S. government's secret plan to save itself – while the rest of us die*. New York, NY: Simon and Schuster.

Granville, K. (2018, March 19). Facebook and Cambridge Analytica: What you need to know as fallout widens. *The New York Times*. Retrieved from https://www.nytim es.com/2018/03/19/technology/facebook-cambridge-analytica-explained.html.

The Guardian. (2019). *The Cambridge analytica files*. Retrieved from https://www. theguardian.com/news/series/cambridge-analytica-files.

Homeland Security National Preparedness Task Force. (2006, September). *Civil defense and homeland security: A short history of national preparedness efforts*. Retrieved from https:// training.fema.gov/hiedu/docs/dhs%20civil%20defense-hs%20-%20short%20history. pdf.

Klinenberg, E. (2015). *Heat wave: A social autopsy of disaster in Chicago*. Chicago, IL: University of Chicago Press.

Kondō, M., and Hirano, C. (2014). *The life-changing magic of tidying up: The Japanese art of decluttering and organizing*. Berkeley: Ten Speed Press.

Kutner, M. (2017, September 19). War with North Korea? People are building nuclear bunkers and shelters again because of Trump and Kim Jong Un. *Newsweek*. Retrieved from http://www.newsweek.com/nuclear-fallout-shelter-bunker-north-korea-japan-667680.

May, P. J., and Williams, W. (1986). *Disaster policy implementation: Managing programs under shared governance*. New York, NY: Plenum Press.

New York City Department of Emergency Management. (2018). *Close to home: An urban model for post-disaster housing.* Retrieved from https://www1.nyc.gov/assets/whatifnyc/downloads/pdf/close_to_home.pdf.

New York City Department of Emergency Management. (2019). *Get prepared.* Retrieved from https://www1.nyc.gov/site/em/ready/get-prepared.page.

Osnos, E. (2017, January 30). Doomsday prep for the super-rich. *The New Yorker.* Retrieved from https://www.newyorker.com/magazine/2017/01/30/doomsday-prep-for-the-super-rich.

Peirce, N. R. (1972). *The megastates of America: People, politics, and power in the ten great states.* New York, NY: Norton.

Schwartz, N. D. (2016, April 23). In an age of privilege, not everyone is in the same boat. *The New York Times.* Retrieved from https://www.nytimes.com/2016/04/24/business/economy/velvet-rope-economy.html.

Smith, R. N. (2014). *On his own terms: A life of Nelson Rockefeller.* New York, NY: Random House.

Toner, J. (2013). *Roman disasters.* Cambridge, UK: Polity Press.

United States Bomb Data Center. (2017). *2017 Explosives Incident Report.* Retrieved from https://www.atf.gov/resource-center/docs/report/2017-explosives-incident-report-eir/download.

Vanderbilt, T. (2003, March 16). Urban tactics; in duck-and-cover times, shelters get a fresh look. *The New York Times.* Retrieved from https://www.nytimes.com/2003/03/16/nyregion/urban-tactics-in-duck-and-cover-times-shelters-get-a-fresh-look.html.

Weiner, T. (1994, April 18). Pentagon book for doomsday is to be closed. *The New York Times.* Retrieved from https://www.nytimes.com/1994/04/18/us/pentagon-book-for-doomsday-is-to-be-closed.html.

5 "Bugging out"

Strategic relocation and strategic packing

The horrors depicted in apocalyptic novels and movies are not the first things that come to mind when I think about the dangers urban preppers may face when escaping the city to reach a safe destination. Instead, I find myself reflecting on the Donner Party. These American pioneers, some of whom were city dwellers, prepared for and embarked on a dangerous journey in hopes of making it to a safe haven, struggling to survive in a very real, apocalyptic landscape.

This harrowing historical event serves as a cautionary tale for city folks who must leave their creature comforts behind to bug out in the event of disaster. For urban preppers, "bugging out," refers to leaving a disaster area with a bag of emergency provisions (a bug out bag) to arrive at a safe haven—a pre-determined location or simply a place that is out of the disaster area. The Donner Party epic illustrates the importance of the three critical elements of a bug out: determining a safe haven and methodically planning a route to get there, careful selection and packing of emergency supplies, and the ability to adapt to changing circumstances.

In the summer of 1846, Margaret Reed set off from Springfield, Illinois to start a new life in California with her husband, James, their five children and her sickly mother. For months, Margaret had rejected her husband's requests to leave the comforts of their modern life to move West to generate more wealth. Finally, James was able to coax her into leaving with the offer of traveling in luxury. To accommodate the needs of his wife and his family, who preferred the conveniences of city life, he ordered a custom-made two-story covered wagon outfitted with everything Margaret might need for a comfortable passage: spring seats, a stove, an actual bed for her mother, a small library, her favorite possessions, including a large hanging mirror to help maintain her appearance and six months' stockpile of premium foods including brandy (Reed Murphy, 1891). Well stocked and comfortable, the Reed family wagon was the largest of its kind in a caravan of 500 wagons headed West, led by George Donner. However, the Reed's well-appointed wagon could not protect these American pioneers from the tragedy and catastrophe awaiting them on their journey from the Midwest to California.

Eager to shave over 300 miles off the trip, the Donner Party took a shortcut, the Hastings Cutoff, an alternate route between Utah's Wasatch Mountains and the Great Salt Lake Dessert. However, this proved to be a disastrous error. The shortcut was narrow at points and nearly impassable, which forced the travelers to abandon their wagons. The Donner Party was forced to suffer the winter trapped in the Sierra Nevada mountains fighting arctic temperatures and a series of powerful blizzards. Facing starvation and with little hope of rescue, some of the pioneers turned to cannibalism as a means of survival (Brown, 2009). However, Margaret and her children survived without resorting to such an extreme measure. She was forced to provide for her children alone after her husband was banished from the camp after fatally stabbing a man during a fight. Margaret utilized her resourcefulness and self-sufficiency (prized prepper qualities) in crisis: she left camp in search of food, struck deals that promised future rewards with other survivors to gain food, and even boiled hides that had been used as roof covers to try to make soup that only turned to glue. According to the account of her eldest daughter, Virginia Reed Murphy (1891, p. 422):

> Christmas was near, but to the starving its memory gave no comfort ... but my mother had determined weeks before that her children should have a treat on this one day. She had laid away a few dried apples, some beans, a bit of tripe, and a small piece of bacon ... the delight of the little ones knew no bounds.

The Donner Party appears to have disregarded the three prepping principles: precisely planning and sticking to a designated route, carefully selecting and packing supplies and adapting to changing circumstances. The Donner Party took a great risk by taking a new shortcut to California after receiving scant information about the route. The trail proved to be too challenging as it was mostly uphill and narrow. As a result, travel time increased by several weeks which subjected the group to dangerous weather conditions. The terrain rendered the group's primary source of transportation (wagons) and the majority of their provisions worthless. Their provisions were cached in the ground, but blizzards made it impossible to dig them up. Certain that they would always have their wagons, bulky, heavy provisions were stored in large containers. They did not consider bringing smaller and lighter provisions that could be carried on horseback or on foot. Given the historical period, lighter provisions in some categories such as foodstuffs or tools may have been unavailable. Still, the Donner Party did not fully recognize that provisions must be carefully chosen based on factors such as their utility, durability and portability. One must be ready to scale down supplies if needed. Lastly, one must be focused, adaptable and able to successfully respond to crisis in order to increase one's chances for survival. Margaret Reed's case illustrates the importance of strategic action to protect one's family. It seems that Reed did what urban preppers hope to do: she stepped out of her normal role as a city dweller into the role of a survivor.

This chapter explores the practice of "bugging out": the strategy of leaving an area to escape disaster that is practiced by both HNW (High Net Worth) and everyday New York preppers. In a *New York Times* article on bugging out, reporter Alex Williams (2017) suggests that New Yorkers do a gut check to determine if they are ready to make bug out plans:

> But if you are among the swelling class of weekend paranoiacs of affluent means who are starting to mull fantasies of urban escape following the endless headlines about disasters, both natural and manufactured, you may be starting to see a different image in your mind when you think 'survivalist.' You may no longer see the wild-eyed cave dweller in camouflage fatigues, hoarding canned goods. You may even see one in the mirror.

For the HNW prepper, bugging out practices include the purchase of secret strategic relocation destinations, generally homes in exclusive and remote areas, as well as the acquisition of curated luxury bug out bags containing state-of-the-art survival equipment. Meanwhile, middle-class New York preppers seek to escape disaster through more modest means such as retreating to a second home or a hidden campsite in the tri-state area. Both groups expect to rely on their own bug out bags for supplies until they reach their safe destination. With advance warning, HNW urban preppers may try to leave the city by private helicopter or plane, while middle-class preppers recognize that they may have to leave the city on foot. This chapter focuses mainly on the preparation and plans of independent preppers (both wealthy and middle-class) to examine their different approaches to responding to disaster without reliance on a larger network of preppers.

In prepping literature, establishing a retreat for survival is known as a "strategic relocation." Strategic relocation is a process that involves finding an area with strong long-term security from man-made or natural threats (Skousen and Skousen, 2016). Strategic relocation calls for assessing the continuing safety of a place based on criteria such as geography and climate, crime rate and standard of living, government stability and the likelihood of terrorism or war. Generally speaking, a suitable location for a retreat is an area without an extreme climate or topography, that has a stable government and a high quality of life. Personal preference and familiarity with an area are also important considerations. Some individuals may be drawn to an area with deep forestation that provides cover and natural barriers against attack. Conversely, others may prefer the coastline (despite its disadvantage of being open to external threats), because they are able to operate a boat and know how to fish.

For the wealthy, the locations of hideaway retreats range from remote areas in the American wilderness to exotic destinations in Latin America or foreign countries. New Zealand, with its comfortable climate and remoteness, is a popular destination for HNW American preppers shopping for a strategic relocation site. In response to demand, New Zealand has developed a niche luxury market for HNW American preppers (Osnos, 2017). In keeping with the tactic of reducing risk, some HNW preppers prefer to hedge their bets by securing both a strategic relocation destination and a safe room. For example, Mark Zuckerberg, founder of Facebook, maintains a 700-acre waterfront estate on the north shore of Kauai, Hawaii (Weise, 2017). In addition, Zuckerberg is currently building a fortified compound at his Palo Alto estate in California (Turton, 2016) (a safe estate rather than a safe room). By having both a strategic relocation destination and a fortified compound, Zuckerberg has purchased extra "apocalypse insurance" (Osnos, 2017, p. 39).

While an escape to a tropical, foreign locale sounds dreamy, the process of strategic relocation to another country is complex. First, gaining citizenship can be a lengthy process that requires years of residency. However, for the extremely rich, the process of gaining citizenship in some countries can be expedited by making significant business investments in the particular country (Strauss, 2009). Another roadblock is the considerable amount of time, effort and discretion required to purchase a suitable property that provides protection and resources. Select real estate agents now specialize in the sale of these properties. Beyond interior design and décor, these homes are outfitted with custom security features, and specialized systems such as air filtration to sustain life in the event of a disaster. Security and luxury prepping experts are usually consulted to ensure that homes are properly appointed. These hideaway locations must always be maintained and fully stocked in the event of a disaster. Therefore, staff are often hired to manage the properties.

A hideaway location, however luxurious, is worthless if its owner cannot reach it. As a result, HNW owners must ensure that they will have safe and reliable transportation. To be certain that their family will be taken quickly to safety, hideaway owners often arrange for transportation on private helicopters or planes, and make agreements to provide accommodations for the pilot's family as well as select staff (Osnos, 2017). Without these advance arrangements, it would be reasonable to expect that a pilot or staff member may refuse to leave his or her own family during a moment of grave adversity. Offering the promise of safety and shelter to these critical workers increases their motivation to undertake a dangerous escape. For HNW preppers living in Manhattan, the island's size may make securing arrangements for escape more competitive. Unless one owns a private helicopter and a helipad on one's building, a quick escape might prove difficult. Manhattan has only two public helicopter ports that offer a total of six helipads and one seaplane base with one space (City Data, 2019).[1] Taking off from some skyscrapers in Manhattan may be possible; however, the demand for the limited numbers of helicopters and rooftop space will be tremendous. Given the complex factors impacting all stages of securing, maintaining, and escaping to a hideaway retreat, this approach to prepping for disaster requires significant coordination and trust. And a significant amount of money.

The Simpsons episode, "Frink Gets Testy" (2018), is an absurd yet insightful exploration of a HNW person's difficulty in trying to escape a disaster scenario. After watching a late-night dose of "Apocalypse Week" on television, a fearful Mr. Burns becomes terrified of a future doomsday. He insists on the immediate construction of a spaceship called the "Doomsday Ark." Soon enough, Mr. Burns begins to struggle with the nagging question that might be faced by HNW preppers who have made elaborate escape plans for disaster scenarios: "Who is worth saving?" Professor Frink designs a new test guaranteed to determine one's "Personal Value Quotient" (PVQ)—how valuable someone is based on his or her sense of humanity and resourcefulness. After administering the test across Springfield, Mr. Burns rounds up all the high scorers into the spaceship ark. Once on board, Mr. Burns announces to the group that they will become his slaves and prepares to fly away. The group quickly escapes through an unlocked door. The episode exposes the real question posed by HNW preppers that invest in strategic relocations or safe rooms. With the limited space offered by escaping to a hideaway or by retreating to a safe room, the real question being asked might be: "Who is *useful to me* and, therefore, worth saving?"

My two interviews with HNW preppers echoed Osnos' observation that disaster preparedness is closely connected to this group's familiarity with risk assessment. These elite preppers reached out to me to discuss prepping rather than responding to my request for interviews. In other words, they were interested in confirming their research findings with me. Talking with me was a method of triangulation (Denzin, 1970) to confirm that their approaches to disaster preparedness were satisfactory. The first HNW prepper (who wishes to remain anonymous) recognized me at a Greenwich Village coffee house from a short *Wall Street Journal* article that discussed my project and featured my photo. He introduced himself and suggested that we "compare notes about prepping." He was friendly and gracious throughout our discussion. We talked about possible disasters in the city and we shared our thoughts about a few books on prepping. We even exchanged stories about our September 11 and Hurricane Sandy experiences. Overall, we shared many of the same perspectives. However, we did not share an equal level of wealth, and this significantly impacted our assumptions about the possible experience and aftermath of disaster. The HNW prepper explained to me: "Look, my extended family and I have a plan. We have an agreement about my place. There's no showing up empty-handed. Every family [member] has a responsibility to meet to be let in." I didn't get the sense that he was being cruel, that he really planned to turn people away. However, I understood that there was a serious expectation that everyone must come prepared.

I attempted to clarify his statement by asking if he meant that he expected his family to bring particular supplies, such as a certain amount of food or water. He paused and considered me for a moment. My face burned under his gaze, as he made me acutely aware that I did not live behind the velvet curtain. No, of course he didn't mean that. He meant things like Picassos, necklaces such as the ladies on the Titanic wore, or rare wines from the ancient tomb of Saqqara. Precious items that I will only see in museums. For non-HNW preppers, there is anxiety about not having enough staples (water, food, medicine) to see their families through a catastrophe. Some non-HNW preppers are worried they will not have enough basic provisions because they have been in the position of not having enough to eat. In a disaster situation, most people would hope to show up at a relative's home with a valuable contribution that would go toward helping the group sustain itself. This HNW prepper had very different concerns. His priority was preserving the prized objects his family had spent their lives amassing and cherishing. I quickly corrected myself: "I'm sorry, you probably mean family heirlooms—important works of art or jewelry." He gave me a slight nod. I did understand. His plan was intended to preserve wealth, not just to preserve life. Maybe even in that order.

I met the second wealthy prepper at the *Garden and Gun* Jubilee, an annual exposition that was held near Charleston, South Carolina. Sponsored by *Garden and Gun*, a magazine that covers sporting life and highbrow culture of the South, the event appealed to wealthy magazine readers who were interested in experiencing a range of activities, from sporting dog demonstrations to posh dinners to photography field classes offered by the Leica Camera company. With readership split almost evenly between men and women, the average profile of a *Garden and Gun* reader is a person over 35 with an average net worth of $2.5 million, who also owns two homes and travels throughout the year (Garden and Gun, 2018). As part of the research for this book, I attended the event in order to examine high-end outdoor gear that might be used by wealthy preppers. This level of outdoor equipment would not be readily available for inspection at a sporting goods store in Manhattan. At the Jubilee market, I was able to test a high-powered set of binoculars. They were lightweight with incredible range. At the binocular booth, my husband, (who accompanied me to the event), and I discussed their suitability for a bug out bag. We also compared the portability and ease of these binoculars verses the drones used for surveillance by some preppers, which I characterized as noisy and of limited utility, since the batteries will die. Another visitor at the booth, a trim white man who looked to be in his sixties, gave me a bit of grin and seemed amused by our conversation. He looked like he wanted to say something, but he thought better of it. At this point in my field work, I recognized that any conversation about prepping always drew curious reactions, so I just returned his smile. My husband and I then moved on to inspect the handmade canoe that could be also displayed as art until needed.

Later that evening, I was surprised to see the man I had noticed earlier sitting next to us at the bar of a local restaurant. He introduced himself as Greg, and struck up a conversation with me and my husband. We broke into laughter when we discovered that we were all from Manhattan. He remarked that he was surprised to overhear us talking about prepping at the Jubilee. He commented that he had "wondered what that was all about as we didn't seem like that type." As I explained my research project, Greg tapped his fingers on the bar and kept nodding. He then surprised me with a revelation: he considered himself a prepper, and his family's beach house near Charleston actually doubles as his strategic relocation spot. Greg shared that he attends events such as the Jubilee and outdoor expos so that he can pick up prepping strategies, check out gear, and practice shooting and hunting without being labeled a prepper. He explained that having a second home in the South also allows him to practice his interest in prepping:

> Having a second home here gives me good cover. People trust me. I can't talk about prepping in the city. Hunting? No way. Other New Yorkers judging me, that's one thing. Clients thinking that I'm uneasy about the economy. No way. A word about prepping would be like my shooting up flares as a signal that the market is going to die. Not crash, die.

At the conclusion of our conversation, Greg agreed to meet me for a formal interview and give me a tour of his family's strategic relocation destination. Given the history of severe hurricanes in the Charleston area, I was skeptical of his notion that the location would be ideal for strategic relocation. However, my subsequent visit to his family's beach house decreased my skepticism. As a more recent construction, the large beach home is built to be resilient against hurricanes and it is set back from the ocean. While his wife declined to be interviewed, she was lovely during our brief exchange. Their gorgeous home resembled the ocean getaways usually featured on a home design or travel program, but it was clear that his was not merely a luxury abode, as it was also cleverly designed for strategic relocation. The house could be easily shuttered to protect its occupants against both hurricanes and intruders. Although the owner said that the house did not contain a safe room, an oversized family room on an upper floor was outfitted with items like a large and well-stocked gun cabinet, a walk-in prepper closet (that included both the high-end binoculars and two drones). In beach houses, upper floors are viewed as important real estate because these rooms are protected in periods of high flooding. Therefore, the location of the prepping area suggests that it is significant to the family.

Greg explained to me why he felt that his family might have to flee Manhattan at some point:

> I'm most concerned about two possibilities: Major rioting, social upheaval. Whatever term you'd like to use. No predicting it. Could happen at any time. Everyone mocked the Occupy Wall Street protestors. The younger guys kept making fun of them, but I took it a sign of things to come. Another serious attack. We won't be able to stay in the city. We have everything that we need here. Smooth transition.

I asked him if they had made advance travel arrangements to leave the city in the event of a disaster. After declining to discuss his specific plans, he only said: "All taken care of."

While owning a beautiful hideaway may not be possible for all NYC preppers, strategic relocation is still a primary goal of bugging out for middle-class preppers. In 2017, citywide homeownership was 32.4%, with the lowest rates of homeownership in Manhattan at 24.6% and in the Bronx at 22.1% (Department of Housing Preservation and Development, 2018). Given the high cost of homeownership in the city, many middle-class New Yorkers prefer to purchase modest weekend homes outside of the city in the rural and scenic areas of upstate New York, New Jersey and Connecticut. Adopting this practice, middle-class New York preppers also seek to purchase weekend homes to serve double duty as a place for respite and as a strategic relocation site. Like many other New Yorkers, middle-class preppers may choose to make arrangements to stay with family or friends at their nearby suburban homes in emergency situations.

Regardless of their destination, NYC preppers seek to carefully plan their route to safety. The first priority is determining the mode of transportation for exiting the city. For all New Yorkers, attempting to leave the city by car will be very challenging given traffic congestion and the limited number of exit routes. However, some NYC preppers still consider driving or flying out of the city as viable options, if they heed advance warning. For preppers, advance warning refers to keeping abreast of the news and responding swiftly to their own perceptions about increasing danger rather than waiting for official announcements. For example, if there are projections of a severe hurricane, a prepper will most likely depart the city well in advance of an announced evacuation. Recognizing that some disasters may occur suddenly and without warning, many NYC preppers plan to walk or ride their bikes out of the city to reach the safety of their strategic relocation. Therefore, NYC preppers chart routes and meetup points to guide their journeys. These directions are coded to hide meeting locations and the final destination. Assuming that smartphones will be useless, they plan to use printed topographical maps. As preparation for a strenuous bug out walk, NYC preppers often practice the hike out of the city to become familiar with challenges such as walking across the George Washington Bridge as well as adjusting to walking for lengthy periods of time while wearing a bug out bag. Most preppers expect to walk for several days to reach their destinations. However, some preppers plan to drive once out of the city. For example, one prepper revealed that she had vehicles with supplies hidden in locations just outside of the city in both New York and New Jersey.

Biking out of the city to a safe haven also demands considerable physical stamina. One independent NYC prepper shared that, through training, he and his bug out partner had built up their endurance to riding 100 miles per day to ensure that they would reach their destination, referred to as "Grandma's house," as quickly as possible. Given his athletic physique and his commitment to prepping, I did not doubt his ability. Two other independent NYC preppers talked with me about the possibility of leaving the city by water in an inflatable raft or canoe. Their assumption was that an inflatable raft, one that could be stored in a New York apartment, might not be secure enough for the trip due to strong currents. A canoe might be a good choice, but the challenges of storing and then transporting the canoe to the river discouraged their reliance on this option. During field research, I also observed a prepper test a foldable kayak. It was watertight but seemed about as durable as a paper lantern. It took the person nearly two hours to assemble it.

In any bug out situation, all preppers expect to rely on their bug out bags for survival on their journey to safety. A bug out bag, sometimes called a go bag, is a pre-packed bag with emergency essentials for a five-day period (Charles, 2014). A bug out bag contains critical supplies from the categories of water, food, first aid, shelter, clothing, fire, tools and reference documents (See www.ready.gov/build-a-kit for a supply list). While there are must-have items, many supplies are selected according to personal preference. A premade bug out bag can be purchased with all supplies. However, some entry-level premade bags have significant limitations, placing buyers at risk. For example, one premade bag advertised on a popular shopping website provided a small number of water pouches rather than a water filtration system that can be used repeatedly. Therefore, many preppers prefer to purchase their own provisions to ensure quality and durability. "A bug out bag" is actually a misnomer. Preppers typically have a series of bug out bags at the ready in different locations: a main bug out bag for home, an EDC (Every Day Carry) bag, an office bag and a car bag for those that own cars. Each bag stores a combination of standard items and items specifically needed at a particular location. A main bug out bag typically weighs around twenty pounds. An EDC is the lightest of all bags as it contains the minimum number of items such as a wallet, smartphone, keys, mini-flashlight, a lighter, and medication. Many women and men already carry an EDC; however, these bags are more commonly known as purses or messenger bags. A bug out bag for the office or for the car is similar to the main bug out bag. However, it is left on location to ensure that a prepper always has access to emergency supplies in the event of a disaster

Preppers with families have additional challenges in preparing and packing bug out bags. Few real prepping supplies exist for children. To remedy this problem, many prepping blogs offer advice about preparing bug out bags for children. Charles (2014) recommends that parents with infants or toddlers should make one parent responsible for the infant carrier while the other person carries a bag with heavier items. Young children should carry small backpacks that contain comfort items including favorite snacks, a game or book, socks and at least a sixteen-ounce water bottle. Beyond general advice, parents have few options when it comes to purchasing protective equipment for their children. As Roman Zrazhevskiy, the co-founder of Ready-toGoSurvival.com, a prepping supply company, observes:

Although many parents are interested in protecting their families from disaster, most gear is too large for children. There are no kids' sizes and the smallest adult sizes are still too big. There are no gas masks made in children's sizes. We've lost customers over this. Some parents feel that they shouldn't have all of this protective equipment if it isn't available for their children. It is an underserved market. Special precautions and warnings also have to be issued to be sure that kids' products are being used safely. However, some of us are working to change this.

Zrazhevskiy's new venture, Mira Safety, a gas mask and personal protective equipment company, is now designing gas masks for children as well as infant hoods.

Although pet disaster preparedness is not a focus of this project, protecting one's pet in an emergency is critical to many preppers who feel that pets should be part of a family's disaster plan. The logistical challenges of evacuating companion animals are numerous, ranging from difficulties in finding pet-friendly shelters to a fearful pet running away, or evacuation (Farmer and DeYoung, 2018). To ensure the safety of pets in a disaster, the Center for Disease Control (2019) recommends that owners pack items from five main categories: documents like vaccination certificates and veterinary records, water, food, medication and comfort supplies (including a leash, toys and bedding). Given the size and weight of these items, most owners will carry their pet's supplies in their own bags. However, some pets may be able to carry a portion of their own supplies. Therefore, retailers now sell small bug out packs for dogs to wear.

Generally, in packing a bug out bag, preppers should prioritize supplies according to their area's possible disasters, their fitness level, experience and budget (Charles, 2014). Similar to hikers, most preppers use a high-quality hiking backpack as a bug out bag for its durability, efficient storage and easy carrying. Like new hikers, new preppers must be careful not to overpack their bags. Walking with a pack that is too heavy quickly encourages a re-evaluation of what "essential" really means. Therefore, preppers must streamline their supplies to meet the needs of a five-day period. To reduce weight, preppers remove packaging and reduce amounts to make travel lighter. For example, a roll of duct tape requires too much space and is too heavy to carry, so preppers reduce its size and weight by packing a smaller amount of tape on the roll. One multi-tool replaces a few tools. First-aid essentials are repacked in Sucrets boxes. Trauma kits are flattened and sealed into vacuum-packed bags. Every item is reduced to its smallest and lightest size without compromising its use.

The goal of owning a bug out bag is to provide the peace of mind in knowing that you are prepared for disaster. However, bug out bag preparation is a process subject to continuous revision prompted by experience and the release of new products. Given preppers' interest in planning for emergencies, they are always searching for new and more efficient products as well as new applications for existing supplies. Brian, my neighbor and a white NYC independent prepper in his thirties, met me in Washington Square Park to talk about prepping. He also agreed to bring along his bug out bag to show me its contents. He said:

> Your bug out bag is like a recipe that you're always trying to perfect or an old hot rod that you're always tinkering with. I'm never satisfied. I'm always swapping one thing out for another. Remember how our dads used to tinker around Radio Shack? It's like that only I'm working on saving my family, not trying to fix an old VHS player.

Brian carried a large black military-looking backpack with a sleeping bag roll. In the outside pocket, he stored items that he might need to use quickly, like bug spray, work gloves, N95-breathing masks, a headlamp and small flashlight, a multi-tool, a compass and maps of the city, New York State and New Jersey, all tucked in a plastic bag. He also had a fixed-blade knife and a hatchet hidden in this pocket, given New York's restrictions on carrying these tools. A small first-aid pouch was clipped to the outside of his bag. A large water bottle was tucked in each side pouch. The outside pockets were catch-alls for small items including a bandana, sunglasses, sunscreen, lip balm, a beanie and even two folded up garbage bags. Inside the bag's main section, all supplies were stashed in clear bags according to category. For example, a compact water filter plus water tablets as a backup were stored together. A flint-striker, tinder in the form of cotton balls soaked in Vaseline and birch bark, a bellows and waterproof matches alongside a lighter made up his fire-starting kit. Packed separately was a collapsible firebox. Clothing included lightweight athletic wear used for layering, underwear and socks were rolled into a small tube, again tucked in a waterproof pouch. A toiletry bag included a toothbrush and toothpaste, floss, body wash, toilet paper and talcum powder. His food provisions included packets of salmon and tuna, protein bars, turkey jerky and some dried fruit. Inside his cooking pot were coffee packets, dried creamer and a spork. A folding shovel and duct tape were also stored in this area as well as two tarps and plenty of cordage. Brian carried a hammock rather than a tent to save space. As he unpacked his bag and showed me the items, he often shared his critiques of supply choices to explain why he had decided on a particular product or approach. It was clear that he had spent a great deal of time researching and trying out things to choose the supplies that were the best fit for him.

Preppers gain valuable experience through testing their gear to meet their specific needs. However, given the discovery of new equipment and changing needs, preparing a bug out bag can be a costly investment. Brian estimates that he has probably spent over $2,000 on his main bug out bag and his car bag combined. I have invested around $1,000 on my own bug out bag. The majority of that money was spent on one item, a lightweight tent. My hikes with my bag have taught me that I cannot handle a bag that is more than twenty pounds. Light and high-quality gear comes with a premium price tag. Tailoring a bug out bag to suit your needs is also a time-consuming process.

For HNW preppers, the process of securing and outfitting a bug out bag is much more streamlined. Regular preppers create their own personal bug out bags. HNW preppers have their bags curated for them. Rather than spending time carefully selecting provisions by researching and testing supplies, HNW preppers employ prepping concierge services and buy premade bug out bags offered through boutique internet shopping. Prepping consultant companies such as The Black Umbrella (https://www.blackumbrella.com) offer luxury bug out bags and emergency planning services to help protect HNW families in any crisis. For HNW preppers, these services are important investments because they mitigate risk and save time in a busy lifestyle. According to The Black Umbrella's website:

> During an unusual event, your ES/P [Emergency/Safety Plan Specialist] will help you get in touch with your loved ones when cell phones go down, map out where to go if you can't get home, and help your family stay safe and comfortable no matter what.

A special feature is an indestructible waterproof custom laser engraved go card that lists your family's phone numbers and other pertinent information as requested. The go card looks like a black credit card. It is a convenient update to a laminated information sheet, and it easily fits into the wallets or bags of all family members. Prepping aside, the card is an ingenious idea in everyday life for people like me whose smartphone battery is always on the verge of dying.

Based on analyzing buying patterns on his company's website, Roman Zrazhevskiy, CEO of the prepping supply website Ready to Go Survival (https://readytogosurvival.com), has identified a distinct difference between shopping strategies of HNW preppers and regular preppers. During our interview, Zrazhevskiy said:

> I can always predict what wealthy preppers are going to order. All I have to do is read the morning's *New York Times*. If there's news about a gas attack by terrorists somewhere, then there is a rush of gas masks orders all to be sent to downtown offices, Wall Street companies. Whatever the news is, if they don't have the right gear, they are going to order it. Many of these customers are at the executive level. Financial services people. This is how they operate. Minimizing risk.

As prepping has become more mainstream, Ready to Go Survival and other prepping gear websites have developed marketing strategies to appeal to HNW preppers. Ready to Go Survival offers a curated shopping experience for personalized survival kits, a virtual specialty store within its website. In contrast to the traditional browse-and-click shopping experience on a website, buying a Ready to Go Survival's personalized survival kits is an interactive design process that caters to a client's unique needs. The client creates a survival profile that pinpoints specific needs. Based on this profile, the client receives a personal survival guide made up of a comprehensive list of recommended items with weights, prices and links designed by a Preparedness Specialist. After receiving feedback from the client, the survival kit is curated and shipped. After shipping, the client receives alerts when it is time to change out provisions to keep the survival kit up-to-date.

Quality premade bug out bags and survival kits are not just purchased by HNW preppers. While HNW preppers may purchase more expensive equipment, quality premade bags are also purchased by individuals who are planning to protect their families but who are not committed to becoming preppers. Purchasing a curated bag is a significant time-saver for both groups. One is able to receive quality equipment without investing time in the lengthy process of reviewing and testing equipment. In surveying buyers, Zrazhevskiy has discovered that "some people agree that they should have a bug out bag, but they are not interested in the time investment. They aren't looking for a hobby or a lifestyle."

However, dedicated preppers tend to argue that a bug out bag is valuable only if one knows how to use its contents. For them, watching YouTube videos and television programs about surviving a disaster is of limited value. A central part of preparedness is practicing survival skills to improve one's abilities. Experiential learning is key. Referred to as "bug outs," practice outings are overnight trips, similar to camping expeditions, that require preppers to survive with only the supplies in their packs for a designated number of days. Bug outs give preppers the chance to become familiar with key survival skills such as starting a fire or learning to navigate with a compass and map. During a disaster, familiarity with one's tools and knowledge of basic survival skills allows a prepper to respond and adapt to the situation more quickly. Rather than struggling with how to build a fire for the first time, for example, a well-prepared prepper in a disaster situation will be able to concentrate energy on other matters such as building a sturdier shelter or tending to the needs of others. Most important, bug out trips expose preppers to the stress of surviving in a difficult, unfamiliar situation. NYC preppers are forced to leave behind the conveniences of city life and face new challenges. Living in NY can be an exercise in survival itself, therefore many New Yorkers (and NY preppers) have already cultivated an instinctual alertness and are skilled at negotiating levels of possible danger and threat, which can be quite helpful in a crisis.

For NYC independent preppers, bug out skills and exercises, and prepping skills are learned alone or within small networks of family members or friends. As Brian explained: "Honestly, I don't have the time or interest learning to prep within a larger group. Family and a plan, what else do I need?" However, prepping for a family is complex. I interviewed two mothers about the special challenges of prepping with children. For example, children need to become familiar with long walks if the family has to leave the city on foot. Renee, who lives with her family in Manhattan, plans to shelter in place. However, her husband and their two teenage children still practice bug out walks across the George Washington Bridge. In explaining their drills, she stated that:

> In the beginning, the four of us left from home. Now, we alternate with the kids leaving from a place near their school or near a friend's home to see how long it takes us to meet at our spot. The two who are home bring the bags. We then make our way toward the bridge. I used to be terrified of the walk. I am much better now. My husband has an office bag. If something happens and he is at work, he knows where to meet us.

Leslie, a mother of three grade-school children perceives that living in Brooklyn is less risky; therefore, she assumes they will be able to shelter in place rather than bug out. However, she still wants to teach her children about bugging out. She and her children sometimes take walks in Prospect Park with their bags, and her family camps at Jellystone Campground near the Catskills. Leslie is interested in teaching her children about prepping, but she does not want to overwhelm them: "I don't want to stress them. Kids have way too much of that as it is. I just want them to recognize a few things. City kids have no understanding of the outdoors. This helps a little." In each of the two families, at least one parent is a skilled hiker.

As my research reveals, creating a bug out bag and practicing bugging out, are central components of prepping. However, in studying prepping as a participant-observer, I came to realize that I lack two qualities important to mastering these components. First, I have discovered that I am not a tester-and-tinkerer type of person. I prefer to research items and then purchase them. I lack the patience to enjoy the process of testing items to evaluate their respective performances under different conditions. I am also not good at taking a look at an item and determining how modifications would improve its performance or change its utility. Second, like many other urban preppers, I have limited experience with outdoor excursions. While I enjoy day hiking, I did not have overnight camping skills before conducting this research. Therefore, I have no segue from camping skills into survival skills. My only camping experience dates back to when I was a Brownie. We set up camp in the Den Mother's cramped backyard enclosed by a chain-link fence in our Navy Housing complex. Turned off by the setting and the assignment of latrine duty, I rubbed grass in my eyes to ensure that I went home before sunset. As an adult, I now love visiting National Parks, but I have been reluctant to camp overnight. However, I recognize how strategic preparation and adaptation would be crucial assets in a disaster, and given my own experience with contending with disasters in the city, I was also interested in improving my survival skills in order to discover how urban prepper group members learned these skills together. Therefore, my participant-observation in a prepping group has been key to learning these two elements of prepping.

After reviewing my interview notes for this chapter, my mind kept returning to my meeting with Brian. I thought a great deal about his remark about visiting Radio Shack with his father, how those trips seemed to shape Brian's intellect and interests. Brian's meaningful reference made me feel a little envious. My Radio Shack experience with my father was different. I had never been taught the role of tinkerer. I did go to Radio Shack with my dad nearly every Saturday. Mysterious Radio Shack. All of those little plastic packets of candy-like treasures—smart bows of licorice-like wire in every color, silver button batteries reminded me of the candy coins I had hidden from my sister and the yellow perfboards pretending to be honeycomb. My dad would always leave with a small bag of electronic wizardry to use on his latest project. My dad as the DIYer saving our family, saving the world, one electrical masterpiece at a time.

After one shopping trip, I dismantled my rocket ship radio so I could put it back together. I wanted to be like my dad, the problem-solver, the rescuer. Someday, we were going to need my radio and I was going to save the day. Not exactly. My tweezers, torn from my Operation game, and some dabs of Elmer's glue were not useful in repairing the destroyed circuit board. I needed rescuing. On Sunday, my dad came into my room and saw me, at my desk, puzzling over the broken radio. I explained that I couldn't make it work. He shook his head and brushed the radio into the trash can. He walked over and scanned my toy area. He came back with my Barbie Camper. He said: "Here's what needs some fixin', some fixin' up, that is! This Barbie Camper needs some sprucing up to make sure that everyone's traveling in style. Work your magic!" He hurried away and returned with wallpaper and carpet scraps from his shed. I remember how his face softened when he saw my dismantled radio. I now recognize this expression as his "my kid is a nut" face. And, I loved fixing up the camper.

This memory has made me admit my fascination with studying prepping. Until I embarked on this research project, I had never really had the opportunity to cultivate my childhood interest in gadgets and fixing things. My interest in "boy things" was not reinforced because, well, I was not a boy. I realize now that this memory was an early example of how I was constricted by gender roles and that my dad was, perhaps, unwittingly reinforcing them. I see now that this childhood experience had a big impact on my sense of self as a woman in the future. Whether it is my angst about the missing pieces of myself that were lost due to my conformity to gender roles or my absolute fear about stepping into a new role, I keep bumping up against my own notions of my identity as a woman in this research. As I discuss in subsequent chapters, prepping seems likely to reinforce gender roles, but it may also have the potential to break through those boundaries by encouraging self-reliance. For example, some female preppers who are mothers seem to be merging the traditional gender roles of protector of the family and mother into one complex identity. Other women link their prepping and homesteading practices to carrying on the traditions of their mothers. I am still trying to work through where I fit in. Kohn (2010, p. 186) identifies the power of my unexpected recollection of the past as an important element of ethnographic research that "acknowledges the personal in flux" and steps past reflexivity to "expose the interior self to other selves." Taking on the challenge of prepping is a particularly difficult task because it forces me to confront my short-comings and my own perceptions of gender roles.

Note

1 Given the 2018 tragic helicopter crash into the East River which killed the tourists-passengers, and the excessive noise caused by takeoffs and landings, the city govern-ment has sought to curb the helicopter tourism industry and has halted helicopter travel on weekends. However, some pilots have chosen to ignore these restrictions. In 2012, a billionaire helicopter pilot, Mayor Bloomberg, generated controversy when he was caught flying during the no-fly ban on weekends (Grynbaum, 2012).

References

Brown, D. J. (2009). *The indifferent stars above: The harrowing saga of the Donner party.* New York, NY: HarperCollins.

Centers for Disease Control and Prevention. (2019). *Pet disaster emergency checklist.* Retrieved from https://www.cdc.gov/healthypets/resources/disaster-prep-pet-em ergency-checklist.pdf.

Charles, J. (2014). *Emergency bag essentials: Everything you need to bug out.* New York, NY: Potter Style.

City-Data. (2019). *FAA registered airports, heliports and other landing facilities in New York.* (2019.) Retrieved from http://www.city-data.com/airports/New-York.html.

Denzin, N. K. (1970). *The research act: A theoretical introduction to sociological methods.* New York, NY: Routledge.

Department of Housing Preservation and Development. (2018, February 9). *Selected initial findings of the 2017 New York City housing and vacancy survey.* Retrieved from https://www1.nyc.gov/assets/hpd/downloads/pdf/about/2017-hvs-initial-findings.pdf.

Emergency Preparedness, Emergency Kits and Go Bags. (n.d.). Retrieved from https://www.blackumbrella.com/.

Farmer, A. K., and DeYoung, S. E. (2018). Emergency management: Pets. In L. R. Shapiro and M. H. Maras (Eds.), *Encyclopedia of Security and Emergency Management* (pp. 1–3). Cham: Springer International Publishing.

Garden and Gun. (2018). 2018 Print Media Kit. *Garden and Gun.* Retrieved from https://gardenandgun.com/wp-content/uploads/2018/08/18_07_GG_PrintMediaKit_F-2.pdf.

Grynbaum, M. M. (2012, May 23). Caught violating weekend copter ban, Bloomberg will alter flight plans. *The New York Times.* Retrieved from https://www.nytimes.com/2012/05/24/nyregion/bloomberg-violates-weekend-helicopter-ban-and-will-stop.html.

Kohn, T. (2010). The role of serendipity and memory in experiencing fields. In P. Collins, and A. Gallinat (Eds.), *The ethnographic self as resource: Writing memory and experience into ethnography* (pp. 185–199). New York, NY: Berghahn Books.

Osnos, E. (2017, January 30). Doomsday prep for the super-rich. *The New Yorker*. Retrieved from https://www.newyorker.com/magazine/2017/01/30/doomsday-prep-for-the-super-rich.

Reed Murphy, V. (1891). Across the plains in the Donner party. A personal narrative of the overland trip to California. *The Century Magazine*, 42, 409–426.

Skousen, J., and Skousen, A. (2016). *Strategic relocation: North American guide to safe places*. Orem, Utah: Joel Skousen Designs.

Strauss, N. (2009). *Emergency: This book will save your life*. New York, NY: HarperCollins.

Tiidenberg, K., and Whelan, A. (2017, April 17). Sick bunnies and pocket dumps: "Not-selfies" and the genre of self-representation. *Popular Communication*, 15(2), 141–153.

Turton, W. (2016, May 25). Is Mark Zuckerberg building a doomsday bunker on his Palo Alto estate? *Gizmodo*. Retrieved from https://gizmodo.com/is-mark-zuckerberg-building-a-doomsday-bunker-on-his-pa-1778611834.

Weise, E. (2017, January 27). Mark Zuckerberg drops suits to force sale of Hawaiian lands. *USA Today*. Retrieved from https://www.usatoday.com/story/tech/news/2017/01/27/zuckerberg-drops-kauai-land-suits-hawaii-quiet-title/97152332.

Wikipedia contributors. (2018, December 13). *Frink Gets Testy*. Retrieved from https://en.wikipedia.org/wiki/Frink_Gets_Testy.

Williams, A. (2017, September 23). How to survive the apocalypse. *The New York Times*. Retrieved from https://www.nytimes.com/2017/09/23/style/how-to-survive-the-apocalypse.html.

Part 3

Urban prepping and symbolic interaction

6 New York City Prepper's Network's mission and organizational structure

Interviewing New York's wealthy and middle-class independent preppers offered valuable insight into the motivations for and approaches to prepping but provided limited insight into prepping as a social world. From independent preppers, I understood the importance of a bug out bag as a means of survival but not as a means of communication among urban preppers. To fully understand the phenomenon, I needed to study prepping as human interaction—an ongoing conversation of shared significant symbols, significant in that each symbol means the same thing to all actors involved in the interaction (Musolf, 2003). Joining the NYC Prepper's Network (NYCPN) as a participant-observer provided the opportunity to explore how preppers assign meaning to objects and actions as they interpreted prepping and their identities as preppers. Symbolic interactionism, outlined by Blumer's three premises (1969, p. 2) offers a strong framework for meeting this research goal: First, human beings act toward things based on the meanings that objects have for them. Such objects include everything that a person may note in his or her world: physical things, other people, categories of people, guiding ideals, activities of others, as well other situations that may occur in a person's daily life. Second, the meaning of objects arises from their interactions with others. Third, these meanings are handled in and modified through an interpretative process used by the person dealing with the objects he or she encounters.

This chapter shares the story of this interpretive process for NYCPN group members. For example, trust and responsibility are the guiding principles of the NYCPN. Members are expected to demonstrate a deep commitment to prepping through active participation and developing advanced bushcraft (wilderness survival) skills. As a result, a physical object such as a backpack and its contents are redefined as a "bug out bag" which symbolizes one's competence level in a survival situation. One's "bug out bag" becomes analogous to one's résumé. Sharing in the belief that the government is a weak institution that cannot be depended on for help in a disaster, members look to one another to strengthen their self-reliance by learning and practicing prepping skills together. Categories of members are defined as preppers and non-preppers, core members and regular members. In the NYCPN, a prepper's mettle is tested by a range of activities from workshops to tough weekend excursions. Responses are varied with most members conforming to group standards, and a few members electing to be mavericks or failing miserably. For NYCPN members, the notion of self-reliance and expectation of trust also stems from their own experiences of survival from direct experience as well as other challenges like growing up poor in America's wealthiest city. Each interpretative process is often informed by being a city dweller. The chapter's first section examines the NYCPN's mission and organizational structure. The second section begins the analysis of the NYCPN's activities as crucial social encounters that are "interactional engines that drive concerted social activity" and have significant impact on "maintaining or challenging the identity and personal worth" of actors (Atkinson, 2015, Chapter 5, para. 10).

NYCPN's mission and structure

In 2010, the NYC Prepper's Network (NYCPN) was established as a group of city dwellers interested in learning and sharing knowledge about prepping. As explained on the group's Meetup page,

> The primary goal of the NYC Prepper's Network is to create a community network of like-minded individuals who share their knowledge of all things related to self-sufficiency ... to establish a network of folks to share ideas with, learn from and eventually hope to trust should the need arise.
> ("New York City Prepper's Network", 2019).[1]

Within this mission statement, the NYCPN established the principles that were crucial to the group's foundation; learning from one another, showing commitment by attending events and training, as well as demonstrating trustworthiness. The group's page identifies the unique challenges of urban prepping:

> NYC Preppers Network is an Emergency Preparedness & Wilderness group for city dwellers that are concerned with preparing for disasters. Some of us don't live in a home, have garages, wells, basements or attics to store our survival gear in. Most of us live in apartments. City occupants face a different set of challenges. Space, Food Storage, Water, Security, Sanitation, Evacuation Routes & many other issues are of a great concern for city dwellers.

To facilitate learning emergency preparedness under these complex conditions as well in the outdoors, NYCPN engages in activities ranging from lectures to weekend excursions at various skill levels.

Many of the NYCPN's prepping strategies are grounded in learning bushcraft (wilderness survival skills). In his *New York Times* bestseller, *Bushcraft 101: A Field Guide to the Art of Wilderness Survival*, Dave Canterbury, a wilderness survival expert, notes that practicing bushcraft is a great way to learn the outdoors. If you're feeling trapped in an urban environment, a good tramp is a way to return to the wild, turn off your electronic devices, and escape society's constant pressures. In addition, the abilities that you hone in bush can become life-saving skills when it comes to disaster preparedness and survival situations.

(2014, p.14)

According to Canterbury (2014) all essential tools and knowledge can be organized into "the 5 Cs of survival":

1   Cutting tools to craft needed items and process food.
2   Cover elements to create a microclimate of protection from the weather.
3   Combustion devices for building fire to provide warmth, to cook and preserve food, and make medicines.
4   Containers to carry water across distances and to store collected food.
5   Cordages for bindings (wrapping to protect or secure) and lashing (fastening multiple items together).

(p. 20)

Combined with one's knowledge of first aid and navigation, these tools are supposed to enable a person to survive by helping to control the body's core temperature in various weather conditions and providing comfort and convenience. The NYCPN's own survival skill training is an adaptation of Canterbury's model for survival that includes additional resources such as communication. In my role as a participant-observer, the 5Cs system also served as a metaphor for the experience of being a prepping group member. Depending on the challenge, my core temperature was chilled by fear or miserable cold, or sometimes even hot with frustration. Comfort was that precious treasure that I regretted leaving behind at the start of every excursion and it was the treasure that I longed for in the middle of rough nights such as when I discovered that my tent was slowly filling with icy water due to my poor site selection. My convenience was no longer defined by the amenities of my Greenwich Village neighborhood or my proximity to the internet. Instead, my convenience was determined by my own ability to create, by what I packed or by what I could craft. And, many times, my comfort and convenience were made possible only by what NYCPN members chose to share with me.

Similar to the city itself, the NYCPN's membership is diverse, with the majority of members residing in the most populated boroughs.[2] Given the ability to form connections across different social media platforms, the number of network members fluctuates. In 2019, the number of NYCPN members was listed at 459.[3] The majority of group members were people of color including African Americans, Afro-Caribbeans, Puerto Ricans and Asians. NYCPN members are located across all five boroughs with most members living in Manhattan, the Bronx, Queens and Brooklyn. Some members also now live in

New Jersey, but still participate in the group. No longer in possession of that sense of immortality experienced by twenty-somethings, most group members are in their late 30s and 40s with families. Therefore, they seek to protect their families from physical or economic harm. Members also hold jobs in diverse economic sectors such as emergency response, law, retail, security, technology, tourism and education.[4]

NYCPN recruitment occurs mainly online. The NYCPN utilizes two social media platforms, Meetup and Facebook. The Meetup platform is the method for joining the primary group that physically meets for discussion and outings. Given that the group actually meets for events, membership must be approved. However, membership requirements are minimal and include a short questionnaire about prepping interests and skills. This Meetup platform is a mechanism for announcing events and sending direct messages between members. In addition, the Facebook group page is used to post and exchange prepping information among internet members. The Facebook page is a public group with moderators that provides easy access to general information about specific topics without active participation. In keeping with the methodology of symbolic interactionism, my study focuses on the group that meets regularly to learn and practice prepping techniques to explore their experiences and communication with one another rather than brief responses to posts among the Facebook page's members.

Although the Facebook group page is not the primary method of communication among the smaller Meetup group, it does serve as a valuable introduction to prepping interests shared within the NYCPN. As explained by Allan, the Facebook page's main administrator and a NYCPN member, the Facebook page is

> used to spread information and to hopefully get more people interested in joining and attending events for practice and training. The discussion threads are good for exploring and sharing ideas on prepping and survival in general. Lots of good resources, tips and advice are shared, and it's not just related to NYC specifically.

Created in 2017, the Facebook group page now functions as an information clearinghouse for a small following of preppers throughout the world. In 2019, the page had 195 followers. Beyond the New York area, followers of the page are from diverse locations ranging from Tennessee to France. In its first year (2017), the Facebook page's 345 postings can be classified into five categories:

1　Prepping Gear or Products
2　Skill Development
3　General Prepping Information
4　News Alerts and Warnings
5　Event Announcements.

(NYCPN Facebook Page, 2019)[2]

Postings were nearly evenly distributed among the first four categories: Prepping Gear or Products (28%), Skill Development (24%), General Prepping Information (21%), and News Alerts and Warnings (20%).[5] The gear or products category includes recommendations or questions about equipment and phone apps to be used in emergency situations, while skill development postings offer insight or questions about gaining prepping skills such as proper packing for a long hike (in a bug out situation) or improving home-steading skills such as food storage. General prepping information refers to information that is useful to preppers but not found in the other categories, such as a posting on the challenges of prepping without family support. News alerts and warnings includes current news that suggests possible emergencies or threats. Without requiring face-to-face interaction, the Facebook page represents a low level of engagement for preppers and people curious about prepping.

An advanced level of engagement can only be accomplished by formally joining the Meetup group that meets in-person on a regular basis. For the group, this level of interaction is crucial to successful prepping. According to the NYCPN Meetup page,

> Meeting and training together is [sic] the only way that the NYC Prepper's Network can accomplish its goal of establishing a learning community based on commitment and trust. Prepping takes some sort of commitment. Attending the meetings & events also takes commitment. We know that everyone has a busy life & that life has more pressing issues to attend to but we look for committed members in our group. Commitment shows that you are willing to learn, show, & become a better prepper.
>
> ("New York City Prepper's Network", 2019)

Furthermore, the NYCPN makes it known that it is interested in the practice of prepping rather than meeting to discuss political positions that may drive interest in prepping. The group's description closes with the reminder that "This is NOT a political, religious, or conspiracy group. All are welcome." ("New York City Prepper's Network", 2019). In the effort to gauge the interests and skills of prospective members, each person must answer a very brief questionnaire (three broad questions) to be reviewed by the group leader. The questions are designed to determine why the individual is interested in joining the NYCPN, any skills that one would like to share and any topics that one would like the group to address. An introduction (a bio of a few sentences) is also required.

When I requested to join the group, I recall feeling uneasy and embarrassed when completing the brief questionnaire even though the questions were friendly and reasonable. Although disclosing my position as a Sociologist and as a participant-observer was easy, for me, studying prepping and joining a group was also an admission that I recognized my life in New

York was becoming riskier because I was now forced to contend with unpredictable situations. Second, I felt embarrassed because I realized that I really didn't have any valuable skills in a time of crisis. Yes, I could teach. However, I could not teach skills that I did not possess. I recalled the East Coast Blackout—how my computer skills were meaningless. On that day, I had only $10 in my pocket that I used to buy a hot dog and a drink at Gray's Papaya in the Village, the only place with a manual cash register. I then considered my personal qualities. I know that I have a sense of humor. The role of humor in a disaster is too unpredictable, ranging from tension-relieving to tension-causing. For example, I have discovered that, in an emergency, no one cares that you are listening to a transistor radio that is identical to the professor's radio on Gilligan's Island. As stand-up comedian Kyle Kinane (2016) observes,

> …You don't hear the Doomsday preppers, who are out in the forest trying to disguise an abandoned school bus in the side of a hill, say 'Trish, Trish, before you finish pickling those yams, we must go into the city center and lure us back a clown, because, in addition to preserved foods and fresh water, we must also be able to ensure that we can tee-hee while society crumbles around us.'

Although the questionnaire is useful for identifying the interests of would-be group members, its completion does not mean that a person will immediately become an active participant. The NYCPN has a membership list of 459 people on Meetup.[6] However, NYCPN meetings typically attract between twenty and forty attendees. Three factors could possibly contribute to the sharp difference between the group's membership list and actual attendees. Membership participation levels can categorized as "Drop-Ins," "Monitors," "Insurance Buyers" and the "Core Members". First, some individuals may be seasoned preppers who are not interested in attending meetings or excursions on a regular basis. Instead, these "drop-ins" sometimes attend activities based on their personal interests. As one Brooklyn "drop-in" explained to me on an excursion, "I catch trips when I can and if something interesting is going on. I don't need to practice prepping with the group. I know what I'm doing." Novice preppers also "pick and choose" events based on their skill level, such as attending a meeting on preparing a bug out bag. Second, given that many preppers are reluctant to disclose their identities, some individuals on the list may wish to remain anonymous and not attend meetings, but signed up because they are interested in keeping up-to-date with the group's activities. In other words, they seem to "monitor" the group's agenda to discover new information or to reinforce their own approaches. Third, some individuals may have signed up to the group up as a form of "insurance" security to learn prepping skills or receive help in the event of an actual disaster. Therefore, while regular attendance at meetings and participation in excursions is pre-ferred, the membership list remains large, so that the group can also serve as an information resource for anyone who has joined the list. Rather than frequently culling the list, the NYCPN is committed to welcoming all New Yorkers who have expressed an interest in prepping. In discussing this open-door policy at a meeting, the NYCPN's leader, Jason, said,

> We have people who come to meetings and trips regularly. Those are the people that we practice and train with. That's the core group. However, we have a responsibility to help anyone who comes through that door looking to learn more about prepping.

The NYCPN has a core membership of roughly twenty people. As core members, these individuals regularly attend meetings and/or excursions. Core members comprise the group that practices and trains together.

As discussed in an earlier chapter, Jason Charles, a firefighter, is considered to be the authority on and the face of NYC prepping. America was first introduced to Jason's brawny physique, good looks and straight-shooting manner on National Geographic's record-breaking television series *Doomsday Preppers* in an episode titled "Escape from New York." While decried for its sensationalism and open ridicule of its subjects (Genzlinger, 2012), the show did reveal (if only briefly) that prepping was not a practice confined to the stereotype of rural white men who were suspicious of government and people unlike them. Instead, viewers discovered that prepping crossed geographic, class and racial lines. As an African American male living in New York City, Jason presented a very different image; one that depicts the diversity of preppers. His appearance reminded viewers that preppers can also be city dwellers and people of color.

My research experience has revealed that Jason's dedication to teaching preparedness is not really rooted in the expectation of financial gain. Rather, Jason's high level of productivity stems from his deep curiosity and tremendous energy level. Jason has served for fourteen years as a firefighter in NYC. He has been a prepper for nine years. Within the last four years, his interest in prepping has expanded to include wilderness survival. To strengthen his skills, he has also completed extensive training offered at two leading survival schools, The Pathfinder School in Ohio and The Mountain Scout Survival School in New York. The Pathfinder School offers rigorous survival classes such as its advanced four-day class requiring twenty-mile daily hikes for critical resources. The Pathfinder School is operated by survival expert, Dave Canterbury. Canterbury has also co-starred in two survival-themed television shows (*Dual Survival* and *Dirty Rotten Survival*). Drawing from Native American philosophy, the Mountain Scout Survival School holds traditional wilderness survival classes such as fire making and a specialized series on tracking. The Mountain Scout Survival School is operated by Shane Hobel, a survival and tracking expert. On the television show *Doomsday Preppers*, Hobel was featured as a private prepping consultant for a New York City family. On *MonsterQuest*, a History Channel series, Hobel was featured as a lead tracker trying to locate two panthers that were spotted roaming the Palisades.

After mastering new skills, Jason then teaches them to the group. In addition, Jason improves his prepping knowledge by reviewing new gear and testing out equipment innovations. In the press, his massive collection of prepping bags, supplies and knives appears extreme. However, my research indicates that Jason does not fit the profile of a stereotypical prepper as an alienated and paranoid hoarder leading a group of people with similar neuroses. Instead, he is a passionate learner who dives deeply into all subjects that capture his interest. For example, Jason explores his interest in photography with a similar commitment. As with prepping, pursuing this hobby is all-encompassing. He has experimented with taking photos with various cameras and different lenses at diverse locations and he has earned a drone license to shoot overhead shots. Jason's YouTube channel and Instagram feed serve as resources for beginner photographers and to share his photography.

In 2012, Jason assumed leadership of the NYCPN after its founder was no longer able to oversee the group.[7] He shifted the group's agenda from discussion to action. According to Jason, he sought to "put the lectures into practice by going outdoors and applying ideas to bug out weekends." At the time of the study, under Jason, there were ten co-organizers and two assistant organizers. Co-organizers and assistant organizers made up the majority of the core group members with other group members who often attended events. While Jason was the primary leader, the co-organizers assisted him in managing the group's agenda and activities. Co-organizers were selected based on their seniority in the group, commitment to participation, and their respective skills sets. Appointment as a co-organizer was a special recognition of achievement for demonstrating mastery of prepping skills and a serious commitment to the group. Therefore, the co-organizer level was the highest level of membership and included the group's most senior members. The majority of co-organizers had been in the group since Jason assumed leadership in 2012. Furthermore, they were highly skilled in all areas determined by the group to be of value for prepping, such as bushcraft and first aid. Their role was broad and included teaching and administrative tasks such as designing and leading workshops, planning events, screening membership and scouting locations for excursions. To ensure safety and to reduce the likelihood of injury on excursions, co-organizers led in Jason's absence.

The assistant organizers level was the lowest level of the leadership team. Unlike co-organizers, assistant organizers had no role in decision-making. Being named an assistant organizer was an acknowledgement for newer members with developing skills who have shown a genuine interest in contributing to the group. Assistant organizers were identified as the key resource/group contact for a respective skill or field of knowledge. Assistant organizers developed and taught sessions to share their knowledge on subjects related to prepping. For example, in 2018, two assistant organizers were appointed by Jason. Given his amateur radio expertise, Ben was appointed as communications lead. Based on her expertise in homesteading skills, Inshirah was appointed as homesteading lead. I was also selected as an assistant organizer because I attended activities regularly and I shared my administrative skills (preparing presentation hand-outs) and my knowledge of essential oil use with the group.

From its start in 2010 to 2018, the NYCPN has held 106 meetings. Meeting types included general meetings and topic discussions, lectures and workshops where members learn and practice a new skill, events not sponsored by the group but related to prepping, and excursions, which include two-day retreats and overnight outings to practice skills. My analysis of the NYCPN meeting data (meeting type and frequency) for its eight-year history indicates that as its members have become experienced preppers, the group's agenda has advanced from exploring introductory topics to focusing on practicing prepping skills in outdoor settings. For the first three years (2010–12), the group's activities centered on developing basic prepping and homesteading knowledge such as learning the purpose and contents of a bug out bag and an introduction to canning through lectures, workshops and events. Starting in 2013, the group's agenda expanded to include excursions like challenging "bug out" trips and more complex workshops on homesteading skills, such as making laundry soap and toiletries. In 2014, overnight excursions to practice skills and to develop endurance comprised the majority of the group's activities for the first time. From 2014 through 2018, excursions remained the top meeting type for the group with an average of six outings per year. As the categories of activities suggest, the NYCPN offers a broad range of prepping events that would appeal to preppers at all skill levels. Each of these NYCPN's activities should be considered an interpretive process in which members were continuously engaged in mindful action whereby they manipulated symbols and negotiated the meaning of situations (Mead, 1934).

Lectures and discussion now occur less frequently than in the group's early meetings. Rather than overviews of large topic areas related to prepping (such as fire safety), topics also became timelier and more specific. With a discussion of Hurricane Sandy in 2012, topics started to be driven by experiences of dangerous events in the city or media coverage of such events elsewhere in the country.

NYCPN's activities

Retreats: Learning the guiding ideals of urban prepping

For NYCPN members, the process of becoming a prepper involves breaking away from the traditional and very singular identity of being a New Yorker—a city dweller. Excursions require mastering survivalist skills and a familiarity with the wilderness. Therefore, for New Yorkers, becoming a prepper requires moving beyond their place identity (Hummon, 1980), which is formed by their understanding of and attachment to urban life to possibly embrace a new and more complicated identity that focuses on the vulnerability of living in the city. This move requires stepping beyond "life on the X" to returning with a new approach to living in the city informed by changed notions of self-reliance and sustainability. Becoming an NYCPN member also allows one to break free from the stereotype of a prepper as a rural white male by claiming the identity of prepper as a city dweller and often as a person of color.

The NYCPN's retreats are important introductions to prepper culture for newcomers and a chance for seasoned preppers to teach or learn new skills. Typically, twenty to twenty-five people participate in the retreat. Usually held at a New Jersey State Park near the Delaware Water Gap, the two-day retreat consists of training sessions and exercises ranging from fire making to first aid. Conducted by Jason and the co-organizers, these sessions are designed to provide an overview of prepping. Attendees stay in a large group cabin or camp nearby. All activities and meals are shared together, with periodic breaks throughout the day. At the retreats and other events, NYCPN members use the codes of dress, equipment and skills to communicate shared meanings with one another about the prepper lifestyle. In training sessions that require the mastery of specific prepping skills or the eagerness to take on new challenges, each group members "looking-glass self" begins to emerge. As Cooley notes, "We always imagine, and in imagining, share the judgements of other minds" (1902, p. 152–3). As the narrative below will show, in practicing prepping skills and rituals, group members imagine how they appear to other preppers. They also imagine how other preppers judge their appearance, and then define their self-worth as preppers according to these two imagined perspectives.

In keeping with previous retreats, Jason was both the event organizer and the group leader for the September 2017 retreat. Throughout the retreat, his duties were numerous. In advance of the retreat, he organized sessions and purchased needed materials (supplies for training exercises and extra food to be enjoyed by the group). During the retreat, Jason managed the schedule which included both daytime activities (sessions with an outdoor component) and nighttime activities (lectures). As a rookie prepper, I expected to observe his expertise in prepping. However, as a professor, I also quickly recognized his teaching practices. During sessions, Jason, like any good teacher, monitored the progress of participants, focusing on their engagement and comprehension. During breaks, Jason, along with the core group members, also seemed to take note of one prepper called Michael, who seemed to be skilled and offered a lot of advice to newcomers even though he was reported to only attend retreats and an occasional trip or meeting. Questions and remarks from this older prepper were addressed politely in and out of sessions. However, even on the first day, I could sense group interest in this prepper shifting from engagement into tolerance. While I did not yet fully understand why this prepper was being pushed aside, it was clear that he was falling short of some standard. Conversely, the questions of earnest newcomers were met with patience and support.

The retreat began on Friday afternoon; therefore, participants had to leave work in the afternoon or leave after work. The drive to the state park took a little under two hours without traffic, so, it took time for people to arrive. I was a little nervous about staying overnight with a group of mostly male preppers. However, I knew that there would be at least two other women there. As I had attended meetings, I knew the women fairly well. They were both mothers, Anne from Queens and Annette from the Bronx. Both women had been with the group since its formation. Their knowledge of prepping and homesteading was extensive. I was relieved because they were also very friendly and supportive.

When I arrived at the large cabin, its cargo furniture/dormitory style décor was a little depressing. However, my spirits were quickly lifted when I discovered that I had my own room. I was relieved. The room had two bunk beds, but I would be the only one in it. The room also had a lock. I felt disappointed in myself that I was concerned about privacy rather than focusing on the group's activities. I was hoping to learn a great deal at the retreat. The group members knew that I was writing a book, so I wanted them to understand that I was earnest and that I respected their mission.

Because people were trickling in due to rush hour traffic and commit-ments, no training sessions were held that evening. Instead, members took this open time to socialize. The preppers caught up with one another and exchanged notes about gear and hikes. As members exchanged greetings and circulated throughout the large cabin, the cohesive nature of the group was reinforced by their appearance. All group members were dressed in clothing that allowed them to work and move around comfortably outdoors. Every-one was dressed in either hiking clothes or in athletic wear appropriate for the season so that layers could be taken off or added as needed. Most members also wore baseball hats. Women wore their hair in ponytails or pulled back. All members wore sturdy hiking boots that were suitable for all types of terrain. Furthermore, most members were physically fit. Com-bined with their bug out bags, their dress signified that they were prepared and ready for any event. The appearance of NYCPN members worked to remind one another that they were committed to preparing for disaster and ready to take on any challenge during the retreat. Therefore, for this diverse group of New Yorkers, their appearance was a cohesive element of identity formation that involved "not only individual self-presentations, but the joint creation of symbolic resources upon which those presentations depend" (Schwalbe and Schrock, 1996, p. 115).

As a late lunch, Jason grilled burgers for the group with a few members contributing snacks such as chips and salsa. Seated at a large picnic table, about six brawny male preppers and I enjoyed burgers as Jason manned the grill. The conversation involved usual barbeque chit-chat about television shows and the eternal debate between the merits of charcoal grilling versus the ease of gas grilling. However, the conversation soon shifted to the rise in shootings across the nation. The remarks echoed many comments that have most likely been made at dinner tables across the nation—dismay over the loss of lives, shock over the failure to respond in some events, critique of local officials for failing to pay attention to earlier concerns about shooters and frustration about the FBI's failure to carefully track already-identified subjects. However, Jason made the most memorable comment, the one that introduced the group's guiding ideals of trustworthiness and responsibility. Jason stopped cooking on the grill for a moment and said:

> Look, some of us here have leadership experience from our workplace—Fire Department, military, whatever. But, what about cowardice? What is it? Culture, race, personality? I dunno. Not everybody wants to step up and be the hero. I think about that every time I go into a fire with a new guy. What's he going to be like? Is he going to stick it out or is he going to run? Is he gonna trust me enough to take my advice so he will breathe better or is he gonna stick with the book and suffer? There aren't enough heroes out there. We all already know—our work experience shows us that this survival thing is all about training and trust between peers.

His powerful statement resonated with the men as they fell silent and took in his words. After a brief moment, the six men started to nod silently and exchanged looks with one another to acknowledge and confirm their commitment to one another in the wake of some future crisis. I thought about how the passengers of Flight 93 on 9/11 probably shared a similar moment of unity. No one exchanged glances with me, which was appropriate given my role as a participant-observer and the fact that they had no real knowledge of me. Did they think that women could be heroes, though? Given that women were part of the group, I looked forward to seeing how they viewed their own roles as preppers.

On Saturday morning, we went on a three-mile hike. Carrying smaller backpacks, the group of nineteen moved quickly uphill through the slippery rocks. I was hardly hero material. Given my lack of experience, I was the slowest member. Kids scurried up the hill past me, the anti-hero. Anne was gracious and stayed behind to chat with me. We talked about family life as she taught me how to navigate the rocky path. Finally, I hit a proper stride. As we continued walking uphill, it started to mist a bit. I noticed that many of us left our rain ponchos in our larger bags. Of course, I seemed to be the only one who was bothered by a little rain. On the narrow cliffside, we had to walk on flat slick rocks, and I lost my footing. Jim, a tall friendly guy, caught my fall. Given the height of the cliff, I was startled. Jim had us stop for a moment. He was nice and he wanted to be sure that I was OK. He said, "Just stay by me. You'll be fine." I thanked him. At the top of the narrow ridge, Jason held a brief talk about hiking guidelines for a bug out situation (having a scout, walking in smaller groups, having the weakest ones walk in the middle for protection).

On the way back down, Steve, another experienced prepper, wanted to talk with me about my interest in prepping. I discussed my research and personal experiences as a New Yorker. He did not share very much about his own experiences. However, he did make a comment that reflected the fear that some preppers have about others who are unprepared for disaster. He said, "The EMT perspective is 'do the thing that helps the most people.' But, think about today, only a few people are present when we are a city of millions. What does that mean?" Without pausing, he began to talk about the value of recognizing plants and then switched to talking about the day's weather report. He raised a good question. In terms of community resilience, those numbers made the idea of prepping in New York futile. However, I also recognized that, given my interviews with independent preppers and NYCPN's large membership list, that there were possibly more preppers in the city than were reflected in attendance at the retreat.

After a short break at the cabin, a fire building workshop was going to be held at the large fire pit in a circular campfire area by the lake. I walked down a little early. The morning's light rain had given way to a sunny, warm fall day. With the orange blaze of the changing tree leaves reflected on the water, the lakeside was gorgeous. Jason and two co-organizers were standing by the lake talking and taking in the view. After a moment, Jason picked up a rock and skipped it across the lake. His rock skipped quite a distance. In response, the two other preppers each took a turn skipping a rock. It appeared to be a lovely scene; three friends enjoying a fall afternoon by the lake. Yet, this interaction offered me a first glimpse into the competitive nature of prepping. While group members were supportive of one another, they also sought to demonstrate that their skills were equal to one another. After the first round, the three men compared distances and then skipped rocks again. A third round was held. The competition ended with Jason as the winner. With more members arriving, Jason and one of the men headed toward the firepit. However, the person in last place stayed behind to practice skipping rocks a few more times.

Jason and Al, a co-organizer, then gave a well-organized and thorough workshop on fire building. In their detailed instructions, they emphasized the importance of a quality ferro rod (a firestarter) and striker as well as suitable tinder. Demonstration stations were placed throughout the campfire area.

Because knives are used to cut small pieces of wood for building fires, Al began the session with a lengthy demonstration on knife safety and proper cutting techniques. After the knife safety lesson was completed, Al demonstrated how to cut a feather stick for tinder. He then invited the group to use their own knives to make feather sticks. As people worked on their sticks, their comments and questions revealed their mastery of fire building. Some members talked about how they always carried white birch as a tinder source. Jason also reminded the group that the fatwood of the surrounding pine trees was also excellent tinder. Anne then discussed the importance of having a firebrick on hand to start a fire in extremely cold temperatures. Anne shared that she relied on a firebrick to build a fire to stay warm during a bug out trip in which the temperature was -17 degrees. Others experimented with starting a fire with a magnifying glass. With some clouds overhead, some preppers predicted that the magnifying glass would cause the tinder to smoke but not ignite. They were right.

As I started to work on my feather stick, I realized that my knife was too small, and I couldn't get a good grip on it. It would work for cutting cordage but not for actual projects. So, I decided to walk around the site to observe the progress of the group members. Noticing Michael by a pine tree, I walked over to him. I watched as he went to cut a piece of fatwood from the tree. Spreading his fingers widely, he placed one hand directly on the tree. He then raised his large knife higher up on the tree as if he intended to slice off a large section of bark in a downward swoop. I could immediately see that everything was wrong but had no time to speak the words. Michael pulled the knife toward his lower hand and quickly sliced the base of his thumb. A stream of blood shot up in the air and I could see the white of the bone of his thumb joint. Anne witnessed it too. We exchanged horrified looks with one another, and both screamed for help. Michael jumped around in pain holding his bloody hand. It was clear that he was in a lot of pain. Marlon and Jason raced over to help. Their facial expressions were both concerned and annoyed. They had "what now?" expressions. Marlon, a co-organizer, had a first aid kit. I called for him because, earlier in the day, he had thoughtfully shown me the equipment that always kept with him on trips. At that time, he showed me his small but well-resourced first aid kit. As a firefighter, Jason has extensive first aid training. Jason quickly applied a bandage to Michael's hand and explained that he must go to the hospital to get stitches. The hospital was twenty miles away. We all headed quickly back to the cabin.

Outside of the cabin, Jason broke out his trauma kit and properly bandaged the hand for the ride to the hospital. Given his first aid training and the severity of Michael's wound, Jason planned to drive him to the hospital. Michael began to argue that he was fine that he didn't want to go to the hospital. Jason argued back and explained that he was losing too much blood and that he needed to go. Michael grimaced and relented. As Jason prepared to leave, he shook his head, clearly aggravated by Michael's injury. He said, "We've got all this going on. A day of training. And, now this asshole."

After the two men left for the hospital, I learned the reason for the frustration. At an earlier retreat, Michael had also cut himself with a knife. I now had a better understanding of why other preppers were not really engaging with Michael. According to Marlon, he was not a real prepper. Michael did not attend events regularly. He showed up at retreats and a few excursions. He did not heed advice or instruction. Instead, he spent time offering incorrect guidance to newcomers or recounting his adventures which may have been fabricated. The group then took their planned lunch break although people didn't seem very hungry. I was grateful for the downtime. I was feeling a little unnerved. The accident's description may seem minor, but it really wasn't— it was sickening. I felt bad for him. I slipped off for a few minutes to be alone. The retreat training sessions illustrated that earning credibility as a knowledgeable prepper is a very serious process and that pretending had dangerous consequences. Michael's careless behavior and Jason and Marlon's shared negative reactions underscored the importance of trustworthiness to the group. Since the start of the retreat, group members had been ignoring Michael because he had already demonstrated a lack of trustworthiness in failing to adhere to safety instructions. His second injury only confirmed their perceptions. By failing to adhere to knife safety rules, Michael, for whatever reason, was unwilling or unable to direct his own actions to conform with the NYCPN's guiding value of trustworthiness (Blumer, 1969).

After lunch, the training sessions continued. Al, a co-organizer and core group member of ten years, was scheduled to give a lecture and demonstration on water purification. At the start of the retreat, one could easily recognize his experience even before his presentation. On a table that ran along one side of the cabin's main room, Jason and a few other preppers had laid out gear and guidebooks for people to peruse. While these materials were interesting, the last section of items on the long table were beautiful, an adjective that I did not expect to use in relation to most prepping gear. This section contained a large collection of finely crafted leather goods and wooden kitchen utensils that Al had made by hand. Using repurposed leather, Al had crafted a variety of bags and pouches, knife sheaths and wallets. Al had also crafted several wooden kitchen utensils of various colors and styles. His leather and wooden crafts appealed to the arts and crafts festival groupie in me. More important, as a researcher, I could see that his talent and approach to undertaking these projects indicated that Al's thinking had advanced well beyond a bug out experience to long-term survival. When I later asked him about his crafts, Al explained,

> I'm also learning blacksmithing, welding. Homesteading things, laundry soap, clothing. Woodworking, making cabinets, cabin building, freehand art crafting, I like going to flea markets, finding things like an impressive fabric or a meat-grinder. The DIY Revolution kind of ruined my career plans as I went to FIT for Woodworking. I'm a perfectionist though. I'm never happy with it. I always think that it could use one more thing.

Al's passion reminded me of Mitchell's (2002) important argument that the needs of future societies extend beyond security and comfort to cultural production and consumption. Mitchell (2002) argues that survivalists' have posed the question of "Who Shall Create?" and in answering this question determined that "ways must be found for people of varied means and imagination to craft culture as wells as consume it" (p. 234). Mitchell's question was brought to bear by studying the complexities of survivalist and separatist subcultures searching to find their identities in the modern world. However, in these earlier groups and in great contrast to the NYCPN, racism was a common theme used by these subcultures to unify themselves against a world in which they felt a loss of dominance and then a loss of place. Therefore, the NYCPN and its members such as Al provide a surprising path for contemplating these questions about a post-apocalyptic future. As city dwellers, and with the majority of the group being people of color, the group has encompassed creativity and production in its mission of learning how to survive disaster. Their interest in prepping may stem from a perceived need to preserve urban life rather than feeling at odds with modernity. Instead, urban prepping may be a response to an odd modernity. In crafting the basic necessities for survival, urban preppers like Al may also desire to maintain an appreciation of artistic production that is common among city dwellers.

At previous meetings, I had observed that Al was often asked for his insight on various topics and that he was always friendly and gave thoughtful advice to members struggling with new skills. Therefore, I looked forward to his presentation on water purification. As expected, his lecture was detailed and well organized. He brought a flip chart that outlined important guidelines for trying to preserve and collect water in the city as well as instructions for purification. He gave his lecture in the cabin's living room/kitchen area as members took notes while seated quietly on the worn and tired couches or fold-out chairs. Seasoned preppers sometimes chimed in with examples or insight. Beyond the expected advice, he explained how to open a fire hydrant and he gave tips on how to collect rainwater by repurposing flowerboxes if sheltering in place. He also discussed several water filtration systems. For the hands-on demonstration component of the session, we walked down to the lake to test a water filtering process. After collecting muddy lake water in the bucket, the water was run through the filtering system. The water looked clear and drinkable. Members were expected to drink the filtered water. Most people did sample the water. Someone even commented that it might be filtered but it still tasted like lake water. Fearful of sampling the water, I tried to fade back into the trees. However, I was soon invited to sample the water by Corey, another co-organizer. He insisted that I try it, but I shook my head no. Corey was a bit annoyed with me. However, I still refused. I just said, "Hey, I teach and I'm giving an exam on Monday. I can't risk it." He seemed disappointed but I hoped that he understood my concern. To draw on Cooley (1902), for a moment, I felt the sting of disapproval based on the imagined judgment of onlookers. Unlike the others, I was unwilling to take the same level of risk.

However, the important finding was seeing how members really appreciated and respected Al's insight. Not only did other core members participate during Al's talk, they also exchanged notes and ideas with one another on the walk back from the lake.

By sharing his knowledge in a meaningful way, Al's position in the group as a co-organizer and experienced prepper was strengthened. For the rest of the retreat, he served as an assistant in most sessions by performing demonstrations and one-on-one instruction as needed. According to Al:

> Preppers tend to be good people, willing to share or learn in my experience. Long-term preppers, they are safeguarding to an extent. They don't want to be taken advantage of. There is an expectation about bringing something to the table to get anything in return, the meetings and outings are a forum, and people have to prove themselves. People find their own way; we are there to nudge and to provide advice. In the group, we assume that people are going in earning. Prepping is about good relationships; preppers are stable, and prepping requires trust.

I thought about the idea of earning, and how it meant contributing something useful to the group. My administrative skills (creating hand-outs, note-taking, recordkeeping) might be useful; however, I also wanted to offer something directly related to prepping.

After the water sampling, a communications session was held. Steve distributed ham radios to the seven of us who attended the meeting. (Not all preppers attended this meeting as some were already familiar with operating a radio.) Steve provided an extensive lecture on the operation and talk protocols of the ham radio. Throughout his presentation, Jimmy asked a lot of basic questions involving the range of radios and verbally repeated the sequence of steps to be sure that he understood it. I started to notice that he seemed to need a lot of confirmation, but he was an engaged participant. As a teacher, I recognized we all have different learning styles. Steve finally gave us the frequency and wanted each of us to say hello (nothing more as we did not have licenses). In my imagination, I had always likened the ham radio to the CB radio. I was completely wrong. I struggled with setting a frequency. Actually, we all did. Annette, Al's wife, was quite funny and broke the tension by singing the word "Hello" into the radio to invoke a few different songs for her listeners.

While grilling dinner, Marlon and I spoke at length about the art of learning prepping. Marlon's comments and actions reinforced the importance of a genuine interest in prepping and the willingness to earn your place. He said: "We are here to test what you can do and you can't do. All in the right way." As he continued to talk with me over dinner, I realized that Marlon was a gatekeeper and monitor of the group. By holding thoughtful conversations with individuals like me who were prepping novices, Marlon was able to gather information about a newcomer's interest in the group and to try to pinpoint any potential issues. In addition to talking with people to gain better insight into their personalities, I had noted that Marlon also worked with members of all levels on an individual basis by modeling and teaching prepping strategies. For example, before the fire making session began, Marlon had spent time reviewing his safety belt with me, which included a first aid kit and a knife. He suggested that I should always carry similar items when outdoors. That's why I sought him out when Michael cut himself. I knew that he could help. During the fire making session, I observed Marlon circulating around the group to offer one-on-one help as needed. He had assessed Michael's skills as weak; therefore, he was very angry with Michael's portrayal of his own abilities. Marlon explained,

> With prepping, people's lives are on the line. This can be a dangerous thing. He was irresponsible. It was taking him double the time to do things and he was the only person not getting his fire going. Don't act like you know. If you do, people who don't know better will have faith in you and it will hurt them.

Since we had started grilling a bit late, the sun had begun to set. It grew darker and I had a little trouble seeing my steak. Marlon had just turned on his headlamp. I asked him if I could borrow it for a moment. He looked at me with surprise and asked why. I confessed that I was worrying that my steak was burning. Marlon reminded me that if I packed correctly, I should have my own headlamp. I was taken back. I was not going to wear it if I was just going to shine it on the grill for a moment. However, I then realized that he was again trying to teach me. In a friendly manner, he suggested that I take my steak off the grill and go get my headlamp so I could get used to using it. As I looked around, most members were already wearing theirs even if the lights weren't yet on. Unlike me, they were prepared. I quickly retrieved my headlamp and our conversation continued. Marlon's monitoring behavior and insightful remarks throughout the retreat were significant because they worked to reinforce the principle of trustworthiness within the group. He relied on his personal interactions with members as a tool for making an appraisal of a person and trying to determine the person's intentions (Blumer, 1969). With this knowledge, he attempted to re-direct a members behavior to conform to group practices, or worked to resolve challenges that would disturb group interaction. Given the seriousness of the core members' approach to their training exercises, this retreat experience highlighted the importance of trust as a core ideal within the group. In addition, it reminded me of the need to establish trust with the group to ensure that my time spent in the field would be productive to my research aims (Gill, 2014).

Weeks later, I brought my gear to "Bug Out Bag", a NYCPN meeting in Washington Heights. The meeting was a sort of "show and tell" to teach newcomers about the purpose and contents of a bug out bag. Members also compared notes with one another about bag types and tools. By sharing the contents of my bag, I sought to demonstrate to members that I was dedicated to learning about prepping and that I respected their interests. I won third prize in the contest for best bug out bags for newcomers (a pair of fire starters). However, the real reward was having senior members comment on the selection of some of my tools. When Jason saw my quality knife, he looked a little surprised. I asked his opinion of it. He smiled and said, "It's not too shitty." I smirked.

After finishing my dinner at the retreat, I had the chance to talk with another new group member, Inshirah. She had arrived before the water purification session. We immediately hit it off. She was a mother and the main prepper in her family. Although this was her first meeting, she had already been prepping for eight years. We talked about how we were glad to meet other women at the retreat. There were four of us out of the nineteen members: Anne, Annette, Inshirah and I. Inshirah shared with me that the group seemed knowledgeable and open. She indicated that this was important to her as she had tried to attend a group outside of the city some years before with limited success. She was a member of a New Jersey group for about two years but ended up leaving because she really didn't feel part of the group. She explained:

> It was a rural group, so they were pretty isolated racially. No matter, even though it was supposed to be about prepping, race was always gonna play a role. They were very cautious ...They were suspicious because of that urban myth of city people coming to take over their town and resources. Here I was, this black female lawyer suggesting that we look at real estate and set up an LLC structure to prepare for the future.

I asked her to elaborate on her comment. She explained that the group was concerned that, in the event of some disaster, city dwellers would leave the city and travel farther out to get food and supplies. As a result, small towns would be overrun by a massive influx of city dwellers, many of whom are black. She also did not find herself compatible with the group because she was interested in expanding beyond the traditional prepping strategies of bugging out or sheltering in place. She perceived that her interest in long term planning was beyond the group's agenda and its discussion was challenged because members seemed to view her as an outsider (not living in the town and traveling to meetings).

After dinner, Jason lead an emergency medicine session in the cabin. Although Jason is not certified to teach first aid lessons by the American Red Cross, he still managed to provide an overview of important first aid skills while respecting those boundaries. He unpacked a large first-aid package and gave detailed advice on the use of each item and identified crucial missing items. He also outlined clotting techniques and how to deal with a deep chest wound. Two EMTs were in the group and offered their own insights. Jason impressed upon everyone the ideals of responsiveness and swiftness, reminding everyone that perfect sanitary conditions were impossible in emergency situations. The goal was to respond quickly with the understanding that you are treating the person with the intention of going to a hospital. He discussed the different types of first aid classes available and explained that he has a large professional trauma pack, which is different. Given Michael's injury, people compared notes about their first aid packs. The group was excited and laser-focused on the discussion because Michael's injury had emphasized the need for this knowledge.

Soon enough, Jason and Allan, a member with EMT experience (and the NYCPN Facebook administrator), shared war stories with the group to underscore the dangerous and stressful nature of responding to emergency situations. Beyond tame stories that reminded the group that victims might have violent reactions to drugs used to save them, they also shared stories about the additional stress of treating victims at crime scenes. Jason discussed the danger of responding to a shooting if the shooter is still at large. When his partner was trying to save someone who had been shot, the shooter remerged to shoot the victim two more times after discovering that he was not dead. Seeing the facial expressions of the group after hearing that story, combined with Michael's self-inflicted injury and the detailed review of first aids items, the gruesome and tragic story seemed to emphasize the importance of being prepared and recognizing that emergencies involve a myriad of stressors. Jason's presentation was another illustration of the value that the group placed on trust. For the group, trustworthiness was rooted in the expectation that members would be able to perform basic first aid tasks, such as wound care, in an emergency situation. Furthermore, members were also expected to maintain alertness and focus in emergencies rather than succumbing to panic.

Jason closed by cautioning the group that prepping was not about "hoarding first aid kits and stacking them to the ceiling." Instead, he argued that "prepping was connected to homesteading and the idea of being 'self-sustaining' and using what is available in your environment." He suggested that people watch the movie *Into the Forest* to gain an understanding of homesteading. He also discussed the use of essential oils to help with healing, such as oil of oregano to prevent colds. During this part of the presentation, I realized that my knowledge of essential oils would be something meaningful that I could share with the group. A few months later, I gave an "Essential Oils" presentation at the meeting. In my talk, I discussed the safe application of oils and shared examples of their use to aid illness or injury in a bug out situation. For example, Helichrysum can be used to control bleeding in a minor wound, and peppermint eases digestive issues. Throughout the talk, I provided samples to familiarize the group with scents and application. I provided detailed hand-outs to the group that identified which essential oils should be carried in a bug out bag. I also brought several reference manuals for members to explore after the talk. Members were responsive to my sincere effort as they were engaged and asked thoughtful questions. Based on that meeting, members came to me with questions about essential oil use. Beyond sharing my knowledge, the talk also gave the group a chance to know me a little better. Rather than just seeing me focus on my research and learning prepping skills, they discovered that I had a sense of humor. Because the meetings were held at a church, we could sometimes hear the music rehearsals. My talk was punctuated with the sound of hymns and organ music. Rather than viewing the interruption negatively, I adopted the voice of an old-time preacher and announced: "That's right, it's time! It's time to open your hearts and come to Essential Oils!" We all had a great laugh.

Jason's first aid session ended around 9:30 p.m. We sat around and talked with one another. Corey, another co-organizer shared a delicious stew that he had made for the group. He had intended to hold a cooking lesson in the outdoors session but decided against it. However, he made copies available of a short "72 Hour Outdoor Cooking Guide" that he compiled for members. The guide contained advice on supplies and methods for cooking over an open flame and cautioned against purchasing a cheap knife that wouldn't last in the double-duty of processing wood and cooking. He was there with his girlfriend (who shortly after would become his fiancé). They looked very cozy together. Watching them, I remembered those days of young love and realized that he probably just wanted to enjoy her company rather than dealing with giving a presentation.

As people started to turn in for the second night, Jason informed me that I would now be sharing the room with another prepper. A male. We had all paid for spots so that was perfectly reasonable. Rather than share the room, I decided to leave. I felt uneasy about sharing a room (even though we had bunk beds) with a man that I did not know. I did not feel threatened in any way; however, he was a stranger to me. Inshirah was not staying overnight so I made my apologies and I readied to leave with her. I also knew that we were all leaving in the morning, so I was not going to be missing any morning sessions. Jason was disappointed and suggested that I bring a friend or my husband on overnights if I was reluctant to bunk up with anyone. Anne and Annette were with their respective husbands and Inshirah was not staying the night. I recognized that, in a survival situation, I clearly would not have had the option of returning home. I held a quick sidebar with Inshirah and we both agreed that leaving seemed prudent. So, I rounded up my stuff quickly and followed her out. Driving home, I thought about what my plans would be in future situations. I decided to take Jason's advice and invite my husband on some overnight outings. On our vacations we often visit national parks, and enjoy day hikes, so my hope was that he would be agreeable to attending some excursions.

On Sunday morning, I woke up to a text message from Jason. He informed me that I had left some undergarments behind. I was mortified. Since I arrived home late, I just placed my bag by the door. After reading his text, I rushed over to inspect the bag to discover that the pouch that held my undergarments was unzipped. His next text asked me what I wanted him to do with them. His question was a clear reminder to be certain that I remembered all of my belongings. I thanked him for letting me know and gave him instructions to please throw them away and to never bring it up again. For a moment, I had inadvertently introduced the element of sexuality (and disorganization) into my fieldwork[8]. I am certain that he had a good laugh about it. Once I stopped blushing, I did too.

On another retreat, the group's rejection of a prospective new member illustrated the seriousness of assuming the identity of an experienced prepper. Eager to be recognized as a seasoned prepper, a new female member, on the first day, circulated among the group and discussed her role in nearly every recent disaster across the globe. Ever quiet, group members listened without making any real comments. A few discrete eyebrows were raised, and glances exchanged when she described being transported by an ancient military cargo plane to the site of a disaster. However, after she recounted her experiences to Jason, he asked her if she had been to Pompeii. As Jason recalled: "She was like, yeah, I've been to all disasters. I'm like, well, Pompeii? That's like the funniest thing ever, but that's a great description of what was going on. That lady, she was exhausting." She did not understand that making in-roads in the group was accomplished by working hard within the group. She was unaware of the group's credo of earning your place as described by Al.

At first, Annette and Inshirah were happy to see another female prepper. However, she did not seem interested in getting to know the other female members. For example, in one brief conversation with Inshirah and I, her primary interest was informing us that she held a master's degree. She merely walked up and randomly announced this credential. Inshirah and I were not having a conversation regarding our respective careers or educations, so any mention of a degree was not relevant. We just merely nodded without comment. Group members actually spoke very little about their respective jobs unless their job skills were relevant to prepping. Rather than bonding over their careers, NYCPN members bonded over their shared identities as preppers. The organization's identity as a prepping group reinforced their self-identities as preppers (Ashforth and Mael, 1996).

At various times during the retreat, I tried to start a conversation with her, but my efforts were fruitless. She really was not interested in engaging on a personal level. Jason later noted that he "watched her walking around trying to be the alpha with the women." He was right. She later tried to commandeer Inshirah's canning demonstration by explaining that she was an expert and attempted to guide the lesson although she was unfamiliar with this homesteading process. However, her antagonism had a wider reach. Following the canning demonstration, she struck up a debate with some of the men including Jason, Marlon, Al and Corey about the strength of women. She argued that, with proper training, she or another woman could win a fight against any man including the group leader, Jason. It was a bizarre challenge given the group's mission to learning survival skills together (not to mention Jason's muscular physique).

The group's overall response to her behavior was illuminating. In a work-place, her antagonistic comments may have been quickly identified as alie-nating by her co-workers. Most likely, she would have been encouraged to exhibit more collegial behavior. However, the culture of the NYCPN does not require a quick redirect to behavior more suitable to the group. The NYCPN's mission involves members preparing to contend with harsh cir-cumstances that may include destruction or chaos. Therefore, an aggressive personality seems to be viewed as an unpleasant obstacle rather than a sig-nificant problem. Furthermore, a particular prepper's challenging personality might be offset by that person's contribution to the group such as teaching a little-known skill to the group. Given their commitment to learning survival skills together, NYCPN members are also committed to discovering a per-son's character. This discovery offers insight into how someone might respond in a future crisis by revealing qualities such as accountability and reliability. Therefore, as preppers, they are interested in how a situation unfolds to collect as many data points as possible. In other words, they are a patient audience who is interested in seeing the complete performance. Goffman (1959) defines performance as "all the activity of a given participant on a given occasion which serves to influence in any way any of the other participants" (p. 15). In this case, the prospective new member's performance refers to her repeated attempts to claim the identity of expert prepper by boasting about her achievements and initiating challenges. As Marlon explained:

> To get to know a person is to break bread with the person. To take time to talk with them, to listen to what they are about. But, not just that, to observe them, to see how they act, to see how they treat other people.

For the preppers, her performance was dismal. According to Jason, she under-stood that her performance was unsuccessful. He explained: "She got it. In the morning, no one said anything to her. I did not want her to think that she could come into this group and spread her bullshit." By misleading the group about her experiences and challenging everyone, her performance commu-nicated to the group the likelihood that she might not be responsible or dependable in a crisis. In keeping with Goffman's (1959) argument that story-telling within a group reinforces its culture, stories of her performance are often recounted when discussing how the group sometimes has to contend with the unexpected behavior of prospective new members. Within the NYCPN, memories of these interactions have now become anecdotes that work as humorous reminders to be truthful in one's claims about disaster experience and to be modest about one's desired role in the group.

The newcomer's actions were also important because they magnify how some people think about disaster. Her attitude echoes responses that I some-times receive from people when discussing my project. Often, when non-aca-demics learn about my book, they tell me that they are fascinated and that they want to hear all about it. That is not necessarily true. People are interested in my project but for a very specific reason. People want to hear about themselves. They want to hear that whatever they are doing is the right thing (preparing or not preparing) and that they need not fear because they will be safe in any disaster. They want to hear that they are in control. Her insecurity and her need to be an expert in all things might reflect the anxiety that is triggered by prepping and acknowledging the possibility of disaster. If a person is in control of all situations, there is no need for fear. By contrast, contemplating the level of preparedness that would be required to protect against most disasters can be overwhelming.

Notes

1 Launched in 2002, Meetup is a website used to organize online groups that host in-person events for people with similar interests.
2 This data is based on my interactions and conversations as a participant-observer. As a group member, I attended all meeting types and had access to Meetup profiles. Given the reluctance of many preppers to be identified or even to disclose basic information, conducting a formal survey was not possible or appropriate in this study.
3 To stay on the membership list, individuals must be active on the Meetup group page. If a member is not active on the page (such as responding to an event announcement or posting a question about an upcoming event) for a year, the person is deleted from the group.
4 My conversations with NYCPN members rarely included discussions of specific salaries. Instead, I learned the type of positions that people held within particular sectors. These positions ranged from mid-level to senior positions. Based on my interview data and informal conversations, NYCPN members view themselves as part of the middle class.
5 The "first year" period refers to May 2017–18. Data analysis was conducted in June 2018.
6 Note that a few members chose to attend meetings regularly, but they did not go on excursions while other members chose to attend excursions but did not attend meetings.
7 Between 2010 and 2012 (before Jason assumed leadership of the group), the NYCPN mainly met to hold discussions about prepping topics. With the start of Jason's tenure, the group's activities expanded to focus on skill development and excursions. The first group leader was unavailable to be interviewed.
8 For a discussion of sexual interaction and ethnographic research, see Martin and Haller, 2018.

References

Ashforth, B., and Mael, F. (1996). Organizational identity and strategy as a context for the individual. *Advances in Strategic Management*, 13, 19–64.
Atkinson, P. (2015). *For ethnography*. London: SAGE Publications.
Belson, K., Medina, J., and Pérez-Peña, R. (2017, October 2). A burst of gunfire, a pause, then carnage in Las Vegas that would not stop. *The New York Times*. Retrieved from https://www.nytimes.com/2017/10/02/us/las-vegas-shooting-live-updates.html?searchResultPosition=2.
Blinder, A., Montgomery, D., and Healy, J. (2017). Texas church shooting video raises an unsettling question: who should see it? *The New York Times*. Retrieved from https://www.nytimes.com/2017/11/09/us/texas-shooting-video-devin-kelley.html.

Blumer, H. (1969). *Symbolic interactionism: Perspective and method.* Englewood Cliffs, N. J.: Prentice-Hall.

Canterbury, D. (2014). *Bushcraft 101: A field guide to the art of wilderness survival.* Avon, MA: Adams Media.

Charles, J. (2014). *Emergency bag essentials: Everything you need to bug out.* New York: Potter Style.

Cooley, C. H. (1902). *Human nature and the social order.* New York, NY: C. Scribner's Sons.

Fichman, N., Gilbert, A. L., and Page, E. (Producers), Rozema, P. (Director). (2015). *Into the Forest.* Canada: Elevation Pictures, Telemovie Canada, Ontario Media Development Corporation, Bron Studios, Rhombus Media, Das movies, Selavy, Vie Entertainment, CW Media Finance.

Genzlinger, N. (2012). Doomsday has its day in the sun. *The New York Times.* Retrieved from https://www.nytimes.com/2012/03/12/arts/television/doomsday-p reppers-and-doomsday-bunkers-tv-reality-shows.html.

Goffman, E. (1959). *The presentation of self in everyday life* (Anchor Books edition). Garden City, N.Y.: Doubleday.

Hummon, D. (1980). Popular images of the American small town. *Landscape,* 24(2), 3–9.

Kinane, K. (2016). *Loose in Chicago.* Comedy Central.

Martin, R. J., and Haller, D. (2019). *Sex: Ethnographic encounters.* Martin, R. J., and Haller, D. (Eds.). New York: Bloomsbury.

New York City Prepper's Network (APN Chapter) (New York, NY). (2019). Retrieved from https://www.meetup.com/NYC-Preppers-Network/.

Mead, G. H., and Morris, C. W. (1934). *Mind, self & society from the standpoint of a social behaviorist.* Chicago: The University of Chicago Press.

Mitchell, R. G. (2002). *Dancing at Armageddon: Survivalism and chaos in modern times.* Chicago: University of Chicago Press.

Musolf, G. R. (2003). The Chicago School. In L. T. Reynolds and N. J. Herman-Kinney (Eds.), *Handbook of symbolic interactionism* (pp. 91–117). Walnut Creek, CA: AltaMira Press.

Santora, M. (2014). First patient quarantined under strict new policy tests negative for ebola. *The New York Times.* Retrieved from https://www.nytimes.com/2014/10/25/ nyregion/new-york-ebola-case-craig-spencer.html?searchResultPosition=3.

Schwalbe, M. L., and Mason-Schrock, D. (1996). Identity work as group process. *Advances in Group Processes* (13), 113–147.

7 Toughing it out over the weekend

While retreats provided training sessions, weekend excursions required members to practice bushcraft skills in order to survive in an outdoor setting. These excursions are particularly important because many New Yorkers have little camping or wilderness experience. For example, some NYCPN members who were skilled in wilderness survival did not go on hikes or camping trips while growing up in the city. Instead, they learned to hike and camp while in college outside of the city or as young adults. Other members went hiking and camped for the first time with NYCPN. For studying prepping, excursions reveal how preppers "craft social worlds, create meaning, accomplish self, define situations and engage in cooperative, situated and structured joint action" (Waskul, 2008, p. 118). On outdoor excursions, NYCPN members practice wilderness survival skills such as hiking with their bug out bags, constructing shelters, fire making and filtering water. Through engaging in these activities, preppers also construct frames of meaning in narratives, discourse and interaction (Martin, 2002). This chapter explores the powerful symbols at work during interactions on NYCPN weekend excursions. The bug out bag, and construction of fire and shelter were interpreted as key symbols of self-reliance or protection. Properly packing and carrying a suitable bug out bag is the first symbol of demonstrating one's self-reliance and dependability. With a properly packed bug out bag, one is prepared for any challenge. The ability to start and maintain a fire is another vital tool for survival. As an expression of self-reliability, it represents one's ability to keep warm and to cook food. Meanwhile, effective shelter construction enables preppers to protect themselves against both severe weather conditions and potentially dangerous individuals.

On my first bug out excursion, we camped at Harriman State Park for the weekend. The weather forecast indicated that there would be some sun and temperatures in the 70s in the day, dipping to the 50s at night. For this trip, members were instructed to carry a bug out bag of no more than twenty-five pounds and to bring their own water supply for the weekend. I carried a hiking backpack filled with supplies, my lightweight tent as well as a water bladder. I also carried a large bottle of water. No restroom facilities were available.

When I arrived Friday morning, Al and his middle-school-aged son walked down the hill to meet me to guide me to the camp about a half-mile away from the parking lot.[1] As we walked back up to the site together, Al explained how to be more mindful of my steps so I could avoid tripping on rocks that were hidden in the tall grass. Al carried a large and beautiful walking stick that he had hand-carved. When we reached the site, I could see that a few people had already arrived. Al, Jason, Marlon and Corey were the leaders in charge of this trip. The leaders' shelters consisted of a collection of green or grey hammocks that were already set back within the trees. Ben, a seasoned prepper who was new to the group, had also already arrived. He had a green tent pitched in the same area. I looked around for a good spot. Seeing me weigh up my options, Marlon called to me from across the camp and pointed out an area that he thought would be flat enough and close enough to the others. At Marlon's suggestion, I placed my tent closer to the center to be tucked within the ring of members. I felt fine about pitching my tent, as I had practiced setting it up several times in my apartment earlier in the week. Still, I was nervous, because this was the first time that I had ever gone camping. However, I had followed the group's instructions, so I expected a safe weekend. If anything went wrong, I would certainly be in the right group. As a beginner, I did not construct a shelter. My set-up was uneventful. I successfully pitched my tent and hung my bug out bag on a nearby tree due to bears.

In the practice of bugging out, building a shelter that provides suitable coverage is an important indicator of one's prepping ability. After arriving at a designated location, a competent prepper will assess the landscape in accordance with the expected weather to determine the best location to set up their shelter. The location is selected based on a prepper's particular set-up and the level of visibility desired. A prepper who sleeps in a hammock and uses a tarp as cover clearly requires two trees in an area that may or may not be very visible. A prepper planning to construct a lean-to must find a suitable tree, branches and forest debris. Building a debris hut requires even more materials, as more branches and leaves are required. Each set-up requires a significant amount of time; therefore, shelter-building is the first priority in setting up camp. For a shelter to be judged by other preppers as successful, it must provide proper coverage for the prepper by protecting them against harsh elements such as rain and snow as well as extreme cold or heat. Furthermore, a prepper must also be skilled in selecting a site that minimizes exposure to bugs or other pests by not setting up in tall grass or selecting a site that will be flooded when it rains. To protect against intruders, a site should also be difficult to spot and not accessible on all sides, if possible.

If a prepper has failed to adequately construct a shelter, he or she is subject to critique by the other group members. New members receive friendly guidance throughout the set-up and a critique when problems emerge. As preppers set-up independently, experienced preppers take note of one another's construction techniques but rarely talk with one another. Among experienced preppers, help is offered freely but rarely needed, as set-up is viewed as independent and somewhat competitive work. However, after set-ups, experienced preppers do informally inspect each other's set-ups to discover new techniques and compare notes. In my experience with the group, I learned that no knot goes unnoticed, so to speak. It is also important to note that as excursions increase in difficulty, preppers are required to pare down their materials. As the challenges become tougher, preppers are restricted to a few items and must pack their shelter materials into a smaller pack. As always, the demonstration of self-reliance is key.

After setting up, I then joined some members (Jason, Marlon, Corey, Al and Ben) to help with campfire preparations. I had Al's remark about needing to "earn" one's place in mind. Anna, a new member that I had met at a previous meeting, was on a short hike with her son. The men sawed off very large branches from trees and carried them to the campfire area. Without a saw, I collected smaller branches for kindling. Inshirah soon joined me in the task. As I watched the stacks of wood to be used throughout the weekend grow taller, I appreciated how the group worked together. We all completed tasks that were most suitable to our tools and our abilities at the time.

Soon, we broke for lunch. A fire was going for those who were interested in cooking. Marlon prepared a great meal of meat and vegetables. He had brought fresh meat with him and even a small cast iron pan. As he showed me his miniaturized kitchen set-up, he smiled and remarked that "learning how to cook and eat well in the wilderness was a survival skill." In the interest of conserving water, I had packed a sandwich for lunch. While we ate lunch, Jason and others discussed the merits of different types of bug out bags and the advantages that military bags offered, such as the ease of carrying a bed roll. During the conversation, I discovered that the core leaders all carried wool blankets for protection from the cold.

I sat down on a ledge next to Ben and asked him about his bag which was quite large by prepping standards. Before the excursion, Jason had encouraged the group to travel lightly with a bag that weighed only about twenty to twenty-five pounds. Ben laughed and said "I know that I'm gonna catch some shit later because my bag is way too big. I was trying to figure out what I wanted to bring on this trip." I smiled and wondered if he would be right. After a few more minutes, Ben looked at me and then pointed to a yellow blur billowing across the grass. I looked at him and shrugged my shoulders to indicate that I did not know what it was. "Anna, isn't that your tent?" Ben asked, trying not to smirk. I could hear him burst into laughter as I scrambled after it. As I began to set it back up, Ben came over to show me how to properly secure my stakes. Marlon came over to inspect my set-up and then showed me how to reinforce my stakes with special knotting. They were both gracious and patient. Despite my initial embarrassment, I came away with the realization that the co-organizers were also conducting their own kind of field research. As a co-organizer, I could see that Marlon was continuing the assessment of members, which he had started at the retreat. In demonstrating how to reinforce my stakes and then monitoring my attempt, Marlon was reinforcing the importance of self-reliance. In our face-to-face interaction, he could quickly determine my willingness to learn and evaluate my performance. In this exchange, Marlon was busy reinforcing the group's belief in self-reliance while I was busy reinforcing my tent stakes. In this process, we were also getting to know one another. We were learning to communicate with and to read one another as we set about learning to distinguish between "one another's eye twitch and a wink" (Geertz, 1973, p. 6).

After a brief session on first aid that included advice about protecting against tick bites, as it was high season, Jason asked everyone to line up their bug out bags so that they could be reviewed for suitability and weight. The lineup of the eight bags was revealing. The majority of preppers (all the men and Inshirah) had large military-style bags with a few add-on packs. Given that most of them were larger men, some very physically fit, the sizes of most bags seemed proportionate. A few members also displayed prepping tool belts that allowed them to keep tools like knives and compasses at the ready. As Jason moved down the line of bags, he pointed out important distinctions between them and discussed alternative tool belts and vests. Two women (Anna and I) carried backpacks with a few bells and whistles. Jason commented that our backpacks were fine for this beginner trip but that we needed to invest in smaller and natural-toned bags for ease and increased protection (to be less noticeable). This was a fair point.

Jason then stopped and shook his head at one military-style bag that stuck out. It was gigantic. It was the size of a large cooler. Jason already knew whose bag it was. He looked at Ben and we all tried not to laugh. It was reminiscent of a classroom when the teacher calls out another student for something embarrassing. After Ben shared that his bag weighed over sixty pounds, Jason cautioned him that there was no way that he could carry that large a pack for very long. Ben nodded in agreement and explained that he had brought some extra things that he wanted to try out. I could see Ben peering into "the looking glass" (Cooley, 1902) and his facial expression let me know that he was disappointed with what he saw. He knew that he had made a misstep. Ben had come to the group with a few years of prepping experience and his selected bug out bag did not reflect the self that he intended to communicate. He wanted to reflect the identity of a seasoned prepper. For the rest of the trip, Ben worked very hard on all projects to demonstrate his skills and contributions. He was set on changing his image. By not following guidelines and carrying a bag that was too heavy, Ben failed to give the proper impression to invoke the preferred response; approval from Jason, the NYCPN's leader (Goffman, 1959). Ben had perceived a negative interaction with his audience.

By contrast, Inshirah seemed to be more of a maverick. Never mind the hammock or tent, she set up a tipi. She intended to test living in it to see if she could use it with her family. (For example, she was concerned that its lack of flooring might allow warmth to escape and bugs to come in). She even brought a compost bathroom unit, a narrow tent that resembled a Porta Potty. She also periodically traveled back down to her vehicle to retrieve something if needed. As these behaviors were against the group's rules for excursion, I wondered if her actions would be viewed unfavorably by Jason and the core leaders. At the retreat and the meetings, it was clear that the group was quite serious about adhering to its value system, which seemed to center on the importance of packing a bug out bag with minimal gear and mastering survival skills. Jason did seem a bit miffed by the amount of the gear that Inshirah had brought. After watching her for a few minutes, Jason grumbled to another member that "The new people are bringing way too much stuff for a bug out."

However, Inshirah shared with me that she was not very concerned about breaking the guidelines. The trip was about learning how to prep for a disaster and that was what she intended to do. She explained that she planned to bring this stuff with her family in a survival situation and her goal for the weekend was to test her equipment. For her, the excursion was the only real time that she had to work with her gear, so she planned to dedicate her time to both the group's plans and her own plans. That's exactly what she did for the weekend. After the first night, she discovered that the tipi required flooring and more warmth. After watching some members cook with fire-boxes,[2] she began thinking over the best approach to installing a small wooden stove in her tipi that would have an exhaust pipe vented outside through the top of the tent. Her actions were an expression of her commitment to self-reliance. She was focused on thinking about what worked best for her in her unique approach to bugging out. Both Inshirah and Ben recognized the significance of the bug out bag to the group as well as Jason's instructions about its particular weight. Although they both understood the bag as a meaningful object, they organized their actions toward it quite differently (Blumer, 1969). In the effort to be as prepared as possible, Ben disregarded instructions and he overpacked his bag. He clearly felt uncomfortable with his actions and worked hard to correct the group leader's impression of him. Inshirah also disregarded the group leader's instructions. She elected to reject the notion of the bag and brought up large items individually to experiment with them. Rather than becoming embarrassed by her actions, she shrugged off any negative responses and prioritized her interest in testing gear. In both cases, each NYCPN still remained committed to the ideal of self-reliance. Ben wanted to demonstrate his self-reliance by ensuring that he conformed to all other expectations during the weekend. While Inshirah might be considered more of a maverick, her focus on testing her equipment for family use also reflected a dedication to self-reliance.

In the evening, Corey grilled a rabbit (that he had purchased at the butcher) for his dinner and shared it with everyone. Others who had brought extra food like hot dogs also shared. Around the campfire, Marlon shared a story of a miserable winter trip in which the core group's survival skills were really tested as an unexpected torrential downpour gave way to freezing temperatures, snow and isolation. At other points, behavior around the campfire was solitary. Al whittled quietly by the fire while Jason sat silently and sent a few texts. Marlon watched a movie on his phone. I spoke with Anna about a presentation that she had given at a meeting (She and Jason had demonstrated how to make your own laundry soap and toothpaste). I also sat with Inshirah. During the night, we all took turns keeping watch over the campsite. In pairs, members wearing headlights and holding flashlights patrolled the campsite every two hours, walking by hammocks and tents to make sure that all was well.

On Saturday, the group was busy with bushcraft lessons on tinder making. Al and Corey helped newer members (Ben, Inshirah and me) practice these skills. Each new member had to demonstrate that they could ignite a fire. Ben lit his fire quite easily. Next, Inshirah ignited her fire. Given that they were already experienced preppers, they had no difficulty in starting their respective fires after a few moments. Conversely, as someone still unfamiliar with the task, I found starting a fire to be challenging. For several long minutes, the group watched me as I struggled to catch a spark in my tinder nest. Corey then helped me to better shape my tightly woven tinder nest into one made of thinner and looser strands. He also taught me how to properly strike with my new knife and showed me the difference between his quality ferro rod and my inferior one. After Corey's coaching, I was finally successful. The fire challenge gave me insight into how new group members must feel when trying to define themselves as preppers, as they struggle with feelings of dismay relating to how they imagine they are judged. Although the group was supportive, the challenge reflected the value of self-reliance. I first had to attempt the task in earnest and without assistance. As I tried to complete the task, my anxiety contributed to my failure because I became unnerved by the group's possible interpretations of my failure. I then received additional instruction. After receiving this help, I was expected to make additional attempts until I achieved success. In a different social setting, someone may have offered to take over my task if I was having trouble with its completion. However, the NYCPN's mission was to promote self-reliance in a disaster.

Marlon also offered a tarp shelter and knot tying session. I was surprised by how advanced and essential knot tying was in survival scenarios (for example, the trucker-hitch knot is used to secure heavy loads and allows for tension to be pulled tight or loosened as needed). Unlike stereotypes promoted in television programming about prepping, sexism was not an issue of concern. With Anne and Annette absent, all of the core leaders/teachers on the trip were male and most of the new members with the exception of Ben were female (Inshirah, Anna and me). Inshirah had also brought along a female friend who did not participate in training. Ben was also new to the group, but he had already mastered many of the bushcraft skills. So, like Inshirah, he was demonstrating proficiency.

However, a bit of sexual tension did surface after the lessons. Some of the woodpile had been depleted. Given their outdoor experience, some of the men recognized that we would need more wood to last the rest of the trip. With the stash of collected fallen branches and large branches already used, the men determined that they should saw through extremely large branches from the woodpile to make firewood. To complete the daunting task, they took turns using a large foldable handsaw to cut the wood. It was a bit competitive as each man challenged himself to saw as much and as quickly as he could. It was warm outside and the labor was intensive. Jason had invited a friend on the trip, a tall, young, muscular Eastern European man. I was surprised to observe that sexual interest arose whenever it was this man's turn to saw. The women briefly stopped what they were doing around the campsite and admired the young man, wearing a tank top, as he worked. The women exchanged glances with one another but made no comments. Their objectifying gaze (Fredrickson and Roberts, 1997) went unnoticed by the man.[3] Jason, always alert, took note of the women and gave an eye roll and a headshake. Later, when we four women were together, one woman said, "Why can't they just let him chop all the wood?" The other women (myself included) laughed and nodded in agreement.

In the late afternoon, Jason suggested that someone make a store run. This surprised me as I expected we were only supposed to rely on what was in our packs. However, it was clear that the group had worked hard on both days, so I got the sense that a store trip for a few indulgences (coffee grounds and a couple of cans of soda) was permitted because we had earned it. Inshirah volunteered with the other women in tow. For a moment, it felt like cheating. Yet I was delighted to join, as I was grateful for access to a restroom. We hiked down the hill and drove to the convenience store in town. Located within a tiny strip mall, the convenience store was next to a takeout Chinese restaurant. Fortunately, the store was swarmed with dusty hikers like us. We bought the requested items as well as a few snacks. We also decided to order some takeout Chinese. We each ordered a plate for ourselves. Recalling how everyone shared food on Friday night, I ordered some fried rice for the group.

We returned to camp moments before sunset. As everyone was cooking their dinner, I announced that I had bought some fried rice to share with the group. Marlon looked disappointed and declined. He reminded me that we were supposed to be cooking on the fire not eating takeout in the woods. I could tell that he was moved by the gesture but that I had gotten it wrong. I did not know the rules. It seemed that there was a continuum of acceptable to unacceptable in store runs. I had overshot. Replenishment of depleted items and the purchase of smaller items such as snacks seemed to be acceptable, but I had gone overboard. I had purchased a large container of rice for everyone. I was embarrassed. However, I learned something valuable. Marlon had clearly noted the other women's meals. However, he only mentioned something to me because I had brought it to the forefront. He observed the behavior of members as I suspected. The difference was that I had invited others to disregard the rules. In contrast to Marlon, Al shrugged his shoulders and said that he really did not mind because he liked fried rice.

After the night watches, Saturday quickly turned into Sunday. On our way out of town, we all met at a diner for breakfast to close out the trip. As the group was seated and awaiting breakfast, they were immediately identifiable as city people. They had a "tell" (a giveaway about their identity). Even though this diner by the highway was filled with all sorts of people such as other hikers, locals and travelers, the preppers looked a bit different. The preppers were tidy, despite their having just spent two days in the woods. Each prepper slipped off to the bathroom before the meal to quickly clean up and look presentable at the dining table. Many other hikers did not make this effort. With this practice, the group members were signaling the close of training and their shift back into city life. In other words, they appeared to be compartmentalizing their identities as wilderness survivalists. With the end of the training, their behavior at the diner represented a move back into adhering to the norms of urban citizenship in public space. Both the meal and the conversation were good. I soon discovered that excursions often closed with a visit to a diner. It was a celebration of a shared experience.

The level of training and endurance required during the excursion served as evidence that NYCPN members were committed to their identities as urban preppers. Furthermore, group members also sought to protect the integrity and the safety of the group. As a result, those who jeopardized the safety of the group and who continually demonstrated a lack of skill comprehension were viewed as risks and shunned by core leaders. Weeks later, an intermediate-level weekend excursion reflected the challenges posed to the group in dealing with weaker members. Within the group, the inability of such members to avoid injury and adhere to safety guidelines is viewed as selfish and as a barrier to self-reliance.

On this intermediate-level bug out trip, preppers were required to carry only Haversacks (small canvas military-style backpacks) and to construct their own shelters (no tents). I was quite anxious about attending this outing because I was fearful of sleeping without a tent. However, recognizing my role as a participant-observer, I decided to try my best while still packing my tent as a backup. Only three members attended the trip due to work and family commitments (Marlon, Al, Michael and me). Given my concern about hiking alone, since bears had been spotted near the area, my husband, Scott, also attended the excursion. Upon arrival, we walked up the hill to the campsite as it was in the same location in Harriman State Park. When we arrived at camp on Saturday afternoon, I immediately noticed tension within the small group of preppers. Michael was sitting down on a log by his hammock with his pants leg pulled up. His right knee looked swollen and uncomfortable. He told me that he had fallen down and hurt his knee. I had a flashback of his knife injury at the retreat. I asked if he was okay, and if he needed help back down the hill so that he could be taken to the hospital. Michael argued that it was just a sprain and that he would be fine. Al and Marlon were busy at their respective shelters, but I could see the frustration on their faces.

In greeting us, Al and Marlon brought us up to speed on their activities. They explained that Michael had actually injured his leg at the start of the trip on Friday. However, he refused to leave the camp with assistance to receive medical attention. Instead, he chose to stay overnight which meant that the two other men were charged with helping him. Although Michael overheard their recount of events, he did not join the conversation and no effort was made to invite him in. As with the retreat, Michael was posing a risk to himself by refusing treatment and holding back the group from achieving its objectives.

The three men had hammocks protected by tarp covers, so I decided that setting up a tent was acceptable. Given the small size of the group, no training sessions were held that afternoon. Instead, I spent my time learning more about Al and Marlon's set-ups. Al had set up a lean-to with his tarp. He had wool blankets rather than a sleeping bag. Marlon had a hammock set-up with the tarp covering to shield both his sleeping area and an outside area for sitting and any other activities. With fireboxes and other equipment, the set-ups of both men were self-sufficient. For example, I recognized members would sometimes sit quietly with their own fires after they turned in at night. Also, early risers would often make their own coffee and breakfast in the morning. Having a firebox at one's shelter promoted self-reliance rather than having to depend upon the large group fire.

Michael also had a hammock set-up. He was seated in front of his hammock. Given his injury, he did not walk around the camp very much. However, he was located almost in the center of camp (near the group campfire) and next to a walking path, so he was not isolated. I chatted with him and asked if he was feeling any better. He shrugged. He looked like he might complain about his knee. Instead, he looked over his shoulder and complained that Marlon and Al had done a poor job of hanging up his tarp and setting up his area. Al was doing something nearby and I saw him shake his head, so it was clear that he had heard Michael. It turns out that when they arrived on Friday, Marlon and Al set-up Michael's shelter because he was too injured to do it alone. I looked at Michael's site and everything seemed secure. I could not identify the source of the complaint. He mainly argued that they used the wrong knots. Given Marlon's previous lesson and demonstration on knot tying, I was skeptical of his assessment. I was also a little taken back by his lack of gratitude. I double-checked to make sure that Michael had medicine and that he was sure that he should not return home. He told me that he had taken some anti-inflammatories and that he did not want to go home.

When out of ear shot of Michael, both Al and Marlon later expressed frustration and concern about Michael. They felt that he was a danger to the group. Al remarked: "He doesn't know what he is doing and always hurts himself." Marlon argued that Michael was "irresponsible by acting like he knows something when he doesn't, giving bad advice, he is always doubling the time to do things like not getting his fire going, he's just dangerous."

Shortly before dusk, Marlon, Al and Scott went to hang our food bags for the night to discourage bears and other animals from nabbing them. They disappeared down the path. I sat by the campfire across from Michael's camp area. My hope was that he might want to talk, but he kept to himself. Michael hobbled around a little bit and rifled through his backpack for something. He lay down in his hammock for a few minutes. Michael tossed and turned for a few minutes and then, suddenly, he flipped himself out of the hammock. Somehow, he had managed to catch air. It was an exaggerated motion like a scene from a Three Stooges movie. Just then, I saw Al standing frozen on the path. We were both shocked. Michael scurried back into his hammock. Al ran past as if he had not noticed. While it was comical, I felt sorry for Michael. With the knife injury, the knee injury and now the hammock mishap, it was apparent that Michael was clumsy. After confirming that he was all right, Al and I quickly fled to our respective shelters to deal with the embarrassment of witnessing the incident.

After that awkward start of the night, we sat around the campfire looking around at each other and blushing for the first few minutes. Michael remained in his hammock. In an effort to change the focus and to gain more insight on prepping, I asked the others what books and movies inspired them to develop an interest in prepping (some selections have already been addressed in Chapter Three). After a brief conversation, Marlon then used his smartphone to play snippets of his favorite classic rock songs from the 1990s (think Guns N' Roses). Al also shared a few of his favorite songs. We each nodded in appreciation or suggested other songs. After about thirty minutes or so, Michael joined the group. He did not say very much and there was not too much of an effort made to encourage him to be part of the group.

In the morning, Al and Marlon helped Michael break down his shelter and pack up his gear as needed. While the two men were disappointed in Michael's performance and lack of gratitude, they still helped him. Al lent Michael his walking stick to help him with the rocky descent back down the hill. As seasoned hikers, Marlon and Al moved quickly down the hill without waiting for Michael. Michael moved very slowly, and he was clearly in a lot of pain, so I walked with him. Marlon and Al did not stop on their hike to wait for other members to catch up as they usually did. Instead, they waited at the bottom of the hill. Even if unintended, they gave a clear message that they were finished with Michael's antics. I wondered what would have happened if this had been a real disaster situation.

In studying my field notes on formal discussions and conversation held during excursions, I confirmed that members observed the group's rule against discussing politics. Conversations centered mostly on the training-at-hand, problem-solving, disaster scenarios, observations about the camp, humorous observations. Some ribbing about mistakes, popular culture (such as movies and songs) and stories about previous trips. As my research continued, I identified these topics as the main categories of conversations for trips. The nature of these topics do not lend themselves to deep introspection or passionate debate; therefore, they work to promote group cohesion. As a result, one critical element about these preppers remained hidden; their personal narratives. In other words, they did not freely disclose their full motivations for prepping. Much of prepper discourse focuses on different acronyms that describe the future moment of grave crisis or disaster such as "WTSHTF,"[4] what preppers are planning for. However, there are no acronyms to reflect the personal experiences that have influenced people to become preppers. These experiences are seldom discussed.

A scene from a winter excursion best symbolized this sense of privacy and protection maintained by some NYCPN members. Located in a remote area of the Catskill Mountains, this excursion was classified as a "tough bug out" as the temperatures at night would be in the 20s with a high chance of rain or snow (all of those predictions proved to be accurate.). The seven members who had signed up to attend the trip were core members—Jason, Al and Annette, Corey, Marlon, Ben and Preston (who usually only attended the more challenging bug outs). The two-and-a-half-mile trek to the camp was rough and beautiful. As my husband and I hiked through the mountains on Saturday, we were treated to the wonders of the mountains in winter—snowy trees, crisp air, sparkling rays of sunshine, rocky uphill hikes and slippery, muddy walks downhill.

After crossing a series of bridges, I was overcome when we reached the campsite. A quick glance around the camp revealed nothing. Almost all was invisible. Only after several moments of study did I make out the shelters that had been erected among the trees alongside a river in the cold wintery landscape. The members' shelters had been completely covered with branches and foliage. I had to travel around the area to spot all of them. I was a bit unsettled. For the first time, I really saw what a campsite of this group of skilled New York City preppers would look like if they had to leave the city. The group was certainly task-oriented, and the excursions provided me with rich data on the shared meaning of mastering survival skills; however, this was a very different experience. To paraphrase Marlon, these members had definitely learned to get comfortable in their discomfort. As I stood admiring Al's amazing tapestry of interwoven pine branches, I realized that this camp seemed to reflect the nature of New York City prepping. The camp symbolized the members' success in mastering the unfamiliar skills set of bushcraft and yet it also allowed them to remain undercover. Their respective achievements were recognized by other group members but not by outsiders.

My role as a participant-observer allowed me to delve beyond task-focused conversations to discover their personal narratives. The themes of protection and coverage were threaded throughout their stories. In framing their identities as urban preppers (Martin, 2002), NYCPN members discussed issues such as their motivations for prepping, the types of disasters they were trying to protect themselves against and their rationales for disclosing or hiding their identity as a prepper. For NYCPN members, this lifestyle is very much connected to their experiences of living in the city of New York. Some members were motived to join due to direct experience with disaster. Beyond such direct experience, interest in joining the NYCPN also stemmed from factors such as contending with the challenges of growing up in poor and unsafe neighborhoods, and an immigrant experience that reinforces family traditions of planning for lean times and emergencies. Members were also concerned with more effectively protecting themselves from the types of disaster that New Yorkers have faced—attacks, hurricanes, blackouts, possible pandemics, economic collapse, to name just a few (See Chapter 2 for a more detailed discussion of these threats). Therefore, they were committed to mastering survival skills in both bug out and sheltering in place scenarios. Some members were anxious about disclosing their identities as preppers for fear of being stigmatized by family members or people within their social network (friends or coworkers).

Exploring members' personal narratives is crucial to understanding their segue into prepping and the adoption of this lifestyle. The personal narratives of Al and Annette, a married couple who have been NYCPN members for seven years, offers some insight into these complexities.

For example, Al linked his interest in prepping to the challenges of growing up in Spanish Harlem, in a poor family raised by a single mom. As he explains:

> Poor family, single mom, growing up in a rough neighborhood, I learned about prepping early, by watching your back, being mindful of your environment.
>
> I learned how to live life on the defense. Neighborhood had gangs, drug dealers, my mom was an alcoholic, so I had to go down to the corner to buy beer and cigarettes when I was ten. People on the street know you. I didn't really have a male figure in my life. I had an uncle, he was the biggest male figure in my life, I guess. We used to watch Karate and Kung Fu movies. For my birthday he bought Karate lessons for me at Harlem Karate School taught by Professor Ernest Hyman. I learned it and went through the whole thing, color belts and tournaments.
>
> My mom was tough, she was in a gang, she knew how to fight, she would always teach me to watch my back, that was her instinct. Her experience, the neighborhood, martial arts, it rounded out everything. It is about being mindful of your environment.
>
> We started [prepping], my cousin and me, around ten. We would make plans in case 'something was going down', what are we gonna do, weapons, stars, knives, not money or food, we were kids. We were thinking about fighting off people, we even had a meeting spot. We had no real name for it. We would just always say, 'we gotta prepare.' The *Doomsday Preppers* show gave it a name.

For Annette, her interest in prepping is rooted in her mother's tradition of stockpiling food and basic supplies to protect the family during times of financial insecurity. She explained:

> For me, it's about 'preparing for life, being smart.' My mom started me on this. My mom always made sure that the cabinets were full. She caught sales on everything like beans. There were seven of us, she was always saving and always stocking. She started me on this. It is about being responsible. After seeing Jason on the show, Al was interested, and we checked it out. We have been members since the start.

For this prepping couple, Hurricane Sandy was an important reminder about the value of prepping. Annette shared:

> Hurricane Sandy didn't really affect our family because we were living uptown in Manhattan, but we saw how it was for everyone else. My sister's father-in-law passed away. Hurricanes are what I am most concerned about, because I know how dangerous they can be. I moved to Florida when I was 19 and stayed there until I was 21. A tropical storm was scheduled to hit. People panicked. Boarded up their homes. Stores were all sold out. But two storms ended up hitting back-to back. I got stuck at work late at night. The electricity was out. I looked outside and I was seeing darkness and water everywhere. There were downed powerlines and my ride was unable to get through. I was young and it was a real eye-opener for me. With added stress, you don't think clearly and make poor decisions. If you have things at home, less stress on you. We now live in the Bronx. We've had two blackouts. We were fine. We didn't have to worry about the kids. We had motion-sensored lights. We had extra. We were prepared.

Drawing on her mother's example, she also advanced her homesteading skills to include canning and the medicinal use of essential oils. Her prepper closet includes the usual items, but her supplies are also supplemented by a stash of several Costco buckets of emergency food rations (designed to feed a family of four for a month) that she bought on sale (at such a low price that they were probably mismarked).

Both Annette and Al worked to improve their prepping skills. As Annette put it: "The whole point of prepping is to figure out the problem, and taking care of it yourself." By going on NYCPN excursions, she has vastly improved her bushcraft skills. Annette is even the hero in a group story that is often told to highlight the value of perseverance. For groups, storytelling is significant because it gives meaning to events and reinforces a group's ideals (MacAdams, 1997). Annette is the member who helped the group manage a dangerous change in weather conditions. During a winter trip to Slide Mountain that turned treacherous due to intense rain and a sharp decrease in temperature, Annette managed to build and maintain a fire in a downpour when other core leaders were unsuccessful. On a rainy and cold excursion that I attended, Annette again demonstrated her perseverance in trying to ignite and maintain a campfire. While she was ultimately unsuccessful in keeping the larger fire going, her efforts were the most productive out of all members.

To increase his knowledge and his endurance under harsh conditions, Al attended the grueling Canterbury Survival Training classes. He has also taken on the tasks of learning blacksmithing and welding. Expanding on his F.I.T. degree in Woodworking, his construction projects now range from making cabinets to building a cabin. Given the labor-and time-intensive nature of these projects, the pair's continued commitment reflects that prepping is a vital part of their lives.

Despite this commitment, the couple still remains cautious about disclosing their identity as preppers. Al argues that being "a gray man" is part of his nature as he has had to be that way all of his life. In prepping culture, a gray man refers to someone who blends in easily and doesn't stand out from the group. In an emergency situation, the ability to blend in is viewed as an asset as it reduces conflict and the discovery of resources. According to Al: "Long-term preppers are always safeguarding to an extent. They don't want to be taken advantage of." For Al, blending in means avoiding the judgement of non-preppers and protecting his family's stores in the event of a disaster. Annette has not disclosed their membership in the group to her family or friends for fear of their negative reactions. She indicated that discussing prepping is difficult due to the stereotyping of preppers and the reality that, as city dwellers, her family and her friends do not really have knowledge of outdoor activities such as camping. Therefore, introducing her practice of prepping is made more complicated because it cannot be discussed in relation to a shared hobby with her family or friends. Like other NYCPN members, Annette feared the stigma of being identified as "a crazy person who thinks that the world is going to end tomorrow."

In discussing her own reluctance to share her identity as a prepper with her family and friends, Inshirah commented that she "knew that [her] family would think that [she] was nuts." Ben was reluctant to reveal his prepping to his co-workers because he believed that "they wouldn't get it and would give me shit about it." While Jason does not conceal his identity as an urban prepper, he often explains that "he wants people to know that NYC preppers aren't the people wearing tinfoil hats." Marlon acknowledged a shift in people's perceptions of prepping by observing that: "Ten years ago, people would laugh at me, you would never have them talk to me, now they ask me for advice."

In contrast to the alienation of stigma, the NYCPN supports its members with an organizational frame (Goffman, 1974) that links social interaction and subjective experience. Based on the shared goal of preparing for disaster, the NYCPN offers its members a forum for discussion about topics such as disaster scenarios and a structured setting for learning the technical skills required for survival. By fostering knowledge of prepping and bolstering one's abilities, these components work to create a new sense of self for each member. Through these organizational features, that foster learning and interaction, each member develops a new self-identity as an urban prepper (Martin, 2002).

The dynamics of being ostracized by outsiders for being a prepper whilst receiving positive reinforcement from other group members sometimes led to conflict. While most excursions were posted on the Meetup page, core members also occasionally went on last-minute bug out trips together to enjoy each other's company in a less structured setting. I attended one of these last-minute excursions to Harriman park included six members (Marlon, Ben, Al, Annette and a new member). The trip was much like the other outings. However, there was flexibility in shelter type and amount of gear. Members packed as preppers rather than regular campers (foregoing luxuries such as coolers and elaborate camp set-ups). Members also continued to focus on developing skills.

For example, Ben experimented with a new tarp shelter set-up that required mastery of a knot and pulley system. When he had completed his set-up, he fashioned a large tent complete with a porch. His impressive set-up could be expanded or reduced as needed. His porch was perfect for the summer day. Ben had brought a new member with him. This member was quiet and seemed to know a lot about the outdoors. He did not share very much, but I knew that preppers are often not forthcoming.

Shortly after setting up my campsite, I started to collect kindling and smaller branches to start a fire. However, I failed at collecting suitable firewood. I did not realize that the dry branches that I collected from the ground were actually wet inside from the previous day's rain. Al walked around the forest with me to help better identify proper wood as well as tall grass that could be used for tinder. I felt disappointed as I had failed at an easy task, but I did learn a great deal. The afternoon sailed by with easy conversation and testing of gear. As the core leaders tended to use hammocks, I had purchased a hammock for myself to test out. Joining me on the trip after a long flight from the West Coast, my husband arrived and spent some of the afternoon sleeping in it. We all broke into laughter when we heard him snoring. It was comical but it also underscored the difference between traditional camping and group excursions. Resting was not a primary component of NYCPN outings. In contrast, NYCPN members did not relax very much on trips. Instead, they chose to spend their time practicing with their gear, engaging in activities such as testing set-ups, trying out water filters or comparing fireboxes.

During lunch, there was more laughter. In response to someone's desire for ketchup on a hot dog, Marlon went to his backpack and returned with a quart-sized bag jammed with what seemed like every type of condiment packet ever produced. It was more of a thick brick rather than a bag. It was not the sort of extravagance that one would expect from a prepper. Seeing people's reactions, Marlon laughed and said: "Hey, when something happens, things are gonna be bad enough. Why make it worse with terrible food?" We all chuckled and nodded in agreement.

In the evening, a non-prepper arrived at the camp. She was a young woman who was a friend of one of the members. She had planned to camp for the night nearby, so the member invited her to join the group for the night. As she arrived after dark, the group had finished dinner and they were seated around the campfire talking. She sat down with the group to a general conversation that was not focused on prepping. After a few minutes, her friend left the campfire for an extended period. Seated near Al and Annette, she inquired if we were all part of an outdoor Meetup group. Before anyone responded, she said: "Yeah, I know he's a prepper, but you all aren't that. You'd all be wearing yellow Hazmat suits." I could see that Annette and Al were taken back by her comments. After pausing for a moment, Annette said: "We are with the prepping group." The non-prepper immediately replied and rolled her eyes: "*Oh*, you are one of *them*..." Annette paused for a moment and said: "We all are. We are all preppers."

As the woman scanned the small group around the campfire, they returned her gaze and remained silent. The easy flowing conversations of the day abruptly stopped and there was only silence. As a researcher familiar with interviewing preppers, I could almost hear the castle's iron gates slamming down to cut off any exchange with her. Reminiscent of Clint Eastwood's famous stare, the new group member gave her a long look as he took a drag off his cigarette. For a moment, I expected the woman to look embarrassed or to fumble an apology. However, she did neither. She seemed defensive and annoyed.

She attempted to change the subject by commenting on Annette and Al's preschooler as he came over to ask his father for help with his video game. Noticing all three children, she said: "Oh look, you've brought your children." Annette gave a slight nod. The non-prepper then said: "Yeah, wherever you are with them, you have to chase after them, right? Because they are always trying to get away from you." Of course, she had no idea that her comments made things worse because this particular family is quite close. "No, we love our children, why would they run away from us?" asked Al. "That's what I'd do. I'd want to get away from you," she said. My guess is that the woman was attempting to make a friendly comment on the freedom of movement desired by children at play. However, combined with her comments about preppers and the absence of her apology, her sharp delivery made her remarks seem more of a harsh criticism of their lifestyle choice rather than an observation about the zaniness of children.

Given the exchange, I expected that one of the preppers, in particular Al or Annette, might express anger or frustration with the outsider. Maybe someone might storm off or something, but that didn't happen. Any such scenario was highly unlikely as she was a guest of another prepper. Instead, they remained silent and refused to relinquish any space at their campfire.

Immediately, preppers began to speak only with one another. She finished her meal and then returned to her shelter to sleep. After learning about the conversation, Ben later commented: "See, that's why I never tell people. People have an image built up in their heads. If there is no need for you to know, why should I tell you? Otherwise, there is all this nonsense and ridiculousness."

Always eager to test his prepping knowledge, Ben proposed that the group take on the challenge of bugging out in a new environment. He suggested that members discover if their approaches to prepping would carry over into a harsh and a dramatically different environment, an isolated beach campsite called Watch Hill. Operated by the National Park Service, Watch Hill is located on the western edge of the Otis Pike Fire Island High Dune Wilderness, directly across the Great South Bay from Patchogue, Long Island. This oceanside wilderness is accessible only by Watch Hill Ferry, private boat and foot. To reach the camping area, one has to walk about 1.2 miles down the beach. The campsite has no water, toilets or other provisions. Given its remote location and limited facilities, Watch Hill is a stark contrast to the ever-popular Fire Island. As a beach lover, I signed on for the trip because I have always had the fantasy of becoming a carefree surfer who lives on some remote beach in a small hut and fishes for my meals. I imagined that surviving on the beach would be easier, so I was curious to see if I was correct.

More importantly, I wanted to see if the group members were willing to break away from their routine of mountainside excursions. Unfortunately, there was not a great deal of interest. Only three members planned to attend this early summer excursion. However, the third member had to cancel at the last minute. So, that left only Ben and me. I was a little nervous about just the two of us going on the trip. I was not worried about our difference in gender. I was worried about our difference in ability. Ben was much more knowledgeable about prepping. As a participant-observer, I was learning a great deal. However, as I was not experienced prepper, I recognized that I was not self-sufficient. Ben and I spoke about this imbalance. He reassured me that he would help me and that he was confident about both of our abilities. He also reminded me that, while we going to Watch Hill to practice prepping, other people were going just to camp at the beach.

We planned to catch the morning ferry to Watch Hill. Weather for the trip looked promising but hot, with a clear sky and temperatures in the high 70s during the day and in the 50s at night. I knew that it would feel a lot hotter on the beach without tree coverage and the sun's rays reflecting off of the water. Given the absence of a water source or restrooms, we needed to pack carefully to ensure that we had necessary items. My concern was being able to carry my pack for such a long hike in the heat and sand. I pared down my pack. I carried 2 liters of water in my bladder plus a bottle of water to use on the walk. I was worried about my water intake, so I tried to stay hydrated before the trip. I protected my face with plenty of sunblock and I even wore a hat. I also wore a thin white hiking shirt and light-colored pants to keep cool.

We also needed to pack clothes and a sleeping bag to be warm during the night. However, I was not concerned about the nighttime temperature. I was now familiar with sleeping in the 50s, so I knew which sleeping bag to bring and which warm clothes to pack. Since Watch Hill is known for its mosquitos, I made sure to pack spray and to wear a long sleeve shirt.

We met at Ben's home. Even though I knew Ben was married, I still imagined the décor of Ben's home to be spartan. I expected it to have severe furniture, all angles, blank walls, a weight bench instead of a coffee table. Instead, his home was Instagram-perfect. The cozy living room was decorated in a cottage style with muted colors and overstuffed couches that demanded naps. Sitting on one of the couches was Ben's wife. For a moment, I felt awkward about going on the trip with her husband. However, in keeping with the perspective of other spouses who are non-preppers, she immediately thanked me for going on the trip because she has zero interest in suffering on her days off.

Her remark made me think about how a member at a meeting once raised the issue of how to deal with the challenges of having a partner who is not interested in prepping. He said:

> I'd like to know what other people do. My wife does not get it. I keep trying to learn more about prepping and all she wants to do is argue about supplies. I would like us to learn this together, but she acts like I am crazy.

This member had recently joined the group. While he did not attend excursions, he attended meetings regularly. He was an active participant. He took careful notes, shared his experiences and sought advice. Members at the meeting laughed and nodded in recognition of his predicament. Jason and Marlon were leading the meeting. Marlon first shared an amusing story about fighting with his wife over space for storing supplies in an apartment. He said:

> We used to argue about it. I was only allowed to have a little space in the cabinet under the sink. So, I had to get creative with my storage back then. I would store cans of soup in the pockets of winter coats. Whatever it took. Put on a coat and there is some soup.

As he spoke, he pretended to put on a coat and pat the pockets. His humorous delivery was a crowd-pleaser. Other members chimed in with advice about reminding your partner that you are trying to protect the family in a disaster. Jason concluded the discussion by pointing out a change in his wife's attitude toward prepping. He said: "My wife used to complain until Hurricane Sandy. With Sandy, we were set. We did not have to worry about anything. After Sandy, she told me that she understood and was fine with it." Again, the group nodded their heads in agreement. His statement was a reminder of the value of their mission. Through learning prepping techniques and becoming self-reliant, they would be able to protect their families.

Before we left, Ben showed me his man cave which made me realize his advanced level of expertise in both radio and the martial arts. One section of the basement housed a ham radio communication workstation that reflected his advanced certifications. Another section of the basement had been transformed into a martial arts studio. I discovered that Ben was a black belt and that he had competed as a young man. He also showed me his prepping gear and emergency equipment.

We left for the ferry. I discovered that Ben was very resourceful in an unexpected way. He was very friendly, outgoing and curious. His friendly demeanor encouraged people to share things with him. He had the gift of gab. Therefore, he was excellent in information gathering. I had not seen this side of Ben during excursions or at meetings because members were very task-driven and the NYCPN events did not require the need to gather information from strangers. First, we drove to the ferry station to be sure that the time-table was correct. As we were quite early, the ferry ticket office was closed. Ben approached a groundskeeper on a riding lawnmower to confirm the departure time. After a moment, the groundskeeper turned off the mower to chat with Ben about the ferry's schedule in relation to the summer season. Because we now had ample time, we decided to drive to a nearby deli because Ben wanted a breakfast sandwich. On the way, Ben explained to me that there are a few delis with the same name that must be owned by the same person and he wondered if they all did well. While waiting for his sandwich, Ben struck up a conversation with the cashier and manager. After a moment of social pleasantries, Ben followed up on his curiosity about the other delis. He made a comment about the differences that he saw between the two places and in a moment he and the manager were joking about how much busier and more challenging it is to operate than the other deli. The manager shared that the other place "needs an army behind the register." He seemed to appreciate Ben's interest in recognizing that they have the same owner but that they were completely different sorts of places.

The ferry ride was quick. We admired the boats and the ocean. After the ride, less than thirty-minutes, we reached Watch Hill. Because it was a late Monday morning and not yet tourist season, we were the only visitors on the ferry, the two other passengers being employees at the park. The marina was beautiful with a new bar, general store and a ranger station. Whilst these amenities were great, I knew that we still had to walk over a mile down the beach to the wilderness camping area. The door to the bar was propped open. Ben immediately struck up a conversation with the general manager. They planned to open in the next few days. He explained that they were still happy to serve us even though they were not yet open for business. We both laughed and explained that it was a little too early for a drink and thanked him for his generosity.

After a short bathroom break, we continued walking on the boardwalk and then down a long stairway toward the beach. Walking down the stairs with my pack was awkward. The beach was empty. It was sunny and beautiful.

However, it was a little tough to walk in the deep sand, so I explained to Ben that it was easier to walk on the hard sand by the ocean. I explained the impact of the tides on the beach. Not a beachgoer, Ben was unfamiliar with the importance of the tide schedule on beach use, especially for walking and camping. I asked Ben about how he developed an interest in prepping. He responded like it was something that came naturally: "With the blackout and Sandy, and everything, we didn't have power or anything, I figured that I needed it. I learned the radio, too." He shrugged his shoulders. According to Ben, it seemed like a logical path because he tended to follow up on his interests and curiosities.

We walked for about half a mile before we came upon another person. From a distance, we had noticed a large tarp shelter with lots of items amassed on an area of the beach. Ben thought that it might be a campsite as it seemed like an extensive setup. However, I disagreed. My take was that it seemed to be a series of four Found Art installations with a tarp to protect the artist against the sun. When we reached the site, we determined that I was correct. A thin older white man in very small swim trunks was the creator. Before we reached his site, Ben turned to me and said that he wanted to talk to the guy because he "bet that he has a lot of good insight about camping on the beach. A guy like that is going to know a lot." I surveyed the site again. The installations included a large red balloon and, affixed to the top of a large branch, a weather vane of sorts with sticks and shells dangling from it, a makeshift pretend solar charging station, and a quartered off section that looked like a too-small livestock pen or a cage for, well, people. Two totem poles made from driftwood were adorned with single feathers that blew in the breeze. I turned to Ben and asked him if he had seen the first season of *True Detective* or the movie *It*. He had not. I said that was obvious and that I did not have a great feeling about his hunch.

Ben was right about the man's knowledge of the beach, though. We discovered that the man had been coming to the area for nearly thirty years. He explained that he used items that he had found on the beach to create things. Ben asked him questions about his tarp arrangement, complimented him on his homemade hand truck to carry items, and asked him how long it took to create a few fixtures. Indeed, Ben was a conversationalist. I did not participate very much in the conversation. I did not want to disturb Ben's mojo with my unease. Ben quickly found out that we needed to avoid being too close to the dunes as there were many ticks, that the mosquitos weren't yet a problem in the area, that our best bet was to position our tents between two dunes to avoid the wind. Ben thanked him and we continued on our way. The man was not an artist but more of an eccentric. Ben wondered if he was homeless, but I did not get that sense as we saw his campsite. He was well-groomed. In addition, he had an expensive tent and high-quality gear.

We walked down the beach for another half a mile. It was hot but bearable. I was very thirsty but only took a few sips of my water. I was trying to preserve it. We agreed on a space that would allow us to tuck our site in between two dunes. We pitched our tents. Ben's tent took only a minute as he had a popup bug shelter that he planned to use as a tent. I had a traditional tent. We experimented with the sand anchors until we had it set up properly. It was a bit windy, but the shelters seemed fine. We took a break to eat lunch. We sat on a log at the site and ate sandwiches. Ben suggested that we continue down the beach to see if we could find the ruins of a house that had been destroyed by Sandy, something that he had read about. He thought that we might scavenge for useful items there. We walked for a bit and soon discovered it. Ben quickly spied two cement blocks that could be used to prop our log off the ground to improve its use as a bench. I was delighted when I saw them too but for a different reason. I saw that someone had already arranged them as a bench to look out at the ocean. I felt a little embarrassed because I realized that my thinking was not inventive. I was not thinking like a prepper. I was thinking more like a romantic. I was trying not to be too fixated on indigo-colored seashells and the purple sea glass. I tried to pick up one of the cement blocks, but it was far too heavy for me to carry back to our campsite. Ben ended up carrying both of them. When we returned to camp, he dropped the blocks by the log. I positioned them to elevate our bench, the horizontal log. It made a big difference in our comfort. We also searched around for smaller logs to position as anchors to prevent the big log from rolling off the blocks. In front of the log we also built a small fire area with a wall to cut down on wind affecting the flame. Open fires were not allowed, but small contained fires such as our jet boiler were permitted. We needed to build the backwall to protect the flame.

We scoured the beach for any other useful material. The level of trash was shocking. The beach was beautiful but there was a considerable amount of strange debris. We discussed trying to repurpose objects. We had already used washed-up logs and wood to stabilize our bench and to build a fire shelter. We also decided that we could use large seashells as plates if needed. However, much of the other trash didn't look particularly useful for our needs. With the high tide now rolling in, the beach had turned into a balloon graveyard. There were several half-inflated mylar balloons scattered along it, and a large laundry basket even washed up at high tide. We both agreed that, in a long-term situation, we could use that to collect and store firewood. Ben tried creating a desalination method that did not work. We discussed the merits of purchasing a desalination system for a prepping closet. It is extremely expensive with limited use. However, given the heat and bareness of the beach, we quickly recognized that trying to bug out on a beach without one would be extremely difficult.

Given that it was now hot and sunny, we decided to spend some time in our respective tents to organize our materials and to get a break from the sun. My tent was a lot smaller than Ben's, so my interest was in replying to emails rather than unpacking. Ben and I then came up with a list of exercises that we intended to do such as practicing radio skills, practicing my knife skills, testing the Jetboil, as it was a new item for us, and scouting to study the dunes and obtain a better understanding of the plant and animal life. Ben had taken a course in tracking, so he planned to share some insight. However, at this point it was extremely hot. Ben's face was quite red with sunburn. Although I am not as sensitive to the sun, I felt that being out in the sun for a few hours would not be a good idea for him or me for that matter. I thought that we needed to wait until things cooled down a bit instead of sitting under the direct sunlight when the tasks were not time-sensitive. Ben looked at me and said: "You know, this might not be the prepping thing to do, but it's really hot. We could always walk to the bar. That'd be okay with me." I was delighted. Yes, walking for a mile in the blaring sun to sit in some AC for a couple of hours worked for me. Did it make a whole lot of sense? Maybe not. However, it seemed like the civilized thing to do. Ben suggested that we might not want to tell the others that this is what we did. I laughed and said that I thought that it was the smart thing to do.

We headed back up the beach in the blazing heat towards the dock. On the way, we noticed that the artist had moved and reassembled some of his installations. We waved hello. Secretly, I brought a tiny brush to fix my hair before we entered the bar. I did not want to scare away customers. It was useless. The general manager was very nice but not really familiar with bartending. After a few attempts, he accomplished a gin and tonic for me and a beer for Ben. He looked a little guilty. Not me. I ordered fried calamari. We were oceanside, after all. Ben and I begin to talk about non-prepping things. We talked about our lives outside of work and friends. I discovered that Ben was a member of four groups dedicated to his respective hobbies. He had even gone to bartending school. I told him that I was relieved because he did not look so bright red anymore. I asked him if he had ever thought about moving away from New York given his concerns about disaster and he said no and that he could not name a place that he was really interested in moving to. We talked about his job, which he asked me not to disclose. He kept long hours and experienced a lot of pressure. He said that he thought about being a cop but laughed and pointed out that "it wasn't like he'd be escaping those two things as a cop." I asked why he hadn't become a cop. He laughed and said, "My mom." We had a second drink and then decided to head back.

The walk back was fine. It was now late afternoon. It was hot and I was a little tipsy. Walking in the sand seemed slightly tougher. As we approached the found art installations, it seemed that the man may have been sans swim trunks. Of course, I observed this first. Ben was too embarrassed to look. As we drew closer, he was making his way to the ocean for a dip. We hurried by without making any eye contact. I laughed and remarked how none of the prepping literature discussed a protocol for dealing with sudden nakedness. I guessed this was more of an etiquette than prepping question. Is there a prepping etiquette? I asked him. Ben's face was beet red so all I could do was laugh at him. It was hot outside, so I surmised that the guy was "tactical naked."

Back at our camp, we worked with the radio to see which channels we could pick up and how far Ben could reach someone. He made contact with someone on the Long Island Expressway. Because I do not have my license, I wasn't allowed to speak. However, Ben helped me with programming my radio and provided an extensive walkthrough on two phone apps to help locate repeaters. After his tutorial, I took the radio more seriously. It made me think about teaching and reminded me to bear in mind that when students are dismissive of something it usually means that they are having trouble understanding it. Some members had been dismissive of the ham radio and I now suspected that their rejection of it might be related to frustration over learning how to operate one.

Next, we walked around the beach to examine tracks. Ben had a great deal of knowledge from his class to share. He talked with me about the process of slowing down and observing the environment. He had me examine our current footprints and then compare them to our earlier footprints. He discussed the impact of time on a print and how it could change a print. Clearly, the wind had a significant effect on our earlier footprints as they were quite worn away by blowing sand which made them less distinct. He showed me different animal tracks, possibly a fox and small rodent, as well as different bird tracks. It was far more interesting than I expected.

We decided to make dinner with the Jetboil. Ben bought a chicken and rice dish for us to share. I brought self-heating meals for us to try. Ben suggested that we try his dish since he had a lot of it and my dish could be used for breakfast or something. His meal needed to be eaten before it went bad. It took about twenty minutes to warm it up on the burner. This seemed long, given that it was already made, and it was room temperature. Even with a wind guard, the flame was really impacted by the wind. As I only had my tin cup, Ben suggested that I use his tin plate and that he would eat from the stove container.

Marlon called during our meal to check in with us. He wanted to be sure that everything was fine and that we did not need any help with troubleshooting any problems. Throughout the day, Ben had sent him photos to update him on our trip. We reported that we were fine and all set. After dinner, Ben suggested that we rinse our dishes, the pan, the tin plate and utensils, in the ocean water. We had some difficulty given that we were wearing hiking boots and trying not to get wet. I decided to dig a small tide pool to fill with water so that I could rinse the tin plate better. Ben warned me that the plate was too light, but I ignored him. He was right. It did not work. The plate was immediately swept away by a big wave. I tore off my boots to try to run into the ocean to retrieve the plate. No luck. I just got wet and more embarrassed.

Since my bare feet were cold and my pants were a little wet, I tried to warm up by drinking a cup of tea. Ben took pictures of the setting sun. We talked about our favorite relatives. Ben talked about how one of his aunts used to read tea leaves. He asked if I had anyone like that in my family. I do not. I then shared some of my family folklore about experiences with the supernatural. We then tried the radios again and Ben was once more able to connect with someone on the Long Island Expressway.

It was getting windier, so we set up my tarp over my tent. Ben had no tarp, so we moved his tent more directly behind mine to give it more protection. Soon, it was dark. I was glad because I was still hot and sunburned from the day despite my use of a hat and sunblock. I wanted to get out of the wind. We decided to retire to our tents to text our families and unwind before sleep.

We said goodnight. We were both tired and we knew that we would be up at sunrise.

After trying to sleep for a bit, I grew very anxious. With the cover and the strong wind, I could not make sense of the strange noises outside of my tent. We often have watch patrols during the prepper outings, so I was uneasy sleeping without protection. Worse yet, it was a bit colder than I expected. Before sleeping, I had put on a sweatshirt. Now, I put my jacket over my sweatshirt. I pulled my hoodie up. I could hear Ben moving around so I knew that he was not asleep. I asked him how he was doing. Same as me. Colder than expected. His phone read 50 though. We talked a bit. I explained that I was anxious about the sounds. He asked if I wanted to come over to his tent. I said that I was not sure. I thought it over and at the next loud noise I scrambled over to his tent with my sleeping bag. It was only 11:00 p.m. so I knew that I was going to be in for a long night.

He pulled up some *SNL* clips on his phone. We laughed at a few. It was not any warmer in his tent because it was screened. I could see every star in the sky. I loved that view. However, it was still really cold. Ben was sleeping in a heavy hooded brown get-up that made him look like Obi-Wan from *Star Wars*. We slept a bit more. Ben offered me his mylar blanket. He decided to use a large trash bag as a cover for his sleeping bag. He put on gloves. I dozed off again. After sleeping for an hour, I woke up once more to check the time. It was only around 1:00 a.m. We both complained about the temperature a little more and decided to take respective bathroom breaks. After a few more minutes in the tent, I explained that I thought that I might be warmer in my tent, so I switched back there. I offered to share my tent with Ben. He declined. I understood as it was much smaller, but I did not think that was the wisest idea, though he said that he was fine. Before going to sleep, I added an extra pair of socks and pants. The mylar blanket seemed useless. I recalled Marlon telling me that I should wrap it around my sleeping pad, but I did not think to do it.

Around 2:00 a.m., we both woke up because we heard some distinct scratching noises. Ben moved a flashlight around the camp but didn't see anything. We went back to sleep. I had additional mylar blankets and feet and hand heaters in my bag, but I did not think to get them out. I even had an additional shirt to use for layering. Later, Ben also reported being cold but still didn't come over. I understood that he was trying to be respectful, but the extra body heat would have been useful. I did not think to ask him again or to insist. I was just tired and wanted to sleep. Sometime later, the temperature really dipped.

Finally, the sun rose. I welcomed the heat in my tent and got a little more sleep. I could hear Ben moving around outside. I stepped out of my tent and walked the few steps to the bench. It was wonderful to feel the sun's warmth on my skin. I was surprised to discover that I had a little bit of a sore throat. Ben asked me to look at the sand to see if I noticed anything. Boy, did I! There were several animal tracks around our tents and throughout our camp-site area. After dinner, Ben had buried our food scraps and animals had clearly picked up the scent. We saw prints of a fox, a rabbit, a few birds, a small rodent and snake tracks. It looked like a completely different terrain compared to when we had inspected the tracks the day before. We both laughed and agreed that the tracks explained the noise. We were surprised to learn that burying the food seemed to have no real effect. You could see where an animal had tried to dig for it without success. We probably scared it off with our flashlights and noise. We packed up camp, as it would be about an hour walk back to the ferry. I was glad to be leaving, because I had a little under a liter of water remaining and was worried about running out. I was so glad to be warm. I felt kind of foolish for being so dramatic about the temperature. However, Ben said that he felt the drop too.

On the way back, we evaluated the beach as a bug out spot. Its short-comings were that there was no water source without filtering water near the reeds by the boardwalk (however, this was not really fresh water). A water filtration system was therefore a must. There was also little protection from the elements, although we might have selected a better spot between other dunes to protect ourselves from the wind. Given park restrictions, we could not camp behind the dunes. We also could not build a fire. In a bug out situation, these restrictions would probably not be enforced. I also argued that we did not try to fish. Fish would be an important resource. However, the lack of fresh water and natural protection outweighed any advantages. We also talked about the temperature drop. We quickly recognized that we had made several missteps because we were so sleepy. We should have woken up to properly evaluate the situation. Instead, we were doing everything piece-meal to no effect. We should have covered our sleeping pads with the blan-kets. Using our stove fueled by a propane canister, we could have filled our bottles with hot water to use as a heat source by tucking them in our sleeping bags, we could have worn additional clothing, we could have slept in the same tent, we could have used my hand and feet warmers, just to name a few easy possibilities. However, in the fog of sleep, we didn't think about these possibilities. That was the scary part.

The next day, Ben called me to share his conversation with Marlon about our experience. He had briefed Marlon on our trip including the drop in tempera-ture. Marlon explained to Ben that we made three strategic errors. First, we should have also considered the Montauk weather report, as we were close by for a more accurate reading. Second, we should have continued to check the temperature throughout the night if we were that cold. We stopped checking the temperature around midnight. If we would have continued to check the temperature, we would have realized that it had dropped to 37. Third, we should have slept in the same tent for increased warmth. Marlon told him and later me that Ben had made a serious error by not sleeping in my tent rather than risking offending my husband. He told Ben that, as a more experienced prepper, he had the greater responsibility of ensuring my safety. According to Marlon, Ben "needed to think about how offended my husband would be when he had to explain that I died because he did not do the right thing."

When thinking through Marlon's periodic check-in calls to Ben and his response to Ben's decision-making process, it became clear that Marlon was monitoring the success of our two-person bug out experiment. Based on Ben's experience, Marlon viewed him as the leader of the trip. By calling or texting to get an update on our activities, Marlon was communicating and reinforcing his assignment of the role of leader to Ben. Before the trip, voicing my concerns about the difference in our skill levels also worked to establish Ben as the leader of the trip and me as the follower. In defining ourselves against one another, Ben and I intended to occupy these respective roles and to behave in keeping with these roles. In fostering joint action, Blumer (1969) notes that: "Each participant necessarily occupies a different position, acts from that position, and engages in a separate and distinct act. It is a fitting together of these acts and not their commonality that constitutes joint action" (p. 70). Therein lies the problem. During the trip, we slipped in and out of approaching the trip as a bug out exercise. We did not carry out the exercise to fruition. When practicing prepping skills such as radio operation or studying animal tracks, we acted as leader and follower in the joint action of conducting a bug out excursion. However, we also lost our focus through joint action. Through engaging in friendship rituals such as having drinks, we shifted into the roles of new friends getting to know one another. Our interactions had undermined the structure of leader and follower. This periodic shifting between the worlds of prepping and beach camping relaxed the sense of discipline and alertness which is usually in place during bug outs.

Notes

1 Children sometimes attended events. However, studying children was not part of this research project. In accordance with IRB guidelines, no field notes were kept regarding the activities of children and no conversations were held with the children regarding this research project or prepping.
2 A firebox is a camp stove. It is a multi-fuel collapsible metal box used for cooking or providing warmth.
3 For an examination of objectification theory's application to men, see Davids, Watson, and Gere (2018).
4 For preppers, "WTSHTF" is an acronym for the phrase "When the shit hits the fan".

References

Blumer, H. (1969). *Symbolic interactionism: Perspective and method*. Englewood Cliffs, N. J.: Prentice-Hall.

Cooley, C. H. (1902). *Human nature and the social order*. New York, NY: C. Scribner's Sons.

Davids, C. M., Watson, L. B., and Gere, M. P. (2019). Objectification, masculinity, and muscularity: A test of objectification theory with heterosexual men. *Sex Roles: A Journal of Research*, 80(7–8), 443–457.

Fredrickson, B. L., and Roberts, T. A. (1997). Objectification theory: Toward understanding women's lived experiences and mental health risks. *Psychology of Women Quarterly*, 21(2), 173–206.

Geertz, C. (1973). *The interpretation of cultures: Selected essays*. New York, NY: Basic Books.

Goffman, E. (1959). *The presentation of self in everyday life*. New York, NY: Anchor Books/Random House.

Goffman, E., and Berger, Bennett, M. (1986). *Frame analysis: An essay on the organization of experience*. Boston, MA: Northeastern University Press.

MacAdams, D. P. (1997). *The stories we live by: Personal myths and the making of the self*. New York, NY: Guilford Press.

Martin, D. D. (2002). From appearance tales to oppression tales: Frame alignment and organizational identity. *Journal of Contemporary Ethnography*, 21(2), 158–206.

Waskul, D. (2008). Symbolic interactionism: The play and fate of meaning in everyday life. In M. H. Jacobsen, (Ed.), *Encountering the everyday: An introduction to the sociologies of the unnoticed* (pp. 116–138). New York, NY: Palgrave/Macmillan.

8 Dodging a bullet

Held at a church in Washington Heights, the NYCPN meetings provided information on disaster preparedness for preppers of all levels. In a meeting room that did double duty as a daycare room for children, preppers met to listen to lectures and participate in workshops. For preppers who did not attend retreats or excursions, the meetings offered insight into the organization's identity and strategy. Identity refers here to an organization's central character and mission; its strategy refers to its goals and activities (Ashforth and Mael, 1996). The group's initial meetings in 2010 focused on general discussions of basic topics such as fire safety or water purification. Today, meeting topics are now often timelier and more specific. Beginning with the group's discussion of Hurricane Sandy in 2012, topics started to be driven by direct experiences with the occurrence of dangerous events in the city or media coverage of such events elsewhere in the country. The "Ebola Outbreak" lecture in the summer of 2014 was given in response to the Ebola epidemic sweeping across West Africa. (Weeks later, a doctor who treated Ebola patients in Guinea was diagnosed as the city's first disease victim.) As tensions heightened between the United States and North Korea, preppers met to learn more about "How to Prepare for a Nuclear Disaster" (2017). In November 2017, the "Active Shooters and Your Response" lecture was scheduled to address the mass shooting at a Las Vegas Outdoor Concert (Belson et al., 2017). However, during the group's meeting, the "Active Shooter" topic was immediately expanded to include the mass shooting at a church in Sutherland Springs Texas as it occurred on the same day (Montgomery et al., 2017).

The "Active Shooter" meeting is a strong example of the NYCPN's organizational identity and strategies. Given the group's interest in preparing for disaster, the meeting was held shortly after the October 2017 mass shooting in Las Vegas. As a response, the meeting was designed to offer guidelines on safety procedures in active shooter situations. Due to the overwhelming public shock over this mass shooting, the turnout for the meeting was relatively large with thirty-two people in attendance. The majority of whom were new members. The session was led by Jason and Ben. Given Ben's technical expertise in amateur radio, he had been assigned to the role of Communications Director. This meeting was his first teaching assignment. I was looking forward to Ben's presentation as I had worked with him in designing it. Ben was new to teaching so I helped him simplify and organize his notes into an audience-friendly presentation. Ben planned to present a mini-case study of possible shooter scenarios and then guide the class through various ways to protect themselves, which included communicating with others via amateur radio. The case was based on Ben's earlier work experience developing personal safety strategies in response to active shooter incidents.

Typically, political opinions are prohibited during meetings. However, due to the outrage over the Las Vegas shootings, Jason introduced the topic by facilitating an exchange of ideas about what went wrong in Las Vegas, revolving around a critique of the police and hotel security's response, including their failure to discover the cache of guns. The conversation then quickly shifted to a heated discussion about some members' perception that New York City Police Department officers lacked expertise in handling their own firearms. Attendees expressed fear that police officers' insufficient firearm training would be detrimental in the event of an active shooter in Manhattan. Jason summarized the group's fears by stating: "The problem is that some cops act like they are scared to do their jobs and act like they have never seen a gun before. They are hesitant to do their jobs because of backlash." The group's frustration over what they felt was an ineffective response to the mass shooting, reflected a core group belief that the United States government is unable to effectively protect its citizens in emergency situations. Expressing a lack of faith in the government's abilities to protect its citizens was a common refrain within the group. In response, NYCPN members sought ways to protect themselves. I expected that some attendees might disclose gun ownership or express dissatisfaction with New York City's strict gun laws. However, no one mentioned private gun ownership as a solution. Instead, they were intent on learning self-defense strategies that could be employed without a gun. Jason reviewed and elaborated on the Department of Homeland Security's (DHS) Run, Hide or Fight guidelines, its advice for protecting oneself against an active shooter. The DHS (2019) guidelines provide three broad tactics:

1   Run — get away from the shooter and help others to escape.
2   Hide — get out of the shooter's view and silence all electronic devices.
3   Fight — commit to carrying out aggression by relying on the help of others and using makeshift weapons.

The group leaders' instructions echoed the group's goal of reinforcing self-reliance and responsibility. Jason first encouraged people to remember that they have a responsibility to others, especially children. He said: "You can't be that selfish jerk. You have to help others if you can. You can't be that guy.

That's the reason why society is breaking down, people are becoming selfish jerks." For each tactic, Jason offered additional "nuts and bolts" advice. He first explained to the group that adrenaline affects perception and that things might appear skewed as a result. If you are running outside of a building, he recommended pausing before going outside to check for bodies to be sure that it is safe to exit. People should also keep their hands in the air and cooperate with the police to avoid confusion in a dangerous situation. Jason paused for a moment and looked at his phone. He then announced that the news had just reported that a gunman had opened fire at a church in rural Texas. A few audible gasps. Silence followed as the group tried to process the coincidence of events.

I thought about my family throughout Texas who were definitely at church and I asked Jason where the shooting occurred. He did not know. Nearly everyone in the group shook their heads and I heard a few sighs of sadness. Here we were in a church learning about how to protect ourselves from active shooters while a shooter was killing people at a church in another state. I checked my phone to discover that the shooting was in Sutherland Springs with twenty-six reported dead (Montgomery et al., 2017). I wanted to call my cousin Eli to make sure that Shelley and the girls were OK. I reasoned that their church's service had changed and that they were now busy praying for the victims in Sutherland. I thought about the absurdity of trying to protect your family from anything if people were now gunning each other down in church.

Jason continued with his lecture. He classified hiding together as a "fish in a barrel" scenario. If hiding together, he advised the group to plan to attack the shooter as a unit. He explained that if the shooter is unable to get into the room, he/she may try to pose as a rescuing officer. Jason cautioned that: "Fighting should always be a last resort, and everyone should attack at the same time from all angles for any chance of survival."

Next, Ben began the in-meeting exercise of strategizing about different scenarios. As we worked through his list, the group debated the best solutions for each scenario. His review revealed a surprising challenge for escaping our own meeting room which was located on the second floor. The adjoining doors to the room were quite heavy and could keep a shooter at bay for a period of time, making it possible for people to attempt to escape by jumping out of the windows. However, the windows of the old church were too narrow for the majority of people to pass through.

Jason concluded the presentation by giving one last piece of advice: He warned the group about taking on the role of victim too quickly. He said: "Don't be the crying asshole. Don't be the victim if you aren't one." He then shared one of his experiences as a firefighter at the World Trade Center on September 11. Standing outside with his back to the towers, Jason heard a snap. From the sound, he knew that the buildings had started to collapse. At that moment, Jason was trying to help a very obese woman up from the ground so that she could get out of harm's way. The woman was uncooperative, screaming and carrying on. Jason was frustrated and concerned because he did not know if they could get far enough away from the buildings if he carried her. Suddenly, when the woman realized that the danger had escalated, she sprung up and tore off well ahead of him. According to his viewpoint, by not remaining calm and working to protect herself, the woman wasted precious time in seeking Jason's help and increased the risk for both of them. For the group, Jason's closing story reinforced the importance of using self-reliance to protect oneself from danger and to avoid the risk of injury to another person.

In most meetings, the lectures or workshops were usually given by Jason with the help of core group members as co-presenters. Meetings covered a wide range of topics with attendees leaving with detailed information or an item that they made during a workshop (such as homemade cough syrup or a leather wallet). A guest speaker from Beacon, NY, Shane Hobel, the founder and lead instructor of the Mountain Scout Survival School, further ignited the NYCPN's enthusiasm for learning more about wilderness survival. Hobel gave an engaging presentation (a pitch for attending his school located in the Hudson Valley), that included his general philosophy about prepping along with exciting tips. Based on his understanding of Native American traditions that honor nature, Hobel offers courses that encompass survival skills familiar to preppers (water, food and fire) as well as tracking and awareness skills. Hobel immediately drew in his audience by describing a core contradiction of modern life: the never-ending cycle of accumulating stuff, only to repack our stuff to make way for more stuff as we all attempt to jam our stuff into our boxes, otherwise known as homes. He compounded this sense of alienation by discussing how we no longer care about the box next to ours (our neighbors). His reference to George Carlin's "A Place for My Stuff" (1981), a commentary on consumption in American culture, was a powerful and prescient intro- duction. The thesis of Carlin's comedic routine is that the meaning of life is trying to find a place for your stuff. For preppers, surviving focuses on the management of stuff, and discarding your unneeded stuff to make space for only the core stuff that you need to survive.

Hobel's message of trying to break away from excess to reveal the essential was not lost on his audience. His comments further resonated with the group as he talked about how prepping is an expression of moving away from autonomy and back into community, as prepping involves the acceptance of responsibility for one another. He reminded the group that they "can't always depend on a badge-wearing person and that they have to depend on them- selves." He closed by arguing that your "'Go Bag' represents what you know and what you don't know," which is probably the best definition of a bug out bag that I have ever heard. Hobel was persuasive because his remarks echoed the group's two most important principles: self-reliance and responsibility to and for one another. He tapped into the group's mission of coming together to share what they know and to learn what they don't, in order to protect their families in emergency situations.

Following his rousing introduction, Hobel shared information about his course offerings. He discussed his tracking experience and the value of situational awareness. To demonstrate the importance of situational awareness, he used a visualization technique on the group by instructing them to close their eyes and then recall different features of the room. He offered valuable advice such as making sure that the printed maps stored in your bag are laminated to protect against moisture and that they are topographical to give you an understanding of terrain to better estimate walking times. He also did a location coding exercise on the board to demonstrate how a group that planned to bug out together could devise a code and key to keep their destinations confidential.

Finally, Hobel spoke briefly about using plants and essential oils to treat illness in the wilderness and to prevent motion sickness from riding the subway. He talked about how he and his crew always applied "Thieves Oil under their noses whenever they went down into the dirty subway." His comment struck me as overly critical, but I decided that I was probably being too sensitive. I love my city, so I sometimes bristle too quickly at negative comments. Regardless, I trusted his knowledge about survival skills, and I planned to attend one of his courses.

Over the summer, I attended the Mountain Scout Survival School's "Urban Prepping" course held in Central Park. My experience did get me a little fired up. Located near the 72nd Street entrance, the course objective was to provide New Yorkers with information about prepping and how Central Park might be used as a resource. However, the morning got off to a rough start. Hobel began by apologizing because he was unable to give us a tour of an area that he usually showed to his classes. It is an area of dense brush that can serve as a temporary bug out location. Once a person moves beyond the first layer of brush, they can move about quietly and undetected in the spring or summer seasons. Hidden by the first layer, there is an open spot that can hold a group of people. However, on this summer day, a group of drunken homeless people had taken over the spot to party and fight. Therefore, a tour was not advisable.

Unfortunately, Hobel had not planned an alternative lesson for experiencing Central Park. Instead, he spoke very broadly about his interest in Native American traditions and shared stories about his wilderness experiences. This approach was ineffective because class members were expecting to learn more about urban prepping, and how to rely on the park as a resource. Class members grew restless and began to people-watch, with some individuals slipping off to enjoy the park on such a sunny day. Hobel provided no discussion of the park's features, such as its treasure trove of edible plants. Instead, he talked about his dislike for the city and shared his displeasure about its filth. He was probably just frustrated, but a few class members looked disappointed. As he spoke, an occasional well-timed shout, which seemed almost like a twisted rebuttal, could be heard from the fighting drunks hidden behind the bushes. The course then broke for lunch. After lunch, Hobel opened his bug out bag and displayed its contents for the class to examine. He provided an excellent discussion of preparedness and the contents of his bag. However, one left the class without any new knowledge about how to use Central Park in a survival situation.

For NYCPN outings, Inshirah was also interested in training in other environments beyond excursions to the mountains. According to her perspective, now that the group was becoming more proficient in bushcraft skills, it needed to spend more time practicing in urban environments. As a part of preparing for the process of sheltering in place after a disaster and then later leaving the city, the NYCPN periodically offered practice bug out walks around and out of the city. Routes included starting from Washington Heights and crossing the George Washington Bridge into Fort Lee, NJ, or walking from Queens across the Triborough Bridge. Members were required to carry their bug out packs to become familiar with their travel time and walking across the bridges. For members such as Anne, this experience was significant. Terrified of heights, Anne faced her fear by walking across the Triborough Bridge.

To further strengthen the abilities of members, Inshiriah argued that the two-pronged training approach of sheltering in place and bug out walks did not address "the likely reality that preppers may be staying in some sort of urban commercial building on their way to a safe haven." Therefore, she suggested to Jason that the group should have a bug out experience in an empty commercial building (such as a warehouse or factory) to learn how to survive in such a setting. She explained: "You aren't going to walk straight out of the city into the country. You are going to have to stop somewhere." To plan this type of excursion, Inshirah researched renting an unoccupied commercial building in or around New York. However, she was unsuccessful given high costs and insurance liabilities. This type of outing posed significant risk. For safety reasons, a fire could not be made within a building. Experimenting with a window stove was also hazardous. Sheltering in place preparations provided solutions for addressing human waste issues, but since this experience was intended to be a bug out, those resources would not be available. One member suggested the possibility of sneaking into an abandoned building to stay overnight. However, that illegal option posed other dangers like negative encounters with squatters and the possibility of criminal charges. Committed to developing new group activities that centered on the city, Inshirah began to devise new teaching methods for the group such as a map exercise that encouraged members to discover and identify safe places as well as houses of worship that might offer help on their way to their safe havens. She also set about designing a new series of challenges and exercises in the city.[1] Her intent was to broaden the group's meeting content and type of training offered in the city.

Drawing from Inshirah's insight, I decided to investigate New York City escape rooms to discover how city crises are depicted and resolved in this type of urban entertainment environment. Escape rooms are team-based games that require players to discover clues, solve puzzles and complete tasks in series of rooms to achieve a specific goal, usually simultaneously escaping the room and saving the public from death, by a specified time limit (Nicholson, 2015). There are currently about 2,300 escape rooms in the US (Kornelis, 2018). With puzzles that involve fast-paced activities like searching for hidden objects or solving riddles, escape rooms provide players with a desired mix of novelty and fun even if they are not the authentic experiences that are usually sought after by urban tourists (Kolar, 2016). Escape room visits are also used by organizations and companies to strengthen leadership and teamwork. In escape room games, group unity is enhanced by collective problem-solving and constructive interactions (Wu et al., 2018). My goal was to see if experiencing these "mock disasters" offered any knowledge or skills relevant to preppers. Clearly, bushcraft would not be useful here. However, I might be able to rely on other prepping skills to help me escape before the time limit. I also wanted to see how a non-prepper group might work together in a stressful situation, so I invited three close friends. The escape room scenario involved stopping a speeding subway line to prevent the deaths of all passengers. We were given sixty minutes. Without disclosing any game secrets, my prepping skills definitely came in handy. Situational awareness in the form of keen observation helped me identify clues much more quickly. Teamwork was essential in performing tasks. As close friends, we were in sync with one another and brainstormed our way through each step. Much like members of the prepping group, we trusted one another. However, there was one distinct difference: we all worked on one task together and then moved on to the next task. The members of the NYCPN tended to work on independent tasks simultaneously, reinforcing the sense of self-reliance and one's contribution to the group. In other words, they probably would have approached solving the puzzle by dividing tasks and working simultaneously. The experience was empowering, until the last puzzle, that is. We could not solve the last clue despite the group's collective total of nine degrees. Instead, we stood embarrassed and confused as the buzzer rang indicating that we had failed in our mission. The "mock disaster" had turned into a social disaster.

After the time expired, the room monitor (the employee assigned with watching our game and providing guidance if needed) entered our room to explain the problem. There was a flaw. Moments before we entered the subway to begin our game, a technician made a hurried exit after completing a repair. He left behind a screwdriver, the same screwdriver we had attempted to use to unscrew all available screws. Worse yet, the technician had failed in making the repair, so the completion of the last puzzle, (something our group had successfully done), never triggered the end of the game. Shocked, the monitor remained silent during the game because he did not know what to do. I estimated that we had completed the game with about seven minutes remaining. Yet, we still lost the game.

The technician's actions revealed the challenges of practicing a philosophy of preparedness. The mission of prepping is protecting against the harms of disaster. Therefore, preparing for different types of disasters demands extensive planning. This high level of preparation reinforces one's sense of control. However, this sense of control may be false. Preparedness may help one respond more quickly and efficiently to disaster, but it cannot eliminate all potential threats or unforeseen circumstances After my experience, I suggested to Jason and other members that visiting an escape room might be a good team building activity for the group. However, there was little interest. Most members preferred testing their abilities to respond to real-life situations encountered during outdoor excursions. As Ben explained to me, "Rushing around a room and trying to figure out clues made up by someone isn't teaching me anything other than how to think like that person. That's not gonna help me in a disaster situation." Other members had also previously attended escape rooms on family outings or as part of team building events for work; therefore, they were not interested in attending again.

At the conclusion of the research project, I thought a lot about the bonds among the members of the NYCPN. How strong were the interpersonal ties between members beyond group training exercises? I thought about the idea of a real bug out. The group trained together, but, in the event of a bug out, how many members would actually organize a plan to leave the city together (or to meet at a designated point outside the city)? There was not much talk of it during group meetings. Ideas and suggestions were made, but no real plan was ever established. When I asked Jason about it during an interview, he said that there was no real plan. However, his facial expression told me that he might have organized a plan with others and that it did not include me. This was expected, as I was a participant-observer. I also lacked his superior skills. Besides, he lives uptown and I live downtown. The group's mission was to teach preparedness and it met its goal. Its mission was not to develop a detailed plan for surviving together. That was a different agenda involving creating a unified plan for all phases of surviving disaster, with the most important phase being establishing a safe haven together. A few members probably had pacts together that they were not disclosing to the group. Still, I expected that, in the event of a disaster, their training and mutual trust would bind members together without the need for a pact. The hurricane season of 2018 did, in fact, reveal the strength of bonds within the group. However, I did not expect that I would be the one relying on the bond. Alone and preparing to evacuate from Charleston, SC, during the impending Hurricane Florence, my phone conversations with Ben were crucial in making certain that I was prepared for disaster. The following chronology of my evacuation from Charleston in September 2018 has been adapted from my personal journal.

Sunday:

It looked like there was a possibility that the hurricane might hit Charleston by next weekend. At the coffee shop, I heard locals laugh and brush off the storm's possibility. "Oh, we have been through this a million times. Calm skies and smooth sailing. I'm not worried." I understood. It was a gorgeous day. Sunshine abounded. Still, despite my best efforts, I was now thinking like a prepper. Okay, if this storm happens, I need to be out of here before the crowd. Tuesday morning at the latest. I bribed myself with a bike ride on the beach if I booked my "just in case" ticket for Tuesday morning.

At home, I searched for ticket prices. Monday: $218, Tuesday: $323, Wednesday: $218. I was aggravated that Tuesday was $100 more than the other days. Monday was too early to retreat but if I waited until Friday, I could be dead. I cursed the airline for charging extra on September 11; it was already a terrible day. I convinced myself that the hurricane would bypass the area.

Sunday night:

There was now talk of the hurricane hitting Charleston straight on. It would be a Category 2. However, the European Hurricane Model predicted that it would hit Wilmington. Although I was in denial that the hurricane would hit, my prepper training started to kick in. I ordered a car service to take me to the airport on Tuesday, just in case. I also took a quick peek at my supplies just to be sure that I had everything that I needed. I had enough food and water for three days.

Monday morning:

I got up at 6:00 a.m. I planned to do some writing and maybe bring in some furniture and stuff off the porch. Suddenly, there was a knock at the door. A vacationer had locked herself out of her condo. She wanted to use my phone. I invited her in. She saw that I had brought my porch stuff in. My luggage was lying open and I was clearing out my fridge in case of a power outage. My emergency lantern and headlamp were also on the table. By chance, I also happened to have a gas mask on the counter. (After interviewing a gas mask manufacturer, I had ordered it. I had received it in the mail and unpacked it the previous night.) My long hair was also in a bun. In girl world, that means business.

"Wow, you are up so early to do this! Aren't you?" The vacationer remarked as she spied around.

I pretended not to notice her staring at the strange mask. I smiled and handed her my cell.

Monday afternoon:

The mayor announced that there would be an evacuation of Charleston beginning at 12:00 p.m. on Tuesday. My flight was at 9:47 a.m. Great. So much for that head start. I contacted the driver and asked him to pick me up an hour earlier, at 6:30 a.m., even though it only takes forty-five minutes to get to the airport. I also came up with a backup plan to drive my car and leave it in the long-term parking if I decided that I needed to leave earlier or if he was a no-show. Having grown up in the South, I knew that most locals would not leave until the storm got closer. I checked ticket sales and discovered that all flights to New York City were sold out for Tuesday. I immediately started packing all my notes and research for my manuscript.

After the evacuation was announced, I got a text from Ben: "You are getting out of there, right?"

Monday late afternoon:

Since they were doing construction nearby, I had recently hung a tarp on the inside of our screen porch to block out dirt particles during the workday. Using a trucker's hitch knot, I hung the large tarp like a curtain. I could move it up and down as needed. Thinking that a tarp might protect the porch from severe rain, I lowered it down and stapled it into place. I wasn't sure if it would really do anything, but the hammering and stapling made me feel a whole lot better.

Monday night:

I grew more nervous as I began to get calls and texts from concerned friends. The news was now predicting a Category 4. I packed my research materials in a carry-on and a tote. I also packed a large bag to be checked. I kept thinking of Jason's reminder that nothing is sentimental in an emergency situation, and that one needs to be agile and quick thinking. I told myself that I could leave everything but my research behind. Still, my heart was not entirely convinced.

At 8:20 p.m., I became antsy. I started to second guess everything, which was very unlike me. I started to think that maybe I should just cancel the car service and leave for the airport even earlier. If the line was too long, I could leave my luggage in my trunk. I did not want to be weighed down by stuff. Hiking with the group on weekend excursions had taught me that over-packing is never a good idea. Yet, I continued to struggle with the thought of replacing expensive items and feared the loss of sentimental items. I grew irritated with myself because I thought that I should be willing to let these things go. I then started to worry about how I was not permitted to board up the windows in my condominium. I also became worried that something would happen, and I would be stranded at the airport alone with the hurricane rapidly approaching the city.

I called Ben to get a reality check on my approach. I explained that I wanted to troubleshoot. I wanted to make sure that I was leaving soon enough (by prepping standards), that I wasn't packing too much, and that I had done all the hurricane prep I could do given my condo association's restrictions. I was also frustrated because I really did think that I would be ahead of the game in case anything happened. Now, I was with the chase pack. Category 4. Category 4.

I sent a text: "Call me whenever you can. It doesn't matter how late."

Ben called around 10:00 p.m. I gave him the rundown. I explained my hurricane preparations, my packing and my departure plans in exhaustive detail. He was patient. As I reviewed my list, he asked questions.

"Are we talking about the tarp that you put up to block out dust?"

"Yes."

"You know, with that sort of wind, that you have just made a parachute, right?"

"Yes."

"Can you take it down?"

"Can't reach the top. No ladder."

I could not exactly hear the chuckle, but I could sense his smile and his effort to suppress it.

"Well, I guess there isn't too much you can do about that. If it is the only thing on the porch. It's fine."

"About the packing…"

"OK, we are only talking about one checked bag. That's nothing. Look, you gotta remember. This isn't a bug out. You have time to plan more and to bring more. Why wouldn't you do that? That just makes good financial sense. You aren't hiking to the airport, right? You aren't gonna be walking seven miles to the airport. You've got all of your important stuff in your carry-on. It's a flight. This really isn't a bug out. You've got more time to prep. Well, hold on, this is really a bug out, I think. Category 4. You can take more stuff though."

I paused while I also debated the question. Yes, this was a bug out.

"I'm worried. I know what to do. I just want to make sure that I'm not missing anything."

"How early are you leaving again?"

"Two hours earlier than normal. 6:30 for a 9:47. Takes about 45 minutes to get there."

"Did you suggest that time? What did the driver say?"

"Driver thought that we should leave at 7:30 a.m. I wanted 6:30 a.m."

"He seemed calm and okay with the trip? Didn't think that there was going to be a lot of traffic?"

"No, he was very relaxed. He is older. I know him. A really nice guy. He is a local so he would know about traffic patterns."

"It's not New York traffic either, Anna. You are probably thinking of that."

"Agreed. I just don't want to miss the flight. I would drive to my dad's, but they live in Virginia Beach which is going to be hit too. It is too late for me to get ahead of anything."

"You won't. You are fine. You just have enough time now to second-guess yourself. Time to pack and then repack. Look, you did everything that you could now you just gotta get outta there. Why won't you drive yourself to the airport?"

"Who knows when I will get back and I will have to pay the long-term rate? If everything is okay, I don't want the added expense. The car is paid for. I will just leave it here."

"Yeah, I definitely wouldn't do that. Look, remember when we could have gotten hypothermia at the beach that night because we were really tired and super cold? We weren't thinking straight. This is like that but different. Right now, we are going through the list. We're able to do that. You've got this."

I nodded.

"You are right. You aren't trying to kill me. You are helping this time."

We both laughed.

I sighed.

"It is gonna be fine. I just wanted to talk and make sure that I'm not missing anything."

"You are not. You are just like me. You are gonna go through that list again. That's okay. You've got a plan. You can take your car to the airport if you need to."

"Yes, you're right. Thank you so much. I feel better."

"Text when you get back."

Tuesday morning (6:20 a.m.):

Patrick, the son of the scheduled driver, arrived to take me to the airport. I was ready but I was struggling with the lockbox. I could not seem to lock it. Patrick tried to help but he could not lock it either.

I recalled something that Jason had once said to explain the importance of practicing bugging out: "…if the shit hits and your home burns down to the ground or whatever … That's why we do the bug out weekends to let people realize that bag is your bank…"

I told Patrick, "Let's leave it. We gotta go."

I had to accept the real possibility that "the shit" was probably going to destroy my home. I had to recognize that, in this case, my "bank" was not just my bag (my luggage) but my strength to leave my home to seek safety. Driving away from my place that day felt worse than any tough hike I had ever been on with the group.

After a few minutes of quiet, we began to discuss the storm and evacuation plans. I apologized for wanting to leave an hour earlier than his father's suggestion, but I was concerned.

"Your dad seemed calm, but I was worried."

"When did he want to leave again? 7:30? Probably would have been still okay, but 6:30 a.m. was the way to go. My dad is way laid-back though. Listen, my dad missed the last two big storms. The first, he was in Canada and the second, he was in Paris. That's why he sounded so calm."

We both laughed.

"Listen, my dad lives in Virginia Beach. He should probably evacuate. He's not. He is a Vietnam vet. He isn't going anywhere."

We both shook our heads and laughed.

My husband called to check in. I was relieved to speak with him. After we hung up, I passed on my husband's best wishes for safety to the driver as they know one another.

"I think that we left at the perfect time. I have to see the doctor this morning after I drop you off."

"What?"

"My wife. She is due to have our first baby. Anytime. They might induce this morning. That way she won't be having the baby in the middle of everything."

The delivery of a baby. My worries were now trivial.

I stared at the driver to make sure that he was not flipping out and I had not realized it. Patrick looked like he always did. Friendly and stable. I was surprised because he looked a little more dressed up than usual. He was wearing a very nice suit. He had dressed up for the delivery of his baby.

Patrick dropped me off an hour later. I wished him well.

Checking my bag only took about fifteen minutes. The TSA Pre-Check line also only took a few minutes. I walked down the corridor to see the waiting area. It was a zoo. People milled about, jittery and rude. A woman yelled at me in the queue for the restaurant. She was behind me and complained that I "wasn't standing eagerly enough" to get the interest of the hostess. People scurrying about consumed with their own agendas was a stark contrast to the NYCPN process of dividing tasks and working together. Instead, they reminded me more of independent preppers trying to survive without connecting with anyone else. I regretted the absence of a Platinum Club at the terminal because, for a brief moment, I imagined that people would probably be more civilized there. However, that was flawed thinking; entitlement has never been the best predictor of civility. Suddenly, I realized the value of being able to be comfortable in your discomfort. People zoomed around and some called everyone they knew on their cell phones to assure them that they were being evacuated. I called my parents and spoke for a minute or two. I understood their feelings. I was worried too. I was concerned that my flight would be cancelled. I spent the next couple of hours reading. I prayed for Patrick and his family as well as my friends that had yet to evacuate. When our plane took off, the passengers all clapped.

After returning to the city, I called Ben to thank him for his help in keeping me organized and calm. He told me: "It wasn't a big deal and that's what preppers do. We help each other out in a time of crisis." I thought about how his interpretation was vastly different from the public perception of preppers. As an NYCPN member, Ben had demonstrated the group's principles of trustworthiness and reliability. By coaching me through an evacuation, Ben had affirmed the bond between us.

Note

1   At her request, I have not shared any examples.

References

Ashforth, B., and Mael, F. (1996). Organizational identity and strategy as a context for the individual. *Advances in Strategic Management*, 13, 19–64.

Belson, K., Medina, J., and Pérez-Peña, R. (2017, October 2). A burst of gunfire, a pause, then carnage in Las Vegas that would not stop. *The New York Times*. Retrieved from https://www.nytimes.com/2017/10/02/us/las-vegas-shooting-live-updates.html?searchResultPosition=2.

Carlin, G. (1981). *A Place for My Stuff*. Atlantic Records.

Kinane, K. (2016). *Loose in Chicago*. Comedy Central.

Kolar, T. (2016). Conceptualizing tourist experiences with new attractions: The case of escape rooms. *The International Journal of Contemporary Hospitality*, 29(5), 1322-1339.

Kornelis, C. (2018). Unlocking the business secrets of escape rooms. *The Wall Street Journal*. Retrieved from https://www.wsj.com/articles/unlocking-the-business-secrets-of-escape-rooms-1524838226.

Martin, D. D. (2002). From appearance tales to oppression tales: Frame alignment and organizational identity. *Journal of Contemporary Ethnography*, 21(2), 158–206.

Montgomery, D., Mele, C., and Fernandez, M. (2017, November 5). Gunman kills at least 26 in attack on rural Texas church. *The New York Times*. Retrieved from https://www.nytimes.com/2017/11/05/us/church-shooting-texas.html.

Nicholson, S. (2015). *Peeking behind the locked door: A survey of escape room facilities*. Retrieved from http://scottnicholson.com/pubs/erfacwhite.pdf.

Sanger, D. E., Sang-Hun, C., Buckley, C., and Gordon, M. R. (2017, March 7). North Korea tensions pose early, and perilous, test for Trump. *The New York Times*. Retrieved from https://www.nytimes.com/2017/03/07/world/asia/korea-missile-defense-china-trump.html?searchResultPosition=36.

Security, D. O. H. (2019). *Department of Homeland Security*. Retrieved from https://www.ready.gov/active-shooter.

Wu, C., Wagenschutz, H., and Hein, J. (2018). Promoting leadership and teamwork development through escape rooms. *Medical Education*, 52(5), 561–562.

Part 4

Urban prepping as a new reflection of citizenship

9 Future directions for NYC prepping

As Goodall (2016) reminds us, qualitative research writing, "is a joint effort, as how we construct our narratives influences how readers bring in *their own interpretive resources* to make sense of them" (p. 143). For this qualitative project, writing a concluding chapter is especially challenging because the conversation about (and among) NYC preppers does not stop with the ending of this book. Instead, much like the city of New York, the conversation of their lived experience is dynamic, ever-changing and unpredictable. At the conclusion of studying the NYCPN, the conversation of their lived experience changed to reflect tragedy and, in its aftermath, a new start.

"I know that you are going to write about this, that you have to. Just be nice. Be nice. This is an awful thing." Those were Ben's words to me on a terrible day. He was right. Even though my research had concluded, I did have to write about it, because it was significant to the study. I promised Ben that I would treat the matter sensitively and respectfully. And, yes, it is a very awful thing. On July 30, 2018, a person loosely associated with the NYCPN, James Shields, shot and killed his six-year-old son, his ex-wife, his current wife and himself (Southall, 2018). Discovered inside his apartment were two loaded 9-millimeter Glock handguns and about seventy rounds of ammunition which Shields was licensed to keep at home. Shields and his ex-wife had been in a costly legal battle over their son. His ex-wife, his son and his current wife were all Dutch citizens. His ex-wife and son lived in the Netherlands. Nearing the end of a trip to visit Shields, they were scheduled to return home the following week, Shields shot his family when they tried to leave his apartment in Astoria and then himself. In April, Shields had created a GoFundMe page titled "Child Kidnapping" to help pay for legal expenses and described how the custody battle was "destroying my current marriage and my life" (Celona et al., 2018). Shields also had a history of domestic violence that included an ex-girlfriend and both wives.

Shields' story is significant to this study because, during my time as a participant-observer, he occasionally attended prepper group events and meetings. In my narrative, he is referred to as Jimmy, the friendly guy who catches me when I stumbled on the cliffside. In my year-long study, he attended three events, two outings and a meeting. Jimmy and I had informal exchanges. However, I did not conduct an in-depth interview with him, as he was a peripheral member of the group. Therefore, there was little opportunity for me to establish a level of rapport with him for an extended interview. After hearing the tragic news, I reviewed my notes and studied a photo of Jimmy smiling that was published in the newspaper. I was searching for a clue or hint, something that I had missed, but there was nothing. Regardless of his limited contact with the NYCPN, his actions had a great impact on the group. First, there was a genuine sadness and shock about the senseless loss of life, especially the loss of a child. Given his employment at the New York City Fire Department, Jason was the first to hear the news. When we talked about it, he shared that he was "very sad and angry" about Jimmy's actions. After speaking with other NYCPN members, it was clear that Jason's feelings reflected the consensus of the core group. Echoing other preppers, Marlon said that,

> When a guy shows up to the group bragging about his guns or knives and his fake military experience, you can quickly see that something's up. I didn't know about the extent of the problems with his first wife; this kind of thing shows you don't know what a person is capable of under tremendous pressure and trauma.

Anne shared that she had always felt uneasy around him and that he did not seem to be genuine. She told me that she had a picture of the six of us, Jimmy and his new wife, Anne and her husband, and my husband and me, all seated together having dinner on an outing. Any semblance of the objective and somewhat detached researcher in me vanished for a few minutes. My stomach flipped as I thought about how I was delighted to learn that they had just married. As my conversations continued with core leaders, a few other curious details began to emerge about Jimmy's periodic participation in the group. On one excursion, Jimmy arrived at the campsite unprepared. He had no supplies, including no food or water for the overnight excursion. On another trip, he violated the group's ban on alcohol at a retreat. While these actions did not meet the group's expectations, his behavior did not indicate that he was capable of harming his family.

In the aftermath, Ben expressed concern that Jimmy's criminal actions would reflect negatively on the group by reinforcing stereotypes about preppers as "gun-carrying whackos." He also observed that the group's mission carried a risk for attracting certain types of people. Ben said: "Look, we're a strange group, we could be called a little paranoid, we get together and plan for stuff that may not happen, so it makes sense that we might get some crazies." To improve group safety, conversation among core members moved quickly toward developing a stronger vetting process for new members. One member circulated a think piece outlining security concerns and suggestions including a tiered-membership that allowed only senior members (members with advanced skills who regularly attended events) to attend outdoor excursions. While open to discussion, Jason was skeptical about the effectiveness of a stronger vetting process. He argued that some employers have extensive screening tests that are ultimately unsuccessful in eliminating mentally unstable people from these professions, therefore, any vetting process implemented by the group could also be unsuccessful. However, the other core members felt that designing and implementing a new vetting process was vital. As Ben explained, the "ultimate goal isn't to find out if the person is a super prepper. It is to find out if they are trustworthy and willing to learn and improve."

My conversations with core leaders identified two main categories of high-risk members. First, core leaders were concerned about individuals who were mentally unstable and may threaten the lives or well-being of group members, demonstrated by dangerous or erratic behavior, misrepresenting prepping skills and knowledge, and disregarding group rules, such as no alcohol. Second, core leaders were also concerned about individuals who overstated or mispresented their prepping skills and knowledge. By exaggerating their knowledge, these members subjected themselves and others to possible injury. Core leaders had devised two broad types of security measures designed to protect the group: a more thorough vetting process, and stricter safety protocols for excursions. The screening process for prospective members would include a questionnaire on skills and health conditions to be completed before acceptance in the group. Strategies for protecting members during outings included disclosing exact excursion locations only to those planning to attend, and being more diligent about employing watch teams to monitor the camp throughout the night. These possible security changes seemed to suggest a closer-knit group, a group less open to members who occasionally attended excursions and meetings.

Through enduring the challenges of excursions and improving their prepping skills together, the core leaders had bonded and developed a sense of trust in one another. As personal reflection and conversations continued, it seems that a structure of feeling (Williams, 1958) arose with the core group. In this process, core members engaged in "taking meaning from experience" (Williams, 1958, p. 323). The knowledge of Jimmy's crimes pushed the issue of screening members to the forefront of the group's agenda. The core group members seemed to interpret his limited participation in the group to mean that their security measures were flawed. For the core members, the dialogue about security seemed to indicate that something much larger was at stake for the group. The interests of the majority of the core group had now diverged from the mission of the broader NYCPN. The NYCPN's mission is centered on teaching New Yorkers about the principals of disaster preparedness. Accomplishing this goal requires an open-door policy and a broad range of events to address all levels of prepping knowledge. As core leaders spent years practicing prepping together, their knowledge base and skills advanced and they drew closer. Perceiving an incompatibility between the group's mission and their interests, the majority of the core leaders departed and began to organize a new group. Their departure actually represents the success of the NYCPN as an important forum for learning about prepping. If formed, a new smaller group comprised of seasoned preppers with advanced skills would be remarkably different from the NYCPN. If established, this type of new group would represent a transition from a group of urban preppers working together to learn survival skills to a group of urban preppers working together to learn how to survive together. That is a very different group with a very different mission.

This transition points to an important direction for symbolic interactionism research in studying shifts in meaning and rituals in the evolution of small groups. For example, the organizational structure and dynamics of the new group are likely to differ from the original group. Given the importance of the NYCPN's founder in establishing the original group and his role as a spokesperson for urban prepping in the media, the NYCPN is anchored by its founder in a hierarchical form of leadership. With a different focus and similar skill level among members, would the leadership style within a closed group remain the same or will approaches to collaboration be different? Within the NYCPN, an important demonstration of self-reliance was possessing a bug out bag packed with appropriate survival tools and knowing how to use those tools. Within a close group of seasoned preppers, other objects and rituals may also develop significant meanings similar to the bug out bag and its use. For future research, the formation of new types of prepping groups will bring new meanings, values, and practices (Bryson, 2008).

To draw on Becker (Lu, 2015), studying the rise of prepping in New York has enriched my understanding of urbanism by "finding new problems that I hadn't imagined, new aspects of that world I haven't imagined, new ways of thinking about phenomena of everyday life wherever it occurs" (p. 128). Researching urban preppers has been like reading against the grain of urban studies. The identity of an urban prepper, a city dweller who prepares and trains to protect his or her family against disaster, is a sharp contrast to the classic depiction of an urbanite characterized by a blasé attitude and overstimulation (Simmel, 2002). Rather than tuning out the chaos and rhythm of the city, NYC preppers tune in to become mindful of potential dangers in the city. In the 21st century, NYC preppers supplement their knowledge of city life with learning about homesteading and bushcraft skills that seem to harken back to the sense of the rural that Simmel feared was lost. However, I argue that, at least for some New Yorkers, prepping may reflect a new city sensibility. With the perception of an increased risk of disaster or attack, some New Yorkers now feel that city life demands "street smarts" and "survival smarts."

NYC preppers differ from preppers in rural or suburban locations in several important ways. First, most NYC preppers have direct experience with disaster. After experiencing traumatic events such as September 11th and Hurricane Sandy, NYC preppers have sought to protect their families against harm. Subsequent events, such as the discovery of a bomb hidden in a car at

Times Square (2010) and the minor explosion of another bomb at a subway stop near the Port Authority (2017), have only reinforced their interest in preparedness. For these New Yorkers, prepping is a reality-based exercise rather than one driven by fantasy. While rural and suburban preppers have houses (and land) to store their provisions and to shelter in place, most NYC preppers are forced to contend with the limitations of smaller dwellings like apartments. Therefore, they must be more strategic about creating prepping closets and planning to shelter in place.

Based on the limitations of sheltering in place, NYC preppers plan to leave the city rather than stay in their apartments if disaster strikes. However, given traffic congestion caused by high population density, evacuating the city by car to avoid disaster will be unlikely. Public transportation, (subways, trains or buses), might also become overly crowded or inoperable. Also, there are only a limited number of exit routes outside of Manhattan. As a result, many preppers plan to walk out of the city. Unlike rural and suburban preppers, many New Yorkers often lack significant outdoor experience such as camping or hiking. Therefore, many NYC preppers are required to push past their familiar boundaries of city life by simultaneously tackling experiencing the outdoors and learning bushcraft skills.

In contrast to the media stereotype of preppers being primarily white males, many NYC preppers are often people of color who believe that, in the event of a disaster, government response will be ineffective and slow to respond to the needs of their neighborhoods. As a global financial capital, New York is also the home of extremely wealthy preppers. Familiar with minimizing risk and skeptical of the government's capabilities, these preppers plan to escape to secret locales or retreat to safe rooms during disaster.

In the event of a disaster, New York preppers with middle class incomes have sidestepped the global city bypassing its nodes and connections to link with one another at designated points like parks, streets, or other public spaces in the physical realm of the city. In contrast, some of the city's billionaires have doubled down on their faith in the global city and its electronic infrastructure for survival. With plans to flee the city or lock themselves away, some of NYC's billionaires intend to hold fast to all the promises of modernity. However, by locking themselves and their precious belongings away in impenetrable cases, these elites also seem to be harkening back to ancient times: Like the ancient Egyptians tucked away in the Pyramids, some of New York's royalty plan to bury themselves with their riches in hopes of emerging again one day to continue their rule. The different survival strategies between New York's elite and New Yorkers with middle-class incomes is a revealing symbol of class division within cities. Yet, the difference in preparing for disaster is only a recent and novel representation of the class division in cities that has affected all areas of life from housing to education to medical care and now to survival planning.

However, these two groups share a commonality: they do not rely solely on government aid in disaster, but place a premium on practicing self-reliance.

For wealthy preppers, plans of escaping to a safe haven or retreating to a safe room are beyond the measures taken by the state to protect private individuals. Government protections are too slow and too ordinary for this set. Given their extreme wealth, these preppers do not need to depend on the help of government. However, for civil society, the cost of elites simply opting out during a crisis might be tremendous. The argument might be made that, by fleeing to a remote location or retreating to a safe room, elites may deny the country (those locked out of the room) two assets: leadership and philanthropy. However, if an elite's first inclination is to disappear or hide in a time of great crisis, then fostering community has probably never been a core principle for that group. Middle class NYC preppers also do not plan on much government support in times of disaster. According to these preppers, the government cannot be relied upon to provide disaster relief due to mismanagement and limited resources Their suspicions about the government's ineptitude that arose from watching Federal Emergency Management Authority's (FEMA) response to Hurricane Katrina were reinforced by watching the aftermath of Hurricane Maria. With diminished faith in government, these preppers now work to become self-reliant in moments of disaster. While independent NYC preppers create bug out bags and prepping closets, NYCPN members also develop and test their survival skills within a group to further strengthen their self-reliance.

In writing about my participant-observer experience with the NYCPN, I viewed my narrative as an epistemology, a way of understanding (Goodall, 2016). Through storytelling, I have aimed to share with readers a particular type of knowledge, not focusing only on "traditional forms of knowledge (knowing *how* or knowing *that*) but on knowing *what it is like*" (Goodall, 2016, p. 13). This goal seems inherent in symbolic interactionism as it seeks to trace the production of meaning within small groups. My hope is that I have communicated the complexity of what life is like for a NYC prepper, as it seems to be both empowering and still somewhat isolating based on negative stereotypes.

Symbolic interactionism has provided a valuable lens for examining urban prepping group culture. To become a valued group member, a prepper must be able to demonstrate that he or she is trustworthy. For the group, trustworthiness is defined by being earnest in learning about preparing for disaster and demonstrating a sense of reliability that can be relied on in an emergency. In the group, the merit of a prepper is initially measured by one's ability to properly pack a bug out bag and to use its contents (or possessing a willingness to learn). Core leaders watched for these qualities at retreats and excursions. New members were offered advice and instruction to improve their prepping strategies and equipment. Next, a member also needed to communicate their trustworthiness by working hard and making an important contribution to the group. On excursions and during workshops, group members worked hard to learn bushcraft skills. Members contributed to the group's knowledge base by specializing in areas such as fire building, communications, knot tying and first aid. This level of contribution was reinforced by regular participation in excursions and at meetings. As one member explained, a person must "earn the right to be here." Beyond having a firm command of survival skills, trustworthiness also meant demonstrating the ability to remain calm in stressful situations. On excursions when hazardous weather occurred or a member sustained an injury, group members were expected to remained calm to assess and address the new situation. The expression of political opinions was discouraged to avoid disagreement and to maintain focus on prepping during excursions and meetings

Another important direction for future research is to explore the role of gender in prepping culture. Within the NYCPN, there was no real tension regarding gender roles, as self-sufficiency was the primary concern; group members were responsible for their own survival through relying on their own bug out bags and skills. However, during the period of study, this group was led by a man, and there was no specific programming for female preppers. As the NYCPN now incorporates some programming for female preppers (such as personal hygiene), the group's agenda will most likely expand. Possible approaches for new research might include studying the agenda and leadership practices of a female-led prepping group as well as an all-female group. A large study of in-depth interviews with independent female preppers could also be conducted. Would their approach to prepping be different than male prepping group members? Beyond bushcraft, what skills would be foregrounded? Would there be an increased emphasis on topics such as homesteading, personal safety, women's health, reproduction, and prepping with children? Central to these studies would be exploring if there are differences between the agendas of urban female preppers and female preppers who live in other areas.

As American anxiety seems to be heightening in an increasingly uncertain future, the expectation that one should plan to be self-reliant in a disaster may now be becoming part of American culture. Owning a bug out bag has even recently received a stamp of approval from one of America's arbiters of fashion and home goods, Oprah Winfrey. Oprah's "Favorite Things" 2019 holiday gift guide features a luxury emergency survival bag. In keeping with a New Yorker's need to save space, *The New York Times* gift guide promotes a small tin box of survival items. A review of the current American news cycle also confirms that the anxieties present during the midterm elections are mainstays. To fuel support for tightening borders in the south, President Trump has posted more than 2,000 Facebook ads referring to the "invasion" by undocumented immigrants as part of his re-election campaign (Kaplan, 2019). Three mass shootings have occurred across the country in span of less than three weeks, beginning at a garlic festival in Gilroy, CA (Fry and Winton, 2019) which was following by two shootings at a Walmart in El Paso, TX (Romero et al, 2019) and a bar in Dayton, OH (Robertson et al, 2019). Concern about fair elections continued after Senate Majority leader

Mitch McConnell blocked a security bill designed to protect against foreign interference in US elections (Kane, 2019). Due to climate change, July 2019 was the hottest month ever recorded across the globe with the year possibly being the hottest ever (Fountain, 2019). Lastly, Navy pilots have confirmed observing and recording unidentified flying objects traveling at supersonic speeds over the mainland US from the summer of 2014 through March 2015 (Cooper, Blumenthal, and Kean, 2019). No doubt, an entrepreneur has viewed this admission as justification for trying to develop a new niche in the prepping market.

Now that the possibility of a Doomsday may be a very real and present fear for many people, rather than an unimaginable fiction, not only will the approach to protecting against disaster change, the perception of life following disaster may also shift. A conversation I recently had about prepping with a young moviemaker, Sydney Clara Brafman, hinted at this new reality. Her latest project is a short movie on prepping from a fresh perspective. Her movie traces a day in the life of a young woman whose life has been relatively unchanged by catastrophe. Because she prepared for disaster (and is agoraphobic), she experiences little disruption in her life. She slides right into her singular post-apocalyptic life. Set in a glass box apartment in a global city, the movie depicts urban prepping in a minimalist and crisp aesthetic (a Muji store and Marie Kondo inspired approach). Brafman's interpretation of a postapocalyptic future is significant because horror and destruction are not focus points. Instead, this post-apocalyptic narrative is about the business of getting on with it, imagining what the everyday might look like in such a future. And, I really think that is what prepping is about, the business of learning how to get on with it.

I close this book with a sincere note of gratitude to the NYC preppers who agreed to help me "get comfortable in my discomfort." In this project, I required a lot of help because there was a lot of discomfort. Some types of discomfort were predictable with this type of project. The challenges of tough excursions were compounded by miserable weather or my own lack of experience. Sometimes both factors came into play. For example, freezing rain is much colder when it streams into your tent late at night because you set up in the wrong spot. Those fiascos are to be expected; they are part of the experience of being a participant-observer. The NYC preppers also aided me in overcoming another discomfort: when discussing my research, individuals would sometimes try to nudge me into stating that preppers are crazy people who are obsessed by conspiracies theories. When I refused to make that broad claim and confirm their suspicions, I could sometimes actually see their perception of me shift—a raised eyebrow, an almost imperceptible nod of misunderstanding, or the faint trace of a smirk. At the start of the project, I misinterpreted these signs as expressions of ignorance or a false sense of superiority because I had clearly "gone native."

However, as the project progressed and I listened to more reactions, I came to recognize negative comments as expressions of fear. Talking about the possibility of disaster and measures to protect against harm is a dangerous subject. A genuine conversation about this topic requires a person to name their fears and to examine what they are doing to protect themselves (and their families). Worse yet, the person may discover multiple fears to protect against or a fear that cannot be protected against. This research invites non-preppers to go down that rabbit hole. Rejection is the best defense for maintaining the status quo. By sharing their world and their stories with me, these NYC preppers encouraged me to face my own fears in taking on this experience and increased my appreciation of the struggles of others in attempting to confront (or even acknowledge) their own anxieties. A reporter recently asked me about my own personal journey with this project. I spoke about the outdoors and talked about how the project forced me to become tougher. However, that is not really the whole answer. I have become tougher and more sensitive all at once. Vulnerable. I never thought about how so much of the world is just that, vulnerable. In thinking about preparedness, there is an important piece that gets lost. To prepare for disaster implies that you recognize the preciousness of something.

One recent summer evening in New York underscored this vulnerability. I received a text from my best friend who lives in NJ. Her text read: "All good? Got your bug out bag ready?" My friend is not a prepper, so I recognized that her text was an alert that something was wrong in the city. In my Greenwich Village apartment, I turned on the news to discover that Midtown from the West 40s to the Upper West Side to 72nd was without power. Jason had already sent an alert to the NYCPN on social media accounts. I sent back a "Thumbs Up" emoji. However, technically speaking, I should have told her that, if needed, I would be relying on my mini-prepping closet rather than my bug out bag.

Due to machinal failures involving a substation, 73,000 Con Edison customers were without power for about three hours (Barron and Zaveru, 2019). Throughout the brief power outage, New York demonstrated its adaptability and resilience. Unable to perform for the evening, Broadway casts sang to their audiences in front of their theaters. After the evacuation of her concert at Madison Square Garden, Jennifer Lopez sent an Instagram of appreciation and apology to her fans. Star Wars fans used the force and their lightsabers to direct traffic at busy intersections. A few bodegas and local grocery stores remained open in the dark and accepted IOUs from regular customers. The blackout reminded me that I will never really leave my fieldwork. Whether someone used their emergency supplies or directed traffic dressed as a Jedi, that night, New Yorkers of all stripes seemed ready to rely on their street smarts and their survival smarts.

Now, in March 2020, our city has become the epicenter of the coronavirus pandemic in the United States. At the time of writing, New York has nearly 10,000 cases of people who have tested positive for the coronavirus and 63 people who have died from it ("New York has 5%," 2020). At the federal level, weak leadership and early inaction resulted in a vague plan for containment, and stymied the flow of resources (Konyndyk, 2020). Critically short on supplies and hospital beds, the New York state and city governments are struggling to bolster our soon-to-be overwhelmed healthcare system. Amid all this, I am confused and doubtful about what type of help (if any) to expect from the government. However, I am confident about one thing— my prepping knowledge might just save my life. When the virus was first reported in the US, I remained calm as I already had proper safety equipment and provisions. Rather than panicking in front of the television, I did what many preppers did; I reached out to my friends and neighbors to offer advice about how to protect their families and themselves. Tomorrow begins day five of sheltering in place.

References

Barron, J., and Zaveri, M. (2019, July 13). *Power restored to Manhattan's West Side after major blackout*. Retrieved from https://www.nytimes.com/2019/07/13/nyregion/nyc-power-outage.html.

Bryson, J. (2008). Dominant, emergent, and residual culture: The dynamics of organizational change. *Journal of Organizational Change Management*, 21(6), 743–757.

Celona, L., Pagones, S., Sheehan, K., and Musumeci, N. (2018, July 31). Dad says son suspected in family murder-suicide was 'good man'. *New York Post*. Retrieved from https://nypost.com/2018/07/31/dad-says-son-suspected-in-family-murder-suicide-was-good-man/.

Cooper, H., and Blumental, R., and Kean, L. (2019, May 26). 'Wow, what is that?' Navy pilots report unexplained flying objects. *The New York Times*. Retrieved from https://www.nytimes.com/2019/05/26/us/politics/ufo-sightings-navy-pilots.html.

Fountain, H. (2019, August 5). How hot was July? hotter than ever, global data shows. *The New York Times*. Retrieved from https://www.nytimes.com/2019/08/05/climate/july-hottest-month-climate.html.

Fry, H., and Winton, R. (2019, August 6). *Gilroy shooter's target list prompts domestic terrorism probe by FBI Los Angeles Times*. Retrieved from https://www.latimes.com/california/story/2019-08-06/gilroy-garlic-festival-shooting-domestic-terrorism-probe.

Goodall, H. L. (2016). *Writing qualitative inquiry: Self, stories, and academic life*. New York, NYCA: Routledge.

Kane, P. (2019, July 29). McConnell defends blocking election security bill, rejects criticism he is aiding Russia. *The Washington Post*. Retrieved from https://www.washingtonpost.com/politics/mcconnell-defends-blocking-election-security-bill-rejects-criticism-he-is-aiding-russia/2019/07/29/08dca6d4-b239-11e9-951e-de024209545d_story.html.

Kaplan, T. (2019, August 5). How the Trump campaign used Facebook ads to amplify his 'invasion' claim. *The New York Times*. Retrieved from https://www.nytimes.com/2019/08/05/us/politics/trump-campaign-facebook-ads-invasion.html?searchResultPosition=2.

Konyndyk, J. (2020, March 7). Trump, his eye on the border, overlooked the coronavirus threat. *The New York Times*. Retrieved from https://www.nytimes.com/2020/03/07/opinion/trump-coronavirus-us.html.

Lu, W. (2015). Sociology and art: An interview with Howard S. Becker. *Symbolic Interaction*, 38(1), 127–150. doi:10.1002/symb.139.

New York has roughly 5% of coronavirus cases worldwide. (2020, March 22). *The New York Times*. Retrieved from https://www.nytimes.com/2020/03/22/nyregion/coronavirus-new-york-update.html?action=click&module=Spotlight&pgtype=Homepage.

Robertson, C., Bosman, J., and Smith, M. (2019, August 4). Back-to-back outbreaks of gun violence in El Paso and Dayton stun country. *The New York Times*. Retrieved from https://www.nytimes.com/2019/08/04/us/mass-shootings-dayton-el-paso.html.

Romero, S., Fernandez, M., and Padilla, M. (2019, August 3). Massacre at a crowded Walmart in Texas leaves 20 dead. *The New York Times*. Retrieved from https://www.nytimes.com/2019/08/03/us/el-paso-shooting.html.

Simmel, G. (2002). The Metropolis and mental life (1903). In G. Bridge and S. Watson (Eds.), *The Blackwell city reader*. Oxford and Malden, MA: Wiley-Blackwell.

Southall, A. (2018, July 31). Queens killings stemmed from custody dispute in the Netherlands. *The New York Times*. Retrieved from https://www.nytimes.com/2018/07/31/nyregion/queens-killings-custody-netherlands.html.

Williams, R. (1958). *Culture and society, 1780–1950*. New York: Columbia University Press.

Index